£5 £7:00 MP

TASMA

Tasma

The life of Jessie Couvreur

Patricia Clarke

ALLEN & UNWIN

Frontispiece: Jessie Fraser (née Huybers) adopted the name Tasma when her first stories were published in 1877 to honour the colony where she spent her childhood. When she began lecturing on Australia in Europe after separating from her first husband, she used the name Madame Jessie Tasma. (*Queen. The Lady's Newspaper*, 13 January 1894)

© Patricia Clarke 1994

This book is copyright under the Berne Convention.
No reproduction without permission. All rights reserved.

First published in 1994

Allen & Unwin Pty Ltd
9 Atchison Street, St Leonards, NSW 2065 Australia

National Library of Australia
Cataloguing-in-Publication entry:

Clarke, Patricia
    Tasma: the life of Jessie Couvreur.

    Bibliography.
    ISBN 1 86373 519 4.

    1. Tasma, 1848–1897—Biography. 2. Authors, Australian—19th century—Biography. 3. Women authors, Australian—19th century—Biography. I. Title.

A823.1

Set in 10.5/12pt Goudy Old Style by DOCUPRO, Sydney
Printed by South Wind Production Singapore Private Limited

10 9 8 7 6 5 4 3 2 1

Contents

Acknowledgments

Tasma—Jessie Huybers-Fraser-Couvreur—had no direct descendants. Initially, it was hard to trace personal material she may have left. Early in my research for this book, I wrote to every Huybers in Australia whom I could conveniently locate in an effort to contact people from her family. In this way I was fortunate to come in contact with Dr Kenneth Huybers in Hamilton, Queensland, and through him heard of other relatives.

I am extremely grateful for the very generous help I have received from Ken Huybers and his wife Billee, Mrs Enid Jones and her husband Dudley, Burradoo, New South Wales (descendants of Jessie's eldest brother William Huybers), Dr Renée Erdos, Neutral Bay, New South Wales (descendant of Jessie's sister, Maria Theresa Loureiro); and Lt-Colonel Douglas Morris, East Knoyle, Wilts, England (descendant of Jessie's brother, Edward Huybers). Renée Erdos, Enid Jones and Ken Huybers very kindly welcomed me when I visited them during the past few years, and could not have been more generous in ransacking their memories, showing me family heirlooms, and lending me or allowing me to copy diaries, letters, photographs and other material in their possession. It would have been difficult, if not impossible, to write this book without their help. Renée Erdos very generously lent me for an extended period Jessie's Brussels diary, and the diary she kept on the *Windward*, as well as collections of reviews, photographs and much other material. Enid Jones allowed me to copy family letters and documents in her possession, and Ken Huybers has provided records, photographs and many leads to other material.

Material held by the Morris family was deposited some time ago in the Fryer Library, University of Queensland. It includes diaries kept by Edward and Edith Huybers, which provide invaluable information of family movements and events, as well as collections of cuttings and other material. I am very grateful to Douglas Morris for permission to use this, and to Margaret O'Hagan, Fryer Librarian, for making the material available to me and helping in having copies made. Some associated material, as well as the results of his own research, have been deposited in the Fryer Library by Ray Beilby who, fortunately for later researchers, became interested in Tasma at a time when there were still people living who had known her. I am very grateful for his generosity in making the results of his research available, and for talking about Tasma with me.

Through Renée Erdos, I met Fred McGrath, for whose help in research in London I am unable adequately to express my thanks. He has been a most persistent, imaginative and enthusiastic researcher, who has assiduously followed every possible lead in tracing births, deaths, marriages, wills, probate etc. of Jessie's ancestors and many other matters, including the connection of her grandfather with the Simeon family. I am also grateful to Sir John Simeon, Vancouver, Canada and June Roughley, Kenthurst, New South Wales (a Simeon descendant) for their generosity in helping me to research this elusive link.

I am grateful to Bill Falkiner, St Lucia, Queensland, a descendant of Charles Fraser through his second marriage to Lucy Benson, who provided me with invaluable Fraser family information, as well as a copy of a letter written by Tasma. The great value of this can be seen from the fact that I have located only four letters of any length written by her, apart from this one, a letter written just before her death to her brother William (E. Jones), and two written to her niece Fauvette Loureiro (R. Erdos).

When researching Tasma's childhood in Hobart, I received great help from Geoffrey Stilwell, Allport Librarian, who apart from help on the spot in locating Highfield, sent me many leads on items in Tasmanian newspapers. Don Norman, Sandy Bay, Tasmania (author with Margaret Giordani of *Tasmanian Literary Landmarks*) was, as on previous occasions, a great help in my research and with photographs. For research on Highfield I also thank Frank Harris, Kingston Beach, Tasmania, and the present owner, Paul Wilkinson, North Hobart, Tasmania. For information on old St David's, I thank Betty Hibberd, Lindisfarne, Tasmania.

I am grateful to Agnew descendants (Jessie's relatives by her first marriage) who provided me with information about the Agnew, Degraves and Fraser families: June Buxton, Hobart, Tasmania; J.P. Agnew, Oatlands, Tasmania; Philippa Woodward, Kooyong, Victoria; and Colonel Simon Agnew, Farrer, Australian Capital Territory.

In the Kyneton and Malmsbury districts where Tasma lived during her marriage to Charles Fraser, I am very grateful for help from Maurice Gentry, Kyneton Historical Society, Barbara Slimmon, Malmsbury Historical Society, Steve Marriott of Skelsmergh Hall and Mrs Coutts of Pemberley.

In researching Jessie's short connection with Oakville, I am grateful to Gillian Hibbins, Richmond, Victoria (author of *A History of the City of*

Springvale); for her connection with Degraves's stations on the Burdekin in Queensland to Damien Cash, Historian ANZ Group Archive, Melbourne; and for her connection with Blairgowrie, to Betty Malone, Prahran Historical and Arts Society.

In London I was fortunate to be able to visit Tasma's birthplace, Southwood Lodge, Highgate where the owner, Mrs Sue Whitington, was most hospitable and informative about the history of the house.

Melanie Aspey, group records manager at the London *Times* Archives (News International) and her staff were wonderfully helpful in guiding me to the valuable records of Jessie's employment as London *Times* correspondent in Brussels. They even provided my husband Hugh and myself with overalls while we handled the 100-year-old dusty letter books which contain the records of Jessie's relationship with her employers, and the bound volumes of the *Times* in which we found her articles ringed with blue pencil, with her name written across them.

Before I went to Brussels I received the greatest assistance and advice from my neighbour Belgian-born Fleur Kenyon, Deakin, ACT, who advised on many matters and who obtained valuable information concerning Jessie's second husband, Auguste Couvreur. I also thank Joris Couvreur, a diplomat formerly with the Belgian Embassy in Canberra and now stationed in Brussels, who was extremely helpful in obtaining information about Auguste Couvreur.

I am grateful to the Belgian Ambassador in Canberra, His Excellency Jacques Scavée and his staff, for help and advice before our trip to Brussels, and to a staff member, Catherine Hill, for locating a descendant of a relative of Auguste Couvreur, Jetty Couvreur, Castle Hill, New South Wales, who also provided me with information about the Couvreur family and the Ecole Couvreur.

In Brussels, residents of chaussée de Vleurgat where Jessie lived were surprised to find two Australians on their doorsteps. Chantal Radoux-Rogier and Eric Petit graciously showed us one of the houses in which Jessie lived. I also thank Carlos Van Lerberghe, Catalogue Room Printed Works, Bibliothèque Royale Albert I, Brussels, for his help in locating articles and stories written by Tasma.

The Cultural Attaché at the French Embassy in Canberra, Gérard Guillet, the Australian Ambassador in Paris, His Excellency C.R. (Kim) Jones (a descendant of Jessie's brother, William Huybers), and Fleur Kenyon were of great assistance in facilitating our research at the Bibliothèque Nationale. I am grateful to J. Beaucourt, Secretary General of the Association of Members, for information on l'Ordre des Palmes Académiques and to Jacqueline Laude, Marnay, France for information concerning her great-uncle Eugène Jean-Charles Reverdy.

In Athens I was grateful for help from Nelly Economou.

I would like to thank Joy Hooton for her friendly advice and encouragement of my work; Dr E.W. Ringrose, Red Hill, Queensland, for advice about Jessie's fatal illness; Dale Spender, who lent me copies of some of Tasma's novels; Tim Hewat, Axedale, Victoria (author of *Golden Fleeces. The Falkiners of Boonoke*); Paul Greenhalgh (author of *Ephemeral Vistas*); Jane Clark, Curator of Australian Art, National Gallery of Victoria; Bronwyn Rose, Forrest, ACT; Gerard Vaughan, Oxford, UK; and officers of National Trusts and similar bodies for information and assistance.

I am grateful to the staffs of the National Library of Australia, particularly in the Petherick Room, Pictorial and Newspaper/Microform sections; Fryer Library, University of Queensland; Tasmanian Library and Archives; La Trobe Library, State Library of Victoria; Mitchell Library, State Library of New South Wales; British Museum; British Museum Newspaper Library, Colindale; Bibliothèque Royale Albert I, Brussels, and the Bibliothèque Nationale, Paris; and I also thank the staffs of the Land Titles Office, Melbourne and the Tasmanian Land Records Office.

It would not have been possible to undertake my research in London, Brussels, Paris and Athens and during travel in Australia without the very generous support of my husband Hugh. I thank him for this, and for the great interest he has taken in the book.

Introduction

In her lifetime in the second half of the nineteenth century, Tasma—born Jessie Huybers—was a famous woman. Her first novel *Uncle Piper of Piper's Hill* was 'the book of the season'[1] when it was published in London for Christmas 1888. After publication of her second, *In Her Earliest Youth* (1890), the London *Times* said she was 'surpassed by few British novelists'.[2] In New York, a bookseller told a customer Tasma's *Uncle Piper of Piper's Hill* was 'a great success'.[3] She was variously compared to George Eliot[4] and described as the Australian Jane Austen,[5] and her characterisation said to equal that of Charles Dickens.[6] At this distance these seem hyperbolic, even sad comments. If she was so remarkable, why was she forgotten so quickly?

In recent years, Tasma has been 'relegated to museum status in literary histories'[7] and in the blurb for one publication she was bracketed with 'little known or forgotten writers'.[8] Obliteration began quite soon after her death. In the 1930s, a respondent to a question and answer column in the Brisbane *Courier* asked 'Who was Tasma?'. The paper was unable to offer very much help until a nephew living in Brisbane, Alfred Stutzer Huybers, supplied some biographical information.[9] My own experience is similar. When I told people I was writing a biography of Tasma, apart from those with a particular interest in nineteenth century Australian literature, they asked the questions: 'Why?' 'Who was she?'

Not alone among women writers, Tasma has been virtually removed from Australian consciousness. The usual explanation for her obscurity is that like other Australian women novelists of the nineteenth century who wrote about love, sex and domestic relationships and whose main characters were women, her reputation has been overtaken and submerged by the *Bulletin* school of almost exclusively male writers who emerged in the 1890s. They glorified the traditions of the bush to establish what came to be seen as the authentic picture of Australia.

Perhaps Tasma's later obscurity was influenced by the fact that she died at a relatively young age, that for the second half of her life she lived in Europe, and that she had no direct descendants to keep her memory alive. Other nineteenth century Australian women writers, such as Ada Cambridge and Rosa Praed, lived much longer, the former in Australia and survived by children. This did not save them, however from similar obscurity. The same reason can be given: the devaluing of the scope of women's writing.

Tasma's life deserves to be much better known, and not only because of her now almost forgotten fame as a novelist. Just as interesting and more gender-defying, she was also an acclaimed public lecturer in Europe and a foreign correspondent for the London *Times*. These were both roles that contradicted the perception of women as solely domestic creatures. In her personal life also, Tasma defied the stereotypes of the nineteenth-century woman, and even those of much later eras, by separating from, and divorcing, her first husband and earning her own living in ways not normally pursued by women.

In Europe she made an extraordinary career as a lecturer on Australia, becoming so widely known that King Leopold of Belgium telegrammed, inviting her to the Palace to talk about the subject of her lectures. The President of France honoured her with a decoration rarely given to foreigners, and even more rarely to women.[10] Today it is difficult to convey how sensational were her appearances as a lecturer. Large audiences applauded enthusiastically as she spoke in an exuberantly nationalistic way about the Australia she had left behind: the culture and material progress of the cities; the life of the squatters, carrying on the traditions of the European pioneers; the opportunities for migration and increased trade between Australia and Europe. In effect she carried out the promotional work that in this century would be undertaken by a trade commissioner or government official.

Simultaneously, she wrote articles published in Australia about Europe. She reported on European culture—the latest developments in art, literature and the theatre—and the latest philosophical theories. She reported on the radical issues of the day: experiments in collectivist living, Communism, moves towards reform of divorce laws, and cremation. She also wrote on charitable works among the poor, who always engaged her sympathy. Through her articles, her readers in far-off Australia could feel part of the intellectual world of Europe.

Her achievements reached their peak in 1894 when she became Brussels correspondent for the London *Times*, an extremely prestigious, demanding and unusual position for a woman. In other accounts of her life, it is dimissively stated that she took over the correspondent's position held by her second husband, following his death. The London *Times*, however, regarded its foreign correspondents as an élite group, and jealously guarded their standing and reputation. Tasma had to fight hard to be appointed correspondent in Brussels, and the demands of the position took a great toll on her health. Nevertheless, she was so successful that Holland, where there was previously no *Times* correspondent, was added to her domain. She reported not only domestic news, but the crises of Belgian involvement in King Leopold's colony, the Congo. She also became a participant in one of the great intrigues of British colonialism, the Jameson Raid.

Tasma lived the life of a 'New Woman', the independent woman then beginning to appear both in real life and fiction, one who refused to conform to a traditional female role, and who questioned conventional ideas on marriage and the male oriented view of society in which women had been entrapped. For six years before her second marriage she lived an independent life in Paris, earning her own living, and involved in the radical issues of the day. She was not a woman 'to hide the light of her militant Radicalism under a bushel', an interviewer wrote. When pressed to talk about her method of writing novels she spoke instead of the latest developments in collectivism, and made 'an impassioned plea for the poor'.[11]

Tasma's interest in and great knowledge of European art and literature, and of philosophical, political and scientific theories, came from her upbringing in an unusual family of Flemish, English and French ancestry. Her mother in particular had a passion for teaching, and venerated European culture. When she finally succeeded, in taking most of her children from Australia to Europe, it was not the standard overseas trip of a well-to-do Australian family intent on 'doing' the Old World. The Huybers family returned in Europe to their roots. Ever after, they found the ties inescapable.

As a young woman in the early 1870s, Tasma attended a meeting on the issue of women's education in London. Straight from her colonial upbringing, she instinctively held more advanced views on the right of women to education than the distinguished speakers on the platform. Like her mother, an independent-minded, forceful woman, she was even then in the vanguard of thought concerning women's rights.

A few years later Tasma was to write a vehement defence of women who killed husbands or lovers who had mistreated them over prolonged periods. Her arguments, presented over a hundred years ago, were on a subject that is still topical today.[12]

In her novels and other writing she often expressed antagonism to 'Mrs Grundy', the narrow-minded character excessively attached to conventional behaviour who became a short-hand way of expressing disapproval of unconventional behaviour after she was introduced in Thomas Morton's 1798 play *Speed the Plough*. In her own life, Jessie was to find Mrs Grundys just as active in Brussels as in Australia. She felt at ease in Paris, because there she could live free from the notice and admonitions of such women. The Left Bank was a place where everyone did as they pleased, and from where they went where they pleased. 'There could be no Mrs Grundy where people did not even acknowledge the existence of that formidable abstraction.'[13]

Her ultimate defiance of Mrs Grundy was to obtain a divorce from her first husband. This was at a time when Victorian laws made it almost impossible for a woman to sue for divorce, and when it was so socially unacceptable that the number of divorces granted in the colony in any one year was rarely above single figures.

Tasma's novels also had heroines who defied convention or questioned existing attitudes. In *Uncle Piper of Piper's Hill* (1889), Laura Lydiat, the forerunner of women characters in her other novels whose interests were intellectual and cultural, questioned the institution of marriage. Portia Morrisson in *The Penance of Portia James* (1891) ran away from her husband. Linda Robley in *A Knight of the White Feather* (1892) gave lectures on Positivism in country halls in Victoria. Eila Frost in *Not Counting the Cost* (1895) attempted to support herself and questioned conventional moral standards. Tasma's heroines were intellectual women interested in art, literature and philosophical ideas. They rebelled against the philistine attitudes of the men in their lives, interested only in horseracing and gambling. But none rebelled as much as Tasma herself.

From Laura Lydiat in *Uncle Piper of Piper's Hill*, who hated the idea of marriage but eventually married George Piper; Pauline Drafton who, although tempted to leave her husband, was reconciled to him (*In Her Earliest Youth*); Portia, who returned to her philandering husband in *The Penance of Portia James*; to Linda Robley in *A Knight of the White Feather*, Eila Frost in *Not Counting the Cost*, and Ruth Fenton in *A Fiery Ordeal* (1897), all of whose husbands die, her heroines decide against or are saved from having to take the drastic steps Tasma took in her own life.

I began following Tasma's life with not much more than a sketchy outline of her childhood, her two marriages, her achievements in journalism and lecturing, and an acquaintance with her novels. I found it exciting to discover details of her family background in England and her childhood in Hobart. I found the background of the man she married so hastily at the age of eighteen, and discovered that her life as Mrs Charles Fraser was by no means confined to Kyneton and Malmsbury in Victoria. She lived also on the Murray, at Oakville, and at Ebden House in Collins Street, Melbourne. I discovered her brief connection with Queensland, and the important part her brother-in-law William Degraves played in her early married life.

Once Tasma began her public career as a lecturer, then became an acclaimed novelist and achieved a prestigious position as a journalist, there were more public records to follow. It was exciting to discover in European newspapers and other places records of her previously unknown lectures,

Introduction

articles and stories. There was even a translation of a book from English to French, on American federalism.

Often by following hints, I have discovered many aspects of Tasma's life not previously known. There remain gaps, however, in discovering her motivation and reactions at important moments in her life. Why, for instance, did she marry Charles Fraser, who proved so incompatible? Why did she leave him and then return, temporarily, three years later? For some periods of Tasma's life there is no direct evidence of her personal life, apart from laconic and scanty reports from her young diarist brother, Edward.

Two notable exceptions are the periods for which her diaries exist. The first is the diary of a young woman, which she kept during her voyage to Europe on the *Windward* in 1873. It was a memorable day when I was handed this previously unknown diary. The second is the diary of a sophisticated woman, by then a successful author with triumphs as a public speaker behind her, which she kept in Brussels in 1889–90.

When I began researching Tasma's life and sought information from descendants of her sisters and brothers they directed me to her novels. *Not Counting the Cost* is the story of the Huybers family, they said. Madame Delaunay of *In Her Earliest Youth* is Grandma Huybers. George Piper, George Drafton, and so on *are* Charles Fraser. It is unfair to Tasma's talent to take her fiction so literally as a recreation of aspects of her life. Nevertheless, the parallels between some of her characters and the situations she describes and her own life became more striking the more I discovered about her. Without wishing to compromise her creative ability I have included in different chapters speculation concerning possible correlations between the reactions of her characters and her own thoughts and emotions at particular moments in her life.

There are some aspects of Tasma's personality that remain elusive, if not contradictory. She was an important public figure acclaimed both as a novelist and a lecturer, yet her confidence in her ability was easily fractured. A woman of great charm and beauty, she was constrained during the years she was separated from Charles Fraser, but still legally married, to confine herself to superficial relationships with men. She had many admirers and herself sought and welcomed the admiration and company of men. But she remained wary of entanglements. It is doubtful whether her second marriage brought any fundamental change to this long habit of wariness. It is possible to suggest that she never forgot or in fact overcame the traumas of her first marriage; that despite the public acclaim for her great achievements and the relative security of her second marriage she had been damaged by her first, and by the strain of the following years when she led an independent life in the most insecure of environments. Was this the cause of the ennui, the tiredness with life, the incapacity for deep feeling, upon which she often commented?

This book is a life of Tasma. It is not a study of her literary works although it records her great public success as a novelist. *Uncle Piper of Piper's Hill*, an inspired portrayal of the life she had observed in Melbourne among the *nouveau riche* of the post-goldrush era, remains Tasma's most successful novel. It has been reprinted twice in the twentieth century, in 1969 and 1987, and was listed among the 101 best Australian novels in the *Bulletin* in 1991.[14] Tasma's other novels have for nearly a century been unavailable except in major libraries, and her articles have never been collected.

1

How magnificently well my dear one taught Koozee and Eddie

London, Hobart, 1848–66

In a section of her novel *Not Counting the Cost*, Tasma described a boisterous escapade on the slopes of Knocklofty, a hill on the outskirts of Hobart, the capital of Tasmania, in the 1860s. The family in the novel, the Clares, live at Cowa, a rambling property on the side of one of the steep hills clustered around Mount Wellington. Below the house the blue waters of the Derwent estuary glisten in the sunlight. Haystacks scatter the great paddock, which slopes down to a rough mountain road leading through straggling outskirts to Hobart lying in a hollow below. Beyond the town, mountains hedge the broad harbour.

In the bright summer sun of Christmas week a group of young people run wild. With shrieks and jumps they emerge from haystacks tumbled and dishevelled, their hair full of straw, like a tribe of gypsies. The eldest, Eila, a girl of nineteen, encases the other children, Willie, the twins Dick and Mamy, and the youngest, Truca,[1] in bundles of hay and at the signal: 'Bell-horses, bell-horses, what time of day/One o'clock, two o'clock, three and . . .', the bundles give convulsive jerks and roll down the steep hill. To Eila's horror they show no sign of coming to a stop when they reach the level ground at the bottom of the paddock. As she races down the slope after them, they stop within a few feet of the rubble wall which divides the paddock from the road below. When she catches up with them, they tell her not to be so concerned.[2]

As the sun glows in the late afternoon, they gather at a haystack to eat strawberries swimming in thick cream. With the touch of unconventionality that distinguishes the Clares from their conformist friends and acquaintances, Mamy serves the strawberries in soup plates from a soup tureen. Later, they gather on the verandah at Cowa to eat a 'delightful and scrambly tea' of hot scones, eggs, jam and dough cake.[3]

Eila, like Tasma, is a tall, dark-eyed, vital young woman. Her description fits her creator's. She has 'rich colouring', 'magnificent dark hair', and a 'peculiar dusky darkness of the eyes, a certain heavy-lidded, thick-lashed environment' recalling the oriental Lalla Rookh or Byron's 'Bride of Abydos'.[4] She has an 'untamed suppleness and elasticity, more Oriental than English' and the 'spring and elasticity' of a kangaroo as she runs headlong down the slope after the others with 'a freedom of movement' of 'an undeniable grace'.[5] Like Tasma, she has an engrained devotion to her younger brothers and sisters. She has a willingness to ' "fetch and carry" to the little ones of the family', so that from their birth 'she never thought of revolting at their commands'.[6]

Not Counting the Cost was written many years after Tasma left Tasmania to live half a world away from the wild beauty of the home of her childhood. Yet the memories of her family and Hobart summers remained vivid. This recreated scene of happy, boisterous family life represents an idyllic aspect of Tasma's childhood and adolescence. Other aspects, however, were to cast dark shadows.

It was an important moment in researching this book to discover Highfield, the country home of the Huybers family on the outskirts of the Hobart city area. I stood beside the house and looked down over house tops to the Derwent below. I saw the resemblance to the paddocks at Cowa, the name Tasma gave to the country residence in *Not Counting the Cost*, and in her short story 'An Old Time Episode in Tasmania'.

The woman who was to become the famous novelist, writer, lecturer and foreign correspondent Tasma was born Jessie Catherine Huybers, on 28 October 1848, at Southwood Lodge, Southwood Lane, in Highgate, north London.[7] Now set in closely settled suburbia, Southwood Lodge was then a substantial home on the northern outskirts of London, surrounded by a few acres of land. Then it faced Southwood Lane, a thoroughfare since medieval times leading north from Highgate to Muswell Hill past Highgate Common and through woods on either side. Now, with its entrance on the opposite side of the house, it faces a suburban street, Kingsley Close; this was introduced during subdivision in 1968.[8] Then and now Southwood Lodge was situated on a commanding rise overlooking Hampstead Heath. Looking east on a clear day there is nothing between it and the European coast.[9]

The size of Southwood Lodge, a substantial, three-storeyed, almost square Georgian house, its full-length windows flooding the house with light and air, belied the status of Jessie's parents. The family had moved there before Jessie's birth from the inner London suburb of Shoreditch so that her mother Charlotte, who had a passion for teaching, would have room to run a school. Charlotte was a woman of unusual talent and intellect with a great love of learning, a wide-ranging interest in ideas, a devotion to

European literature, art and music, and a single-minded and independent character. She was the child of an English father, Charles Ogleby, and a French mother, Marie Adelaide, the daughter of an emigré family, her father, Captain de Troye, having fled from Paris during the Revolution.[10] Jessie's mother, Charlotte Sophia Ogleby, was born on 11 November 1817 at Caroline Place, St Pancras, Co. Middlesex, and baptised in the Anglican Church on 14 February 1818 at St Pancras Old Church.[11]

Charles Ogleby was a wine and spirits merchant at Salvadore House, Bishopsgate Street, a business in which he was in partnership with the wealthy Edward Simeon, brother of the baronet, Sir John Simeon, Member of Parliament and Senior Master of the Court of Chancery. When Edward Simeon died on 14 December 1812, he left the very substantial sum of £5000 to Charles Ogleby.[12] The size of this legacy added to the family belief that Charles Ogleby had stronger ties to the Simeon family than mutual business interests. Charlotte was brought up believing in this aristocratic relationship and imparted this belief to her children. Tasma was to use a fictional version of a story about searching for a long-lost rich relative in her novel, *Not Counting the Cost*. Charlotte's youngest daughter, Edith, wrote many years later that 'there existed some near relationship between the Simeon family and Mother's father—probably a left-handed one, or it would have been more openly acknowledged . . . No one could doubt the aristocratic origin of our Mother.'[13]

After Edward Simeon's death, Charles Ogleby continued his mercantile business at Bishopsgate, under the name of Charles Ogleby and Co. In the late 1820s, he moved it and the residence of his family to 7 Lambeth Terrace, Vauxhall on the south bank of the Thames, expanding the business from importing to the manufacture of candles, sealing wax and similar goods, and the refining of whale oil.[14]

Charles Ogleby placed enormous importance on the education of his children. Unusually for the early nineteenth century, he extended this concern to his daughter, Charlotte. Apparently because his business frequently took him out of the country, he placed her at Mrs Swinny's Seminary in Queen Street, Milton, near Gravesend when she was very young. In a letter dated 22 April 1824, Charles Ogleby told his six-year-old daughter that he and her mother would visit her very soon, and bring her favourite doll. He prayed that Charlotte would 'learn all that is required'.[15]

This and subsequent experiences at boarding schools had a lasting effect on Charlotte, who was to keep her own daughters away from both day and boarding schools, teaching them entirely herself. While Charlotte was still a young child, she spent some years living with her mother and younger brother Richard at Neuilly, on the outskirts of Paris, a move apparently made to advance the education of the children, since Richard later returned to Paris to complete his education.[16] Charlotte ever after was to speak and

3

write French as easily as she did English, and to have a passion for French culture.

When she was fourteen, she visited Sir Richard and Lady Simeon at their Isle of Wight estate. Richard Simeon had succeeded to the baronetcy in 1824, and through his marriage to Louisa Barrington, heiress of Sir Fitzwilliam Barrington of Barrington Hall, Essex and of Swainston on the Isle of Wight, had acquired the Barrington estates.[17] For Charlotte, one of the attractions of the Isle of Wight was the opportunity for sea bathing, which her father thought improved her 'good looks'. Until an advanced age Charlotte was to love swimming in the sea, and she passed this love on to her daughter Jessie in an age when it was an unusual pursuit for women. In a letter to his daughter, Charles Ogleby expressed his pleasure about her stay with the Simeons. The major part of his letter, however, was about the need for Charlotte to study hard when she returned to her boarding school at Ryde. '[G]et on with your German for I wish you to know that Language absolutely & if you were inclined to work hard I would go to the expense of your giving a twelvemonth to a little Latin which would give you such a command of all Grammar as would enable you to learn Italian by yourself. In short Dear Girl you must now work—indeed you must—seriously you must . . .'[18]

Very few girls in the 1820s in England would have received such encouragement to study. It was more usual to regard mental activity as detrimental to their health. Doctors had developed theories that reading and writing interfered with women's reproductive functions, causing their uteruses to atrophy.[19] Even as late as 1874, a well-known mental specialist, Dr Maudsley, declared that study was 'the cause of ill-health in women' and made them unfit for 'their duties as women'.[20] Charlotte's children were to inherit from her the devotion to learning that she had absorbed from her father.

When Charles Ogleby became ill in 1832, Sir Richard Simeon wrote offering help to him and his family.[21] After his death on 1 February 1833, he invited Charlotte to stay on the Isle of Wight. Following her father's death at Lambert Terrace, Charlotte inherited one-third of his estate, in addition to a £700 insurance policy left to her in trust by her late godmother, Jane Johnson.[22] Although this may have been sufficient money to live on, Charlotte appears to have worked as a governess, schoolmistress or proprietor of a small school from the time of her father's death, when she was fifteen, until her marriage at the age of twenty-eight.[23] She met her future husband, James Alfred Huybers, a native of Antwerp, while both were teaching at Great Stanmore, Middlesex, north-west of London.

Alfred's foreign birth did not disquiet Charlotte, with her mixed ancestry, her knowledge of languages and her interest in European culture. On 8 July 1846 Charlotte Sophia Ogleby married James Alfred Huybers, tutor, aged thirty-five, at the Parish Church of St John Evangelist, Stanmore.[24] Just before her marriage, Edward Simeon, brother of the second baronet, Sir Richard Simeon, heir of his uncle Edward Simeon of Salvadore House, Bishopsgate, and childless from his two marriages, wrote to Charlotte telling her he intended to leave her £1000 in his will.[25]

Charlotte's husband, Jacques (James) Alfred Huybers had been born on 23 April 1811 at Anvers (Antwerp), then part of Holland. From 1830, it was part of the new country of Belgium. He was the son of Jean Baptiste Huybers of Bergyek and his wife, formerly Anne Marie Lauwers, of Boom in the province of Antwerp.[26] The Huybers reputedly had been merchants and mariners for generations.[27] As a young man Alfred went to live in London, where he worked as a tutor, later as a clerk in a mercantile house and then as an agent for imported wines.[28]

During the next four years, Charlotte and Alfred had three children. They were William Charles Alfred, born at Shoreditch on 16 April 1847, where Alfred Huybers worked as a clerk,[29] Jessie at Southwood Lodge, Highgate and Robert Peel in 1850 at the same place. At Southwood Lodge, Charlotte ran a small boarding school. At the 1851 Census, she had six female pupils, aged ten to fifteen. Alfred Huybers's older sister, Thérèsa, aged forty-five, was an assistant French teacher, and Martha Harris an assistant teacher. Three servants, a nurse, a cook and a housemaid made up the household of sixteen, including the three Huybers children.[30]

If Jessie retained any memories of Southwood Lodge they would have been of her mother teaching her to read and to play the piano on the instrument Charlotte had inherited from her mother. Her lessons would have proceeded to the sound of a multiplicity of languages, her mother's English and French, her father's Flemish, French and English, and the German of both. While Charlotte ran her school, Alfred Huybers began a business as a wine agent, perhaps in conjunction with his brother-in-law, David Morian, husband of his sister Adèle, who lived in Brussels.[31]

The Huybers family's circumstances altered with the death of the younger Edward Simeon of Carshalton House, Surrey on 16 October 1851, at the age of sixty-three. As he had promised, Simeon left a legacy of £1000 from his very extensive estate to Charlotte Huybers.[32] This large sum (probably equivalent to between $100,000 and $200,000 at today's values), paid to Charlotte in July 1852, enabled the Huybers to think about their future.

As a wine trader and with his experience in a merchant's business, it was not surprising that Alfred Huybers should look to the Australian colonies as a place to establish a similar business. It is extraordinary, however, that he should choose Tasmania, then known as Van Diemen's Land, instead of Victoria. News of the amazingly rich gold discoveries at Ballarat and Bendigo in Victoria had been reported in the English press from late in 1851, and within months innumerable ships crowded with eager gold seekers were on their way to the El Dorado of the Southern Hemisphere. None of this influenced Alfred Huybers: perhaps he chose Van

Diemen's Land because of some now-forgotten link with the colony. He certainly believed it would be a good place in which to bring up a family.[33] Whatever the reasons for the choice, Huybers was to find Hobart the most congenial of homes, and was to resist, to within a few days of his death at an advanced age, many opportunities to move.

While Charlotte Huybers's legacy probably provided some of the means for the family to emigrate, she almost certainly was not responsible for choosing Hobart as their destination. She was shocked at the small and primitive town she found, and was never happy at being anchored in an outpost far from the treasures of European civilisation. She was to regard her life in the colonies as exile, and brought up her children to hold a similar view. Although it was to be many years before she succeeded, she was to grasp the first opportunity to escape with most of them from the narrow society of Hobart. Her attitude to her colonial exile was to have a deep and lasting effect on most of her children.

With her black hair hanging in long corkscrew curls and her imperious black eyes, Charlotte must have been a striking figure as she stepped ashore in Hobart from the *Australasia* on 5 December 1852.[34] With her were her husband and three children, Willie, aged five, Jessie, four, Robert, two, and Alfred's sister, Thérèsa. In the cargo, Alfred Huybers brought seventy-five cases of French and Flemish wine, and substantial quantities of liqueurs, sherry, brandy and rum, with which he began to trade in one of the large Georgian stone warehouses in Davey Street, near the wharves. Charlotte brought with her a striking portrait of her aristocratic-looking father dressed in a black velvet coat. This was to occupy a place of honour in her home, just as the painting of the Chevalier does in *Not Counting the Cost*. Charlotte brought her piano and cases of the books she was to use to educate her children, and also brought the wicker coffin that was to accompany her ever after on all her journeys.

The wicker coffin was the first indication to Hobart residents that a true eccentric had joined them. Charlotte had a fear of being buried alive, and a horror of being left to rot after death in an enclosed coffin causing 'emanations' generally supposed to be a cause of epidemic disease. These ideas were not unusual at the time, but few took their fear to the extreme of keeping a wicker coffin within reach. In Hobart, Charlotte's coffin rested beneath her bed. She was to accommodate her fear of being buried alive by specifying that her carotid artery must be cut before her death was announced. Like her other beliefs and attitudes, her attitude to death was to influence her children.

Many years later, Jessie told an interviewer that at the age of seven or eight she had developed a terror of eternity. Becoming tired of playing, she thought, 'one tired of everything', and 'even if one went to heaven and were told there was no stop to it, the terror would make one want to be out of existence. But how to get out of it—how rid oneself of the nightmare of eternity?' The interviewer commented:

> The impression of that moment of dread realisation has left its traces on 'Tasma's' mature work. In a fine passage she describes how on a starlight Australian night, moonless and cloudless, the sense of the black abyss of space sown with suns and systems is borne in upon the mind, and 'we almost feel ourselves giddily sweeping on in a sort of vast monotony; a dread of foreshadowing of eternity appals us, and we want to cling to something helpless as ourselves, if it will only reassure us against our own thoughts'.[35]

This crushing fear of eternity, which had its roots in her mother's fears of death, was to remain a nightmare for Jessie to the end of her life.[36]

She retained only dim memories of the sailing ship on which the family spent three and a half months travelling to Hobart. She had clearer memories of the gangs of convicts with their clanking chains she saw as she walked through the streets of Hobart,[37] the 'lifers' in their dingy yellow jackets chained to carts, the shorter-term men in grey. The Huybers children watched them breaking stones and studied the hardened lines of their faces 'in many instances furrowed with age and an expression set in that peculiar mould—half-fierce and half-sullen—which proclaimed the discipline and privations of prison life . . .'. On afternoon walks, their nurses whispered about terrible events and punishments that had occurred at Port Arthur, the chief convict settlement, and the children wondered which of the prisoners had been involved.[38]

Charlotte thought Hobart was a place fit only for savages. Footpaths were unpaved, there was no organised disposal of sewage, and the streets were dimly lit by lamps fuelled by whale oil.[39] She was horrified at the lack of baths in the houses, and had one built in the backyard.

On 9 August 1853, her fourth child, Maria Theresa (always known as Koozee), was born at Davey Street, eight months after their arrival. Less than three weeks later her third child Robert, aged three, died of scarlet fever in one of the epidemics that ravaged the town. [40] So threatening was the disease that a quarantine post was set up to stop people from infected houses travelling north.[41]

Charlotte had several more children. On 21 July 1855, Edward Alfred was born at Davey Street. Shortly after his birth the family moved a block or so up from the wharves to 4 Trafalgar Place, off Macquarie Street, within sight of the old Hobart Gaol where prisoners were still hung in public view. There Francis Alfred Huybers was born, on 7 March 1858, when Charlotte was forty, and John Alfred Huybers on 5 November 1859, when she a few days short of forty-two. Her last child, Edith Charlotte, was born at Murray Street on 9 June 1861, the year in which Charlotte turned forty-four years of age.

At the end of 1859, the family moved to Cleburne House in Murray

Street, one of the largest houses in Hobart. The three-storey building contained substantial living quarters at the front and a store at the back, the higher levels being accessed by pulleys. Alongside the entrance from Murray Street were large iron gates supported by stone pillars. On these sat two distinctive wood-carved figures known as the Cleburne lions, a delight to the Huybers children. Behind the gates there was an extensive garden with two walnut trees, reputed to be the largest in the colony.[42]

At one time Alfred Huybers's warehousing and merchant's business was the largest in Tasmania. His business flourishing, the family's life was one of ease and refinement. Cleburne House was furnished in a grand manner, with imported mahogany chairs, rosewood tables, marble flower stands and a grand piano. There were handsome carpets and rugs, the walls were hung with oil paintings and watercolours, there were clocks and ornaments in bronze and marble and the dining room was lined with three large bookcases packed with books.[43]

Numerous servants were employed. Nursemaids took the children for walks down Murray Street past old St David's with its Gothic tower, to the new wharf near Salamanca Place, and around to the crabpots at Battery Point. Coming back they walked past a paddock of gum trees, later Franklin Square, then stopped in the city to buy jam tarts and glance hurriedly at a dilapidated landmark known as Rats' Castle, a haunt of derelict and homeless people. On other days they would walk to the Domain, then known as the 'paddock', or to the stone steps at the top of Davey Street. Often they would pass on the way one of Hobart's six postmen, dressed in their red jackets, or stop to look as the guard on one of Page's coaches sounded a brass bugle outside the post office before setting off for Launceston.[44]

With their financial position assured, Charlotte probably felt there was no need to run a school as she had in England. Her frequent childbearing and the education of her own seven children in any case would have left her little time. She had no intention of leaving them to the mercies of a colonial education and had come prepared to offer the artistic, literary and cultural education that would have been available in Europe. In addition to reference books, she had more than three hundred volumes in French of the works of the greatest French novelists, dramatists and philosophers, the complete works of English writers from Shakespeare to George Eliot, and volumes on history, painting and many other subjects.[45]

Charlotte's children regarded her as a strict, authoritarian teacher. Her teaching methods dated from the early Victorian age.[46] 'Insist on a certain amount being read and understood, and a summary of it written from memory', she wrote.[47] Family stories tell of John quaking when he saw his mother getting the French grammars out of the sideboard drawer, and all the children feared her raps on their knuckles as they learnt to play the piano. It was probably with relief that the boys went, at their father's

8

insistence, one by one to Hutchins School. William did not go until he was thirteen, in 1861, Edward in 1865, Frank in 1866 and John in 1868. Under its first headmaster, the Reverend John Richard Buckland it, too, was renowned for strictness.

The girls were taught entirely at home, Charlotte's experience having left her with very decided views about girls' schools. 'I have never seen a private school ([E]nglish) yet where I would place a child of mine', she wrote.[48] Despite her strict methods her children grew up with a love of learning, an openness towards new ideas and philosophies, a great attraction towards intellectual argument, vivid imaginations and unusual talents in many of the arts, particularly drawing, painting, music, dancing and writing.

Jessie was nearly thirteen when her youngest sister was born. Already she had absorbed so much from her mother that she had taken over much of the teaching of the younger children. Many years later, Charlotte wrote of Jessie, '[H]ow magnificently well my dear one taught Koozee and Eddie, and who had taught Jessie?'[49] Most of all, Jessie imparted to them her own love of storytelling and make-believe. Her stories, like those told by Eila in *Not Counting the Cost*, may well have been of 'adventures on desert islands' and 'wonderful narratives of giants' making their hair 'tingle at the roots.'[50] Like Eila she may have transformed Hobart into an imaginary city with magnificent palaces and churches—an indication of the European orientation not only of Charlotte's teaching, but of all colonial education. Ever after, her brothers and sisters regarded with awe Jessie's ability to turn ordinary surroundings into imaginative wonderlands.[51]

For the benefit of the youngest child in the family, Edith, a particular favourite, Jessie created a make-believe method of imparting knowledge. Hidden behind a curtain, Jessie would report to her sister interviews with mysterious postmen who brought descriptions of distant lands and seas. A postman dressed in yellow spoke in a high falsetto key; the scarlet one was loud and formidable; the blue postman was urbane and kindly. Sometimes the visitors would leave letters addressed to Edith. According to the same article in which this reminiscence appeared, Jessie's imaginative childhood 'drew its nurture chiefly from the beauty of nature and from her omnivorous reading. A touch of morbidness might have lurked in her exuberant fancy and impaired its healthy development but for the benign influences around her'. This pleasure in informing others, one of the strongest delights of her girlhood, was to help Jessie overcome the agonies of nervousness she suffered before beginning to give public lectures in later life. After a few minutes 'the old pleasure to amuse and inform others' would reassert itself.[52]

Not surprisingly, with Charlotte's teaching centred on Europe, Jessie's imaginary world was peopled by characters from faraway lands. However, she also absorbed, as her adult writing was to show, a love of the physical surroundings of her childhood and an appreciation of the history taking place around her.

Charlotte was an unconventional mother. Her son, Eddie, the family diarist, described her as 'what the average person calls "peculiar" ' with a 'want of mental balance in dealing with the ordinary affairs of life'. 'There were two ways of doing everything in the world, whether of reading, dancing, eating, sleeping, even breathing', he wrote, 'my mother's way and the way of the outside world; hers was the right way, the world's was the wrong way'.[53] Although her ways were autocratic, her dinners might not be on time, and her housekeeping erratic, Charlotte was, however, at the centre of all the wide-ranging discussions around the table, and visitors flocked to her home to talk with her.

Jessie, who had a little of her father's conformity in her character, was the one who urged Charlotte to maintain minimal social conventions, to return social calls, maybe to 'tie her bonnet-strings according to the prevailing fashion'.[54] Jessie conformed to colonial mores by taking the younger children to Sunday School and, for a time, teaching a class herself,[55] before she developed doubts about religion and became an agnostic. Alfred Huybers, kindly, orderly and regular in his habits, also unobtrusively kept the family to a routine.

Despite their mother's unconventional behaviour, the family's social position was assured by Alfred Huybers's continuing success in his business, and his acceptance into the very small world of government officials and business and professional men who made up the social hierarchy of Hobart. Some of his friends were merchants, others lawyers and schoolmasters. The brilliant John Julius Stutzer, 'the most finished scholar who ever visited Australia', whose father had been a friend of the Oglebys in London,[56] and who after losing a fortune on a venture in the Crimea had settled in Hobart to become an inspector of schools, was a great friend of Alfred Huybers. On Sundays he and Alfred would sit in the Cleburne garden smoking their cigars as the bells of St David's chimed a few blocks away. Other friends were merchant Lavington Roope, the Consul for Portugal; lawyer Charles Butler; lawyer T.J. Knight, Member of the Legislative Council, then of the Assembly and, briefly, Attorney-General; liquor merchant Richard Reeves; schoolmaster T.P. Cowle; and lawyer and parliamentarian Francis Smith.[57]

In 1861, Alfred Huybers and several of his friends were among the 'leaders of life in Hobart or Southern Tasmania' who founded the exclusive Tasmanian Club. The first president was Francis Smith (later knighted), a former Premier and later Chief Justice.[58] The new governor, Colonel Thomas Gore Browne, who arrived in December 1861, often visited the club and members were entertained at Government House.

Jessie and the Gore Brownes' daughter Mabel became friends. Mabel was often at Cleburne House and the Huybers children were often at Government House, Jessie to ride with Mabel, and the younger children to attend drill and dancing lessons. Charlotte's theatrical ability and also her children's made them welcome as participants at private theatricals staged at Government House by the well-known author, Louisa Meredith, and others. Charlotte 'took a prominent part'. Her 'playing and acting were always looked upon as very uncommon', her son wrote.[59] No records remain of the parts Jessie played in these theatricals, but she must have made her mark in acting or writing material for plays, since in 1864 Louisa Meredith took 'a great fancy to Jessie (as has been the case with everybody else)', and took her to her bush home, Twamley, for a long holiday.[60] By then Louisa Meredith was famous in Hobart and known in the other Australian colonies as the author of several books of social reportage, including *Notes and Sketches of New South Wales* (1844), *My Home in Tasmania, during a Residence of Nine Years* (1852), *Over the Straits, a Visit to Victoria* (1861), and the first of her series of books on the plants and animals of Tasmania, *Some of my Bush Friends in Tasmania* (1860). While Parliament was sitting, the Merediths lived in Hobart, where her husband Charles Meredith was a member of the House of Assembly. During recesses they returned to Twamley, an isolated house built in a forest at Prosser's Plains, to the north-east of Hobart. It was to be fifteen years before Jessie was to achieve lasting success with her own writing, but it is impossible to overestimate the importance of this friendship between the fifty-year-old woman person-ifying the successful woman author, and the fifteen-year-old girl already possessed of an overflowing imagination.

When she was seventeen Jessie took her third sea trip. As well as her journey to Australia, she had accompanied her father on a business trip to Sydney at the age of twelve. This time she travelled to Melbourne in charge of her ten-year-old brother Eddie, to visit her eldest brother, Willie. In 1865 when he was eighteen, Willie, the stable, practical family member, had left school and gone to Melbourne to join the office of Alfred Wilkins, who had become Alfred Huybers's partner three years previously. Though not prepared to leave Hobart himself, Alfred Huybers saw a Melbourne office as a means of escaping the severe economic depression in Tasmania, and tapping a much larger market. Melbourne, although not as prosperous as in the boom days of the early 1850s, was a great metropolis compared with Hobart, with its population of only 25 000.

Nothing is known of Jessie's impressions of Melbourne over Christmas 1865. But no doubt she had instructions from her mother to go to the theatre and visit the recently opened Public Library, Museum and Art Gallery. To Eddie, Melbourne was a 'great' city; 'it represented London, Paris and New York, all rolled into one'.[61]

On the way home, they had a great adventure. Travelling on the *Derwent* which, after leaving Melbourne on 3 February 1866, steamed down the wild west coast of Tasmania, Jessie and Eddie were nearly shipwrecked when the ship ran into Needle Rock at the most southerly point of the island. Water came rushing into the saloon as the doors flew open. The seventy passengers, including over thirty members of the Lyster Opera Company, rushed for the boats. Eddie wrote:

> My sister, always calm in danger, helped me to dress and remained absolutely impassive, awaiting the call to go on deck, should the vessel be sinking . . . [and she] continued to hold [my] hand, as the screams of terror-stricken women and prayers of the emotional filled the saloon.[62]

Suddenly, however, the captain regained control, the engines were reversed, and the ship slid off the rock.[63]

Epidemic illnesses continued to plague Hobart. While still attending Hutchins School, Willie was striken by fever and most of the rest of the family moved to stay with the Cowles, and later with the Reeves family, to avoid the risk of disease spreading. In 1866, John and Edith caught fever and after their recovery the family went to live at the Roopes for a time.[64] That year, Alfred Huybers bought Highfield on the western outskirts of the town, where his family could spend the summer months high above the polluted drains and air of the capital.

Highfield was a property of five acres, three roods beginning at the end of Upper Goulburn Street and bounded by Knocklofty Terrace, Poet's Road, Salvator Road (then known as Salvator Rosa Glen) and an adjoining property to the west, later known as Barton Vale.[65] The main house, situated on a steep rise with a commanding view of the Derwent and the town below, was an imposing stone residence of nine rooms. In the grounds at the Upper Goulburn Street end was a smaller manager's cottage, Hillside, and at the back were six-stall stables, a coach house and other outbuildings and large iron tanks holding a plentiful supply of water. The garden was stocked with fruit trees and there were three grazing paddocks. The situation was described as 'most salubrious' in 'to let' advertisements inserted in the Mercury by Mrs Harriet King, widow of Captain George King, RN, port officer at Hobart, a former owner.[66] Huybers bought the property from Marcus Walpole Loane, farmer of North Down, Port Sorell on 17 July 1866 for £700.[67]

While his family moved to Highfield for the summer months, Alfred Huybers continued living at Cleburne House in Murray Street, in effect dividing the family. The marriage of Charlotte and Alfred, happy during their first years in Hobart,[68] deteriorated during the early 1860s into constant quarrelling. Charlotte's frequent childbearing in her early forties may have been a reason. Like the majority of women of the time she was probably ignorant of the few and relatively ineffective contraceptive measures, and may have deeply feared a further pregnancy. By 1866 it was becoming impossible for Charlotte and Alfred to live harmoniously under one roof. Added to the strains of the marriage appears to have been the arrival in the household in 1863 of a servant, Rebecca Chance, who joined the Huybers after having worked in the home of their friends, the Murray

Burgesses. It seems probable that Alfred Huybers at some stage formed an association with her which continued until his death in 1893.[69]

At Highfield, the Huybers family were soon running a small farm supplying their own milk, eggs and meat, and living an idyllic existence similar to that Tasma described in *Not Counting the Cost*. Behind them Mount Wellington was a challenge and a mystery. It became a rite of passage for the adolescent children to climb to the top while suppressing fears that they might encounter escaped convicts and bushrangers. As Jessie was to write, the eons-old Mount Wellington in the few years since the arrival of Europeans had witnessed the destruction of almost the entire race of Tasmanian Aborigines, and watched 'goaded convicts hiding like rats in holes and caves, and runaway prisoners hunted to their doom'.[70]

Highfield became the centre for the exuberant physical life that the family loved. They walked on the mountain, boated and crabbed on the Derwent, rode and played over the paddocks, milked cows and fed animals, combining all this activity with omnivorous reading and interminable family discussions on such a range of subjects that visitors were bemused. Like the Clare family in *Not Counting the Cost*, the Huybers no doubt developed 'a fondness for the wild hills, the great sloping paddocks, the haystacks, the apple-trees, the cows, the pigs, the dogs, the fowls, and the flowers'.[71] But they were also under the constant influence of Charlotte's deepest feeling—that she must escape from Hobart. Where? 'Why, Home with a capital "H", of course. England—Europe, that is to say. What other home is there?'[72] as one of the Clare children tells a visitor in *Not Counting the Cost*.

2

She committed the crowning error of her life

Hobart, 1867

Charlotte Huybers's plan for escaping with her children from the narrow colonial life of Hobart back to the great centres of European civilisation was shattered when her 'best beloved child',[1] Jessie, fell in love.

When Jessie met Charles Fraser during the late summer of 1867, he was a handsome, dashing man of twenty-five, already with a reputation as a horseman, amateur jockey, and breeder of racehorses. He was one of the visitors, including naval officers, heirs to English estates and wealthy mainland squatters, who descended on Hobart in the summer months, an exciting addition to the lists of eligible men. They came for the regatta or the races or, in the case of Charles Fraser, to ride in competitions and visit his family and the friends of his youth. He was on holidays from his position at Kyneton in Victoria, as manager of his brother-in-law's flour mill.

To Jessie's father, Alfred Huybers, Charles Fraser was a suitor from an eminently suitable family. He was the youngest child of Major James Fraser, formerly of the 78th Highland Regiment who had been Usher of the Black Rod in the Tasmanian Parliament until his death in 1865. Two of Charles Fraser's sisters were married to men prominent in colonial life—Louisa Mary Fraser to James Agnew, later Premier of Tasmania and a knight, met when he was a surgeon at the Convict Probation Station where her father was stationed, and Robina Fraser to William Degraves, son of Peter Degraves, founder of the Cascade Brewery in Hobart and of numerous other enterprises, including saw and flour mills. William Degraves himself was well on the way to becoming one of the richest men in Victoria.

Charles Forbes Fraser was born at his father's station Moody Yallock (now the Melbourne bayside suburb of Mordialloc) on 30 November 1841, the youngest child of Major James Fraser and his wife, formerly Christina Gray of Edinburgh.[2] James Fraser was descended from generations of Scottish army officers who had fought gallantly in many wars during the reigns of five British kings. He had joined his father's regiment as an ensign at the age of fourteen, serving with the 78th Highlanders in India and Java; he fought in the Flanders campaign in 1814 and was present at Waterloo as a staff officer. He was placed on half pay but later served with the 34th Regiment until his retirement in 1837 with the rank of major. Altogether, he and his immediate forbears and an uncle had served a total of 117 years in the British army.[3]

In 1839 he migrated with his eldest child, James Lloyd Fraser, to Victoria, then the little-known district of Port Phillip, and with a fellow Scotsman, Daniel Mackinnon, took over a run called Brittania Bay at Moody Yallock on the eastern side of Port Phillip Bay. Fraser was joined in November 1840 by his wife and three daughters, Jane, Louisa and Robina, who arrived on the *Perfect*. The ship also carried Henri Bell, who began a merchant's business in Melbourne and following a shipboard romance married Jane Fraser at Mordialloc's first wedding on 8 September 1841.[4] The celebrant was the Reverend James Forbes, minister at the Scots Kirk, Melbourne, who also officiated at the christening of the youngest child, Charles Forbes Fraser, on 13 December 1841.

Fraser and Mackinnon's station did not prosper. Within nine months Mackinnon had sold out his share of the 5120 acres, a considerable part of it swamp land, and moved to the Western District of Victoria. There he became one of the earliest and most prominent pastoralists. Fraser remained on the station, only to see his position deteriorate further.

Drought, followed by the Depression of the early 1840s, ruined Major James Fraser. Like many other settlers, he lost almost the whole of the capital he had brought to Australia. Looking for employment, he was induced by a friend, the very successful settler William Kermode of Mona Vale, to move to Van Diemen's Land. Through the intervention of the Governor, Sir John Franklin, he was appointed superintendent of a probation station in the convict service. In support of his application, he produced an impressive array of references, mainly from commanding officers during his distinguished army service.[5]

Under the newly introduced probation system, male convicts, instead of being assigned to settlers as labour, worked under severe discipline in gangs in the unsettled districts. Through good conduct, probation passes entitling them to work for wages could be earned. The system was set up for disciplinary reasons, and also to cope with the greatly increased number of convicts sent to Van Diemen's Land following the virtual end of transportation to New South Wales in 1840. Over the following few years, 4000 to 5000 convicts joined the probation gangs each year. More than twenty probation stations were established, each taking about 400 men, the superintendent being responsible for 'discipline and management of the gang', and for keeping costs to a minimum. Soon there were allegations of 'unnatural vice' and 'filthy and sordid practices' in the overcrowded dormitories. The sites chosen for the stations were in isolated areas where the convicts could be employed in roadmaking, cutting timber and clearing land.[6]

Charles Fraser spent his early childhood in the depressing and inhumane atmosphere of the probation stations at Wedge Bay, Slopen Island, New Norfolk, Bridgewater Depot and Brown's River, where his father was successively stationed.[7] In 1847, when he was six, he moved with his parents to the Female House of Correction at Launceston, where his father took charge and his mother became matron of the female convicts. They remained there until Mrs Mary Hutchinson, former matron at the notorious Female Factory in Hobart, took over in 1851.[8] Observing at a young age the constant degradation of women convicts and their powerlessness may have introduced to an impressionable mind a view of women as people without rights.

Jessie was aware of the Fraser family background in the convict service and was to make use of it in her novels. She made Tom Piper's first wife in *Uncle Piper of Piper's Hill* a matron on a convict ship, and she gave Mr Frost in *Not Counting the Cost* a background not unlike Major Fraser's, but giving the character a crueller twist to his nature. Frost, she wrote, assisted 'cheerfully' at the 'flogging and hanging of unnumbered convicts'.[9] In her only substantial writing about convicts, her short stories 'An Old Time Episode in Tasmania', 'What an Artist Discovered in Tasmania' and 'Gran'ma'[s] Tale', Jessie expressed views antagonistic to, and subversive of, the whole idea of the convict system. Her two main characters in 'An Old Time Episode in Tasmania' defeat the system by outwitting the employer to whom they are assigned then escaping to freedom. The convict in 'Gran'ma'[s] Tale' escapes with the help of the heroine and becomes a bushranger. In 'What an Artist Saw in Tasmania', the artist travels from London to Tasmania in search of 'the most hardened criminal face on the earth' to paint. Instead the convict presented to him is a girl of great and haunting beauty.

Jessie also drew more directly on the Fraser family for some aspects of Charles Frost in *Not Counting the Cost*. Frost, the insane estranged husband of the heroine, Eila, after an early wild and reckless life, experiences a religious conversion. It is hinted that his later madness is caused by venereal disease contracted during his youthful excesses.[10]

According to family letters still extant, Charles Fraser's older brother, James Lloyd Fraser, to the dismay of his God-fearing parents led a profligate early life. Among his other unspecified transgressions there is a suggestion in a history of the Mordialloc district that he co-habited with an Aboriginal woman.[11] He later returned to the strict religious code of his parents, joined the 80th Regiment and sailed from Sydney for India in 1845. From the Bay of Bengal, on board the *Royal Consort*, he wrote to his parents expressing 'unspeakable misery' for his 'career of worldliness'. To his brother Charles, then only four, he wrote a 'fearful warning' of the 'misery attending vice', signing his letter 'your loving but unfortunate brother'. James Lloyd Fraser had a premonition of early death, and within a year had died in India.[12]

After his service in the convict service and the end of transportation in 1853, Major Fraser was appointed to the much more prestigious position of Sergeant-at-Arms in the nominee Legislative Council in Hobart. At the inauguration of responsible government, he became Usher of the Black Rod.

From the time his family arrived in Hobart, Charles Fraser attended the High School, a private non-sectarian school begun by Presbyterians and others opposed to the High Church connections of Hutchins School. The High School, a handsome building now part of the University of Tasmania, built on a site in the Queen's Domain, opened in 1849. For many years it was rival to the Hutchins School as the leading secondary school in the colony.[13]

After he left school, Charles Fraser was employed from the age of eighteen by his brother-in-law, William Degraves. At first he worked as an accountant at the Degraves flour mill at Riverview on the Campaspe River a few kilometres north of Kyneton. After its closure, he took a job at another Degraves mill, at Carlsruhe, a few kilometres east of Kyneton. From this time on he lived in Victoria, returning to Hobart only for holiday visits. His mother, Christina, died aged sixty-three in 1863, and his father died at the home of his son-in-law in Hobart in 1865, at the age of seventy-six years. He still held the position of Usher of the Black Rod.

William Degraves, although a brother-in-law of Charles Fraser, was twenty years older. Born in England in 1821 he had arrived in Hobart with his father, Peter Degraves, and other family members when he was three years old. His father began very successful enterprises in brewing, shipbuilding and other fields in which William Degraves worked until he moved to Melbourne in 1849. There, with his brother Charles, he bought an acre site in Melbourne bounded by Flinders Lane and the street later named Degraves Street, and erected a steam flour mill. Soon William Degraves had expanded his interests to warehousing, and was trading in wool and gold from his three-storeyed Free and Bonded Stores, one of the earliest in Melbourne, at the corner of Flinders and Russell Streets.

Simultaneously he began investing in what was to become a vast pastoral empire, stretching through Victoria, the Riverina in New South Wales, South Australia and later Queensland. He expanded his flour milling business by erecting mills in country areas, including the two near Kyneton. By the time he was elected to the Victorian Legislative Council in 1860, Degraves was a very wealthy man, described in a newspaper article as 'another name for the great house of Rothschild'.[14] Jessie portrayed a similar character, Josiah Carp, of *In Her Earliest Youth*, as 'a great station-owner . . . a general merchant . . . president of this board, chairman of that; railway director, bank director, insurance office director, autocrat . . .'.[15]

Around Melbourne in the gold-rush era, Degraves was known as Billie. He was a self-made man with a combative nature. Stories were told about his sharp trading practices and dubious business tactics. One concerned John Phillips, down in Melbourne from the bush to stock up on goods for his station but short of money to pay for them. He approached Degraves, then still living above his flour mill, and was offered three tons of flour on credit provided he agreed to take half a ton of gooseberry jam, recently imported from Tasmania, at Degraves's valuation. Phillips was forced to agree, since it was the only way of getting the flour he needed. He later tried to dispose of the jam by sending it to friends, giving it to Aborigines (who, after trying it, would take no more), and finally by feeding it to a pig he bought for the purpose. He alleged the pig died after three weeks. Years later Phillips told this story when he met Degraves in the company of the Governor, whom Degraves was taking on a visit to one of his stations on the Murray. The Government House party was most amused, but Degraves was not.[16]

Politically, Degraves was a reactionary. He was a fierce opponent of parliamentary reform and outspoken in his distrust of democracy, believing universal suffrage was the cause of all mismanagement of public affairs. He was bitterly opposed to free selection, or any break-up of pastoral empires such as his. In speeches in Parliament, he favoured railway development, locks on the Murray, and the migration of greater numbers of better-class migrants, provided they did not cost taxpayers money. He was against more taxes and any environmental controls on the smoke emitted from his mills. A strong advocate of separation from New South Wales, he attended the celebratory separation fancy dress ball held at St Patrick's Hall on 28 November 1850, dressed as 'a Sportsman'.[17]

At eighteen, Jessie Huybers joined the Fraser/Degraves/Agnew family as something of a cuckoo in the nest. Intellectually curious and bright, her education and the influence of her mother had left her with a questioning mind, used to arguing and discussing any subject from philosophy to politics, religion to natural science. She was accustomed to expressing her radical views on philosophical, religious and social issues. She entered a family with, on the Fraser side, very strong military traditions and a close association with the authoritarian convict system and, through Degraves, links with conservative politics and the squattocracy.

Charles Fraser was dependent for his livelihood on Degraves, with his very conservative views. Because of this dependence, and accentuated by the fact that since William and Robina Degraves were childless Fraser could expect to be at least part-heir, Jessie was no doubt obliged to defer to and accept favours from Degraves. She was to exact vengeance by depicting him in her writing. If there are benign echoes of him in the self-made butcher Tom Piper of *Uncle Piper of Piper's Hill*, he appears in more ruthless form as the character Uncle Josiah Carp, of *In Her Earliest Youth*, and as

Sir Matthew Bogg in 'Monsieur Caloche'. Mr Brewster of *A Fiery Ordeal* appears to have some of his more superficial characteristics.

There is nothing to indicate that Jessie was forced into marriage with Charles Fraser. Unlike the heroines of several of her novels, such as Pauline of *In Her Earliest Youth*, who marries George Drafton because he has saved a child she dearly loves, or Portia in *The Penance of Portia James*, who is propelled by the honouring of an obligation into a marriage she does not want, or Ruth Virton, who in *A Fiery Ordeal* is attracted by the thought of escaping from her dreary life as a student teacher, Jessie seems to have freely entered her own marriage. She ignored protests from her mother and perhaps from her brothers and sisters. She must have had her father's consent, since she was under age. In any case, her father was to remain friendly with Charlie, as he came to be known in the family, and some other family members also came to like him.

Charlotte Huybers was vehemently opposed to Jessie's marriage to Charles Fraser. She thought her daughter was too young to marry and perhaps that she was, as Jessie was to describe Portia in *The Penance of Portia James*, 'that saddest of sacramental victims, a child wife'.[18] Charlotte Huybers also saw the complete incompatibility of Jessie's and Charles's natures and interests. She may have warned her daughter as the French-born Mrs Honorine Delauney warns her granddaughter Pauline, of *In Her Earliest Youth*, 'the emotion of a minute fills not up a life'.[19] Jessie's brother Eddie wrote after Jessie's marriage, 'A step hurriedly taken, and a source of never failing upset to Mother.'[20]

Jessie Katherine Huybers and Charles Forbes Fraser were married in the austere Georgian Anglican Church of St David in Murray Street, a few blocks south of Cleburne House, on 6 June 1867. Jessie was eighteen and Charles Fraser twenty-five. As befitted a marriage between two prominent families, the ceremony was performed by the Lord Bishop of Tasmania, Charles Henry Bromby, assisted by the Reverend Tice Gellibrand. The witnesses were Alfred Huybers and Georgiana Harris, Jessie's mother's friend from her Highgate days.[21]

Jessie was a strikingly beautiful woman, 'one of the most beautiful women of the day'.[22] She had a personality of 'consummate charm', her brother wrote.[23] With her long, flowing dark hair, large, lustrous brown eyes and well-formed oval face, she was a striking bride, more than matching the handsome Charles Fraser, with his sportsman's build and brilliant blue eyes.

Three weeks after their marriage, Jessie and Charlie sailed on the *Derwent* from Hobart to Melbourne.[24] Jessie left behind the family she loved, and the stimulation of the discussions that raged endlessly. She also left the family's enormous library of literature and philosophy, and the influence of her mother.

* * *

I was pleased to discover so much about Charles Fraser's background and his Degraves/Agnew connections, more, I believe, than ever before published. I was particularly intrigued by the gradual realisation that Degraves was portrayed in various guises in Jessie's fiction. I admired her ability to observe so sharply the characteristics of a man who for years held a position of such authority in her life.

My research, however, did not help solve the major dilemma of her choice. Why did Jessie marry the obviously incompatible Charles Fraser? Are there hints in her fiction? Is it legitimate to read anything into the stories of her heroines, written long after Jessie's own marriage?

When Jessie met Charles Fraser he was an attractive man with the glamorous aura associated with his reputation as a splendid horserider. He may also already have been the hard drinker and reckless gambler he was later. Initially, Jessie did not seem to see his faults. Eila Clare, in *Not Counting the Cost*, is 'irresistibly fascinated' by a 'reckless, chivalrous Jack Hamlyn type, with the athletic frame and the wonderful blue eyes trusting as a child's and brazen as a profligate's'.[25] Did Charles Fraser, like Charles Frost, have the worldly wise characteristics that appealed to Jessie's naïve ideas of a man? Did Jessie, like Eila, realise only later that her feelings were 'calf love', that women could not afford to make mistakes, as men could, in their first love affair, that it was 'from the so-called weaker sex that the mature judgment, the cool head, the stoical self-mastery [were] exacted—at the cost of the heaviest penalties should they fail in any of these qualities'?[26]

Perhaps during their short courtship Jessie tried to talk to Charles Fraser about his views on some of the philosophical issues that absorbed her, as Pauline Vyner did in *In Her Earliest Youth* with George Drafton, the man she had agreed to marry. Like Pauline, Jessie may have pleaded to know his views on religion: 'Do you believe in your own heart that there's an Old Nick, as you call him, with a pitchfork, and fire, and suffering souls to torment?' Jessie may have had as much trouble convincing Charles Fraser as Vyner did Drafton that there was a fundamental difference in their religious views. Perhaps, like Drafton, Fraser may have ended the conversation with: '—don't you go talking to anyone about religion. It's not the thing, somehow; and do, for the Lord's sake, let the subject drop between us.' Like Drafton, Fraser may have hoped Jessie would go to church 'when they were in town just for the look of the thing. On the station it wouldn't matter so much.'[27]

Pauline Vyner rides on after this conversation with a look of 'hopeless sadness' at the divergence of their views, and the impossibility of conversing on the same level. She marries Drafton knowing of their incompatibility because of a sense of obligation to him. Jessie ignored any such signals.

Perhaps Jessie's and Charles's intellectual incompatibility meant nothing to a young girl, inexperienced in romantic involvements. Perhaps, like Eila Clare in *Not Counting the Cost*, she believed 'the tumult of feeling he raised in her was spiritual and made no allowances for the influence of six feet of splendidly developed manhood upon the Juliet side of a many-sided nature'.[28] Perhaps only later did she realise that like Eila's, her 'early and ill-considered marriage'[29] was the 'crowning error of her life'.[30]

Perhaps Jessie stood at the altar like Eila Clare 'in a state of semi exaltation, half mystic, half sensuous' and endorsed 'with voice and heart all the impossible vows and promises that the minister put into her mouth'.[31]

Or perhaps there is an element of self-justification in these accounts of fictional marriages that proved as incompatible as Jessie's. Perhaps Jessie, under the influence of strong sexual attraction, merely fell in love and, ignoring her mother's advice, married quickly.

After her marriage Jessie, like Eila Frost, went to live with her husband in Victoria. She appears, like Eila, to have been prepared 'to be as happy as the day . . .'.[32]

3

He showed no power of adaptability to her tastes

Kyneton, the Murray, the Burdekin, Oakville, 1867–72

Soon after settling on a 600-acre selection in Victoria, the heroine of *Not Counting the Cost*, Eila Frost, discovers her husband is subject to epileptic fits. Then she notices signs of madness. These culminate in a scene in which he threatens her with a Bible in one hand and a knife in the other.

No such violent crisis seems to have occurred in the marriage of Jessie and Charles Fraser. If they were more complex and subtle, however, the discoveries Jessie made about her husband's character and interests, ignored during their short courtship, were to prove as devastating. Jessie longed for the intellectual stimulation of her childhood home, to be surrounded by books, to discuss paintings and to talk about philosophical problems among people with the same interests. Charles Fraser, on the other hand, had never disguised the fact that his great interests were horseracing and breeding, and betting.

The couple's movements in Melbourne on their honeymoon are unknown. It is likely, however, that they stayed with William and Robina Degraves at Ebden House, the handsome town residence they rented from Charles Ebden in Collins Street, opposite the prestigious Melbourne Club, of which both Degraves and Ebden were members. Perhaps Charles Fraser, always proud of his wife's beauty, walked her round Block Arcade, the favourite parade ground for the fashionable in Melbourne. He almost certainly would have taken her to Kirk's Bazaar, the horseyards at the upper end of Bourke Street, while he looked over the latest offerings of racehorses.

Then Charles Fraser took Jessie to his home at Carlsruhe, six kilometres south-east of Kyneton. They travelled by train on the line opened five years before, and soon after extended through Castlemaine to the goldmining city of Bendigo. Leaving the train at Kyneton, about 90 kilometres north-west of Melbourne, they went to Montpellier, the large bluestone two-storey mansion William Degraves had built as a residence beside his mill at Carlsruhe. The mill, a huge four-storey bluestone structure, dominated the bank of the Campaspe River. Built like the house of Malmsbury stone, it towered over the landscape, as it still does.[1]

Named Montpellier after the town in southern France where Degraves's Huguenot ancestors originated, the house faced the tree-lined river, its windows overlooking a scene of quiet, timeless beauty. It had, however, an almost frightening aspect. Its dark grey-blue stone walls were of immense thickness. Inside, the design was unusual, with the main entrance, formal entertaining and living rooms on the first floor, opening on to wide, encircling balconies, especially wide where a room was recessed. Internal stairs led down to the ground floor where all the bedrooms except the main one were located. The outside staircase leading to the first floor was guarded by loopholes built into the walls at ground floor level. One of the rooms on this floor had, instead of windows, slanted slits in the bluestone. Approaching bushrangers could be shot through them. Before the opening of the railway, gold on its way to Melbourne was locked in this room overnight.[2]

At the time of his marriage, Charles Fraser was manager of William Degraves's flour milling operations at Kyneton and of Montpellier estate. He bred cattle for Degraves, and racehorses for himself. Although ostensibly holding a good position and accommodated in a mansion, he held both at the whim of Degraves. The Montpellier mill, opened in 1860, had already passed the peak of its productive life. The Riverview mill, on the other side of Kyneton, had ceased operations only a few years after its opening, in 1857.[3] As wheat growing moved further out, to the Wimmera and to more marginal country further north, the time was rapidly approaching when the Montpellier mill would become uneconomic. Less than a year after their marriage, Degraves was to send Fraser as relief manager to one of his sheep stations in the north of the state. Although they were to return to Montpellier for short periods over the next four or five years, Charles and Jessie Fraser could never feel secure in making a home there, and do not appear to have accumulated any furniture or similar possessions.

Degraves made a practice of offering Montpellier to Victorian governors as a summer residence. Whenever he decided to bring distinguished guests to stay at the country property of which he was so proud, the Frasers would have had to move. Late in 1866, before Jessie's arrival, Sir Henry Manners Sutton, later Viscount Canterbury, appointed Governor of Victoria that year, had spent a few weeks there, not long after he had accepted the position of patron of the Kyneton District Racing Club.[4] Early in 1869, William Degraves again made Montpellier available to Sir Henry, his wife and family, for a summer holiday. During a three weeks' stay the vice-regal visitor was entertained by Sir William Mitchell, MLC, of nearby Barfold station to a quail shoot, and Lady Manners Sutton announced in the local paper that she was at home to receive visitors.[5] The Governor and his party were back at Montpellier less than two months later, to attend the St Patrick's Day race meeting, the major event of the Kyneton District Racing Club and one of the most popular in the Victorian racing calendar.[6]

Such frequent visits indicate the attractiveness of the district both scenically and in amenities. Discovered by Major Thomas Mitchell during his overland exploration from Sydney in 1836, it was settled very early in the history of Port Phillip. In 1837, Charles Ebden took up a run at Carlsruhe, the first sheep station in the Port Phillip District north of the Great Dividing Range. Other squatters followed along the Campaspe and Coliban rivers. An associate of Charles Ebden, William Piper, a solicitor's clerk from Sydney and later a Commissioner of Crown Lands, took up Pastoria Station in 1839. Piper's Creek and Piper Street in Kyneton, named after William Piper,[7] were to provide Jessie with the name of the main character in her *Uncle Piper of Piper's Hill.*

Compared with newer country towns, Kyneton had impressive facilities for some basic cultural events. Leading singers, such as prima donna Marie Carandini, performed in the town[8] and lecturers, including Mrs Arthur Davitt,[9] gave talks. Her subject was 'Woman and her Mission'. The Kyneton Young Men's Association held debates and other literary events. In January 1869 the Association debated 'Whether woman is mentally inferior to man', before an all-male audience. Perhaps Jessie would have read in the *Kyneton Guardian* a report of a speech for the negative, in which the speaker gave examples of many illustrious women including Mrs Hannah Moore, Mrs Stowe and Mrs Signourey and, nearer home, 'in South Australia there are a Maude Jean Franc, and a Miss Spence, all which go to prove that woman is not inferior'.[10]

Several early settlers had literary connections. Sylvester John Brown, father of the writer Rolf Boldrewood, began Darlington Station, later taken over by Thomas Baynton, father of Barbara Baynton's second husband. Joseph Furphy, who was to become famous as 'Tom Collins', the author of *Such is Life*, was then a shy young man living on a farm outside Kyneton.[11] In August 1871 Ada Cambridge, who was to become an acclaimed novelist, passed through Kyneton staying at the Anglican Parsonage while on a roundabout route to Wangaratta. It is doubtful, however, if Jessie's path crossed any of these, although she probably met Ada Cambridge later in Melbourne,[12] and was also to know Rolf Boldrewood.

Though she appears to have had misgivings about her marriage from an early date, Jessie made efforts to adapt to her husband's interests, and to conform to the role expected of her as a country matron. A few months after her arrival in Kyneton, aged just nineteen, in what seems a pathetically conformist gesture, she joined eleven other older women in running the tables at St Paul's Church of England annual festival and tea meeting, held in the Kyneton Mechanics Institute.[13]

Painting of Hobart by Haughton Forrest, looking from the port to snow-capped Mount Wellington. Jessie arrived in Hobart at the age of four. Her mother, Charlotte Huybers, thought Hobart, with its population of about 20,000, a small, primitive village when the family arrived from London in 1852. (National Library of Australia)

A present-day view of Southwood Lodge in Highgate, London. When Jessie Huybers was born there in 1848, her mother was running a small school in the house, which was on the northern outskirts of London.

Jessie spent most of her childhood at Cleburne House in Hobart. The family lived on the upper floors of the front section of the substantial building, and Alfred Huybers carried on his merchant's business in the remainder. Then numbered 33 Murray Street, Cleburne House is now the site of the Cat and Fiddle Arcade in central Hobart. (Don Norman)

Left: Charlotte Huybers, with her son Edward, photographed in Hobart in 1863. She was responsible for developing the great artistic and literary talents of her children but, according to Edward, had 'a want of mental balance in dealing with the ordinary affairs of life'. (Kenneth Huybers) Right: Alfred Huybers, photographed in Melbourne in 1863. Born in Antwerp, he became a very successful merchant in Hobart. In 1861 he was one of the founding members of the exclusive Tasmanian Club, and was made a Justice of the Peace in 1871. (Kenneth Huybers)

The well-known Tasmanian author Louisa Meredith, recognising Jessie's youthful talent, invited her at the age of fifteen to spend a long holiday at her country home, Twamley, north-east of Hobart. (Allport Library and Museum of Fine Arts)

Left: William Degraves, who had interests in flour milling, importing, and pastoral properties, employed his brother-in-law Charles Fraser as manager of his flour mill and estate at Carlsruhe near Kyneton in Victoria. Jessie based several powerful, ruthless characters in her fiction on Degraves. (State Library of Victoria) Right: This photograph of Charles Fraser taken many years after his marriage to Jessie, shows him dressed, appropriately, for the races. Horse-racing was his passion all his life. (*Cyclopaedia of Victoria*, National Library of Australia)

Left: Soon after Jessie married, her sister Koozee (Maria Theresa Huybers) stayed with her at Montpellier, and at William Degraves's town residence, Ebden House, in Collins Street opposite the Melbourne Club. (Renée Erdos) Right: Members of the Huybers family photographed outside Highfield during the last summer they spent together in Hobart. The group includes Charlotte, Jessie, Koozee, Edward, Frank, John and Edith, with a visiting officer from HMS *Clio*. (Renée Erdos)

Jessie's first home after her marriage was Montpellier, a two-storey mansion built by William Degraves near his flour mill at Carlsruhe near Kyneton. Named Skelsmergh Hall by a later owner, it and the nearby flour mill are classified by the Historic Buildings Council of Victoria and the National Trust (Victoria), and the mill is registered by the Australian Heritage Commission (wing at left is a later addition).

Charles Fraser also attempted to adapt to Jessie's interests. Soon after her arrival in Kyneton he appeared at a Popular Readings, then a popular form of cultural entertainment, the newspaper report noting it was his first appearance as a reader. The event was organised to raise funds for the Campaspe School, Boggy Creek, a settlement near the Riverview mill.[14]

For a racing man, Charles Fraser also paid Jessie the ultimate honour: he named a horse after her. He had been a member and committeeman of the Kyneton District Racing Club from its formation in August 1866, and his colours were often to the fore at the meetings held on the banks of the Campaspe River. At the Blackhill races towards the end of December 1867, 'Mr Fraser's Jessie' won the second race. Fraser also won the hurdle race with Mailboy, and the fifth race with Whackfalooral.[15] He was to win the Kyneton Steeplechase three years running, twice with Whackfalooral and once with Mailboy. As an amateur jockey, he rode many winners on the Kyneton track and elsewhere.[16]

There were compensations for Jessie in life at Montpellier. She could lead the physically active life she enjoyed. She had a horse to ride, something she was to treasure all her life, and miss when horses were not available. An anecdote published twenty years after she had left the district describes an episode exemplifying both her physical health and the impression she made upon observers by her kind and outgoing nature.

While taking a walk one evening from Montpellier, she met an old, decrepit man, returning from a ploughing match held at Springfield pushing a heavily laden wheelbarrow. The man was well known in the district for earning a living by making and selling heath brooms and selling buns at ploughing matches and other entertainments. When Jessie met him, he was about to push his barrow up the steep Shamrock Hill, and since he had already walked many miles, he showed signs of great fatigue. Jessie grasped the handles of the barrow and, disregarding the old man's protests, wheeled the barrow to the top of the hill. She then resumed her walk. When Jessie became famous as a writer, a subsequent owner of the barrow used proudly showed the handles touched by Tasma to anyone who called at his home.[17] In Kyneton, Jessie's brother wrote, 'her happy disposition made her many friends'.[18]

But whatever efforts she made, Jessie found little in her life there to make up for the rich, stimulating family life she had left in Hobart. She longed for her family. Her brothers and sisters in their turn missed her teaching and imaginative leadership. 'Jessie visited us at Easter or Christmas each year,' Eddie wrote.[19] Sometimes these visits stretched into several months. She also had family members to stay with her. In the winter of 1868, her sister Koozee, who turned fifteen that July, spent some months in Victoria, and Jessie resumed teaching her as she had in Hobart.

Less than a year after their arrival in Kyneton, William Degraves despatched Charles Fraser to manage his station, Burnewang West, near Elmore in the north of the colony, between Bendigo and Echuca. Apparently Degraves wanted Jessie neither to accompany her husband nor to remain at Montpellier, so she and Koozee moved to Melbourne, to stay with the Degraves at Ebden House. A letter Jessie wrote to her husband at this time, one of the very few of her letters known to exist, is enlightening on the state of her marriage, the conventional social life demanded of her by William and Robina Degraves, and her continuing close involvement with her own family and in teaching. She wrote on 12 June 1868, from Ebden House:

> Dearest Charlie
> I received your letter last night, and cannot say it made me very comfort-able. You seem to be playing a sort of double game with regard to Koozee urging me to keep her while you say all that you know is most calculated to make me send her away. However I have made up my mind to go home before long, and shall give to Mr de Graves as a reason for my so doing that I want to prepare my sister's things, and see to her lessons a little before she returns as I must not *selfishly* keep her much longer when I know what a *trial* it is to *both* Papa and Mama to have any of the family away even for a *short time*. I do not expect you to be so long away as you seem to imagine, but since you will be writing to me so often, if it is really settled that you are to stay at Burniwang [sic] until Mr Harrison's return I must try again and see if Mr de Graves cannot be induced to allow me to join you. I went out calling yesterday afternoon with Mrs de Graves, on the Nutts and Mitchells. Mrs Mitchell seems quite well again, and has two or three of her daughters staying with her, but I cannot say much for their place of abode. It is a most poverty striken place. The Motherwells spent the evening here last night, and we had great fun. My ring has come from Kilpatricks. Mrs de Graves makes me show it to every-one of her friends. She says I could not get it for 70 guineas at the jewel-lers and certainly the diamonds are amongst the most brilliant I have ever seen. Today we are going to the Aylwins, and most probably Mrs King will join us and we shall spend the night at the Wells. You have so much to do dear Charlie that you must not be dull. The change and separation will be good for us both as from the time I see you again I mean to begin a new and better life than I have ever led before.
> I remain darling Charlie,
> Your very loving wife, Jessie.[20]

Her comment that she would begin 'a new and better life' suggests that William and Robina Degraves had taken the opportunity of having nine-teen-year-old Jessie with them to mould her to their ideas and to exert pressure on her to conform to the role of dutiful wife.

Jessie may have joined Charles Fraser briefly at Burnewang. It is not, however, this locale but a station on the Murray that she used for her fiction set in country Victoria. After relieving at Burnewang, Fraser appears to have been sent to another Degraves property west of Echuca on the

Murray, probably Tooringabby, a 65,000 acre station downstream from Moama on the Riverina side of the river, and later part of Perricoota Station. Jessie used the background of a station on the Murray for the property Rubria, to which George Drafton took his bride Pauline of *In Her Earliest Youth*, and as the setting for her short story, 'The Rubria Ghost'.

By the time he sent Charles Fraser to the station on the Murray, William Degraves was in grave financial difficulties. Beginning with his purchase of several of Benjamin Boyd's properties in the Riverina in south-west New South Wales at the liquidation sale of that failed entrepreneur's assets in 1855, and then extensive purchases in Victoria, South Australia and Queensland, he had bought on small deposits and large mortgages. Such speculation depended on good prices and favourable seasons. Degraves bought and sold several stations quickly, gaining a reputation as one of the showy land speculators of the day. On other stations he produced some of the highest priced wool in Australia, and became one of the country's leading sheep and cattle breeders, with studs of imported Rambouillet rams and Shorthorn bulls.[21]

The serious and widespread drought which began in 1868 and lasted until the unprecedentedly wet year of 1870 caused Degraves to become heavily overdrawn at his bank. His position was exacerbated by a venture into Queensland pastoral properties. In August 1867, Degraves, then a director of the Union Bank, and John T. McMullen, the bank's inspector and general manager, agreed to buy jointly two huge properties in the Burdekin district in the north of the colony. They were Dotsworth, inland from Townsville on a tributary of the Burdekin, and St Ann's to the south, inland from Bowen, also on a tributary of the Burdekin. He paid £8855.10.0 to the Bank of New South Wales for Dotsworth, and £8000 to the Union Bank for St Ann's. McMullen stipulated that his involvement be kept secret, since it was against the bank's rules for a person in his position to hold an interest in squatting property. Soon he wanted to withdraw. Degraves agreed on condition that the bank agreed to discount his squatting and trade bills at seven per cent.

With the devastation to his finances caused by the drought and a decline in business activity, Degraves had by 1869 run up an enormous overdraft of £100,000. This caused alarm to the Melbourne manager of the Union Bank, John Curtayne. During McMullen's absence in New Zealand, Curtayne pressed Degraves for settlement of the overdraft, ignoring the alleged arrangements between him and McMullen. As a result Degraves had to sell his Queensland properties at a loss, in effect getting nothing for the land and only £2.8.0 per head for his cattle, with 150 horses thrown in. Although Degraves had sent up some of his pure-bred bulls from Montpellier, the stations were at the time of the sale very thinly stocked. The total herd numbered only about 3000 head, when Dotswood alone was capable of carrying 30,000–40,000. Degraves's problems with the Union

Bank are apparent from his interest bill. During the time he held the stations, from August 1867 to arrangement of sale in 1871, and settlement in 1872, he had paid £9742 in interest to the bank.[22]

Degraves's subsequent relations with the Union Bank were sensational. In 1873 in a case before the Supreme Court of Victoria, widely reported in the press, Degraves sued his former partner J.T. McMullen, claiming £30,000 damages for breach of agreement. At a hearing lasting seven days, at which Degraves was represented by several prominent lawyers, a jury awarded him damages of £10,204.17.7, assessed as his loss on the sale of the Queensland stations. However, on appeal the verdict was reversed, although costs were not awarded against Degraves, the Union Bank agreeing to pay McMullen's costs.[23]

At the height of the crisis over the Queensland properties, William Degraves appears to have sent Charles Fraser to Queensland. Probably he wanted him to salvage 2000 of the pure-bred cattle later overlanded through western New South Wales to Victoria.[24] Jessie almost certainly accompanied her husband, probably visiting both Dotswood and St Ann's, though both were far beyond the limits of comfortable access. After travelling north to the port of Cleveland (later Townsville) by ship, the journey to Dotsworth would have been about 100 kilometres on horseback. The journey to St Ann's was much further and more difficult, either south from Dotsworth through rough, virtually uninhabited country across the area later to become the scene of the rich gold find at Charters Towers or, alternatively, a ride of nearly 300 kilometres inland from the port of Bowen. Either journey would have been extremely long and arduous. Whether or not Jessie visited these particular stations, it is obvious from her subsequent writing and lecturing on Queensland, and her descriptions of life in the outback, that she travelled widely in Queensland. She visited inland cattle and sheep properties as well as observing the coastal areas, with their sugar plantations. She was to use a Queensland property, Tarragunyah run, as the locale for Hubert de Merle's sheep station in *Not Counting the Cost*. Queensland was also one of her most popular subjects when she became a lecturer in Europe many years later. She was to enthral audiences with life on cattle and sheep stations, the sugar and cotton industries, and accounts of Aboriginal and Kanak peoples.[25]

To Jessie and Charles Fraser, Degraves's financial débâcle added the instability of a sudden change in fortune and uncertainty about their future livelihood, to growing disillusionment with an unsatisfactory marriage. Apparently in an effort to break free from Degraves, Charles Fraser bought a property known as the Yarraman Grazing Paddocks, south-east of Melbourne and west of Dandenong. It was a short distance inland from the Moody Yallock property on the shores of Port Phillip Bay where he had been born. Jessie was to use the name Yarraman for a property in *The Penance of Portia James*. Now part of Melbourne's eastern suburbs, the property was then within reach of several Melbourne race tracks, particularly Caulfield, where Fraser was to ride several winners. He bought the property, of 1500 acres of scrubby farmland with some access to Dandenong Creek, from absentee owner John Mickle on 15 November 1869, undertaking to pay £3157.1.9. He also made a rudimentary beginning to stocking the farm and furnishing a house by buying four cows, a calf, an oven, a stretcher, a bedstead and a table.

Jessie and Charles went to live on this property in 1870, in a house called Oakville, probably a simple timber country home, since no trace of it has been found. It may have been the residence of twelve rooms, sheds and office described when Yarraman Park was put on sale in 1901.[26]

That winter, Charlotte, Koozee, John and Edith, accompanied by a nurse, stayed at Oakville for five months.[27] John, aged eleven, was withdrawn from Hutchins School for the visit, and re-enrolled later. Charlotte had spent the previous winter in Melbourne, with her younger children staying at the same lodging house as her eldest son Willie. On that occasion the party included Frank, on whom Melbourne made a great impression with its busy streets, railways and shops.[28] These visits, together with her summer stays at Highfield, in effect separated Charlotte from her husband, who remained at the town house in Murray Street. She does not appear ever to have visited her daughter in Kyneton, possibly because Jessie was not free to invite her to Degraves's house. The situation of Oakville may also have had more appeal, since it was relatively close to the cultural opportunities of Melbourne—though not close enough for frequent visits.

The wet winter of 1870 must have been long and dreary for Charles Fraser. He arranged three mortgages totalling almost the whole amount he had paid for his property, and contemplated the deterioration of his investment at Yarraman.[29] He probably buried himself in the racing pages of the *Australasian* while his mother-in-law flooded the home with talk of subjects in which he was not interested.

With the directness and assurance that were part of her character, Charlotte would have talked incessantly to Jessie about the limitations of colonial life, with its lack of opportunities for cultural enrichment. She may well have added the uncertainty of her daughter's financial future with Charles Fraser. She also may have continued the process of inducing Jessie to accompany her on her long-planned trip to Europe. Doubtless, Charlotte would have been pleased that Jessie was not tied down with children to a husband her mother had never accepted as suitable.

Jessie was, nevertheless, to love children all her life. They ranged from her young sister Edith, to whom she was a willing slave in her early years, to her nephews, nieces and children of friends in her maturity. Children have important roles in her novels and their characterisation was one of her great strengths. It seems Jessie may have welcomed what she describes as 'the holy boon of motherhood'.[30] Many years later when charmed by the child of a friend, nine-year-old Jules Philippson, whom she described as 'exactly like one of Velasquez's royal portraits', she wrote:

> It gives me the heartache to think of what my life might have been with a child like Jules for my own. Not that I could have wished to have had children under the circumstance of my life. Dieu m'en défend. But life might have been *so* different.[31]

It is possible that in the early years of her marriage she had miscarriages that left her unable to have children. Some of her characters, like Ruth Fenton in *A Fiery Ordeal*, had problems with childbirth. Ruth Fenton lost a baby at birth and blamed the loss on hearing shattering news about a fortune lost through gambling.[32] Perhaps Jessie sometimes asked herself, as Pauline Drafton of *In Her Earliest Youth* does, whether children would have made a difference to her marriage. Would she then have cared whether her husband discussed 'theology or the solar system when we spend our evenings together?'[33] The absence of children from Jessie's existence was to make feasible a life that would have been virtually impossible for a nineteenth-century woman tied to her home by a family.

It is an unresolved mystery why Jessie's first published writing should be a poem about a dead child, 'A Widow's Lament over Her Dead Idiot Boy'. The text of this has only recently been discovered by Lucy Sussex, although its existence was known beforehand. It was first referred to in an article about Tasma published in 1894[34] in which the poem was said to have been written when Jessie was sixteen, and to have been entitled 'Lines Addressed by a Mother to Her Idiot Son', and published in the *Australian Journal*. Lucy Sussex has established the correct title of the poem, and its publication in the *Journal* not in 1865 (as it would have been had Jessie been sixteen), but in June 1869.[35] The poem is signed with Jessie's maiden initials, JKH, perhaps because it was written some years earlier but more likely because she never associated her married name with her writing.

It is difficult to surmise what may have led Jessie to write on such a subject. There is nothing in family memory to suggest she had lost a child—and no record of any such birth. The poem ends conventionally with a reference to the consolations of religion, but there is an ironic tone in the line 'Religion bids me to repine no more.' As far as is known this is the only poem Jessie wrote. It was to be nearly ten years before her literary career began in earnest. During this time, she almost certainly practised writing. Possibly there is more of her published writing from this period to be discovered.

Charlotte and the younger children returned to Hobart at the beginning of October to more family disputes. Eddie wrote in his diary that 'from here date the most unpleasant times in the household, up to their leaving for Europe'.[36] Less than three months after the departure of her mother with Johnnie and Edith, and less than two months after the departure of her sister Koozee, Jessie followed them, arriving in Hobart on the *Southern Cross* on 23 December 1870 for her usual long Christmas stay with her family.

Jessie's father made several trips to Melbourne during the years when instability in Jessie's marriage was becoming apparent. His business no doubt required many or all of these, particularly at the time of the break with his Melbourne partner, Alfred Wilkins, at the beginning of 1872. The firm then became Huybers and Hammond, Frank Pitt Hammond the head clerk in the Hobart business being admitted to partnership. Huybers sometimes travelled in company with Charles Fraser, either returning to Hobart, or travelling from there to Melbourne.[37] It is possible he attempted to patch up the marriage and help or advise Fraser on his future.

Jessie and Charles Fraser's residence at Oakville did not last more than about a year. On 24 January 1871, in great financial difficulties, Fraser sold the Yarraman property subject to mortgage to F. B. Hann of Emerald Hill, Port Melbourne.[38] Hann had made money as a butcher and become accepted in middle class society. His daughters attended the same private school as Catherine Deakin, sister of the future Prime Minister.[39] Although Jessie would have observed Hann only briefly, she may have remembered his success as a butcher when she created Tom Piper in *Uncle Piper of Piper's Hill*, who became rich through butchering.

By the time Charles and Jessie left Oakville, most of William Degraves's assets had been sold although with help from his brothers he was able to maintain for a few more years the trappings of affluence. He had moved from Ebden House in Collins Street to the mansion Oakleigh Hall in Alma Road, St Kilda. He was to remain there until he resigned from the Legislative Council in 1874.[40] Two of his brothers, Charles and John, took over some of his pastoral properties, including Coliban Park near Malmsbury. He hung on to Montpellier longer than he did most of his other assets, and Jessie and Charles returned there after the sale of Oakville so that Fraser could oversee the sale of stock, and the winding up of the farm. The Shorthorn stud bred by Fraser brought high prices, from 32 to 185 guineas each, when sold in May 1872.[41] Some time later the Montpellier house and mill were sold, to Robert Morton. Degraves's bond store in Flinders Street, Melbourne was sold in 1873, and the Riverview mill in 1876.

Jessie was again with her family in Hobart for Christmas 1871 and stayed on during February when the British warship *Clio* was in port. The Huybers had made friends among the officers during previous visits and they were invited to Highfield. 'The visit of the "Clio" made us very lively in the beginning of 1872, as we knew most of the officers on board, and Jessie was spending Christmas with us,' Eddie wrote.[42]

During 1872, Jessie and the Charles's income seems to have depended on the uncertain amount the latter could win at the races, either in prizes or bets. He also made efforts to make money from equally uncertain mining speculation.[43] Generous when he was winning, he probably did not give up his extravagances: trips to Melbourne for important race meetings, staying sometimes with the Degraves at Oakleigh Hall, at other times at Scott's Hotel in Collins Street. This was where Jessie's heroines always stayed for race meetings.

Either the steady accumulation of Fraser's money problems, his continuing to bet on 'certainties' and drinking whether he won or lost, or crises arising from these habits, precipitated a separation. Jessie sailed for her home in Tasmania in December 1872.[44] Charles Fraser could offer her little support, and at the most only tenuous ties bound them. Once back with her family, inevitably Jessie must have compared the richness of its life with the aridity of that with Fraser.

When she left Melbourne it is unknown whether Jessie intended to return as usual after a few months. Fraser remained at Montpellier, horsebreeding and training his main occupations.[45] Late in 1873 the new owner took over, renaming the mansion Skelsmergh Hall, its present name.[46]

Charles Fraser and his horses were homeless. He had no employment and little money, and Jessie had left him.

It was an exciting moment when I found Jessie's revealing letter written in 1868 to Charles Fraser among a descendant's memorabilia of the Fraser family. It provided an important glimpse into her personal feelings at a time for which, otherwise, only external evidence was available.

It was rewarding for me to visit Montpellier and experience the beauty and brooding solidity of the house and mill. It was rewarding also to come across a short phrase in Edward Huybers's diary mentioning Jessie's residence at Oakville. I traced Charles Fraser's brief ownership of the property through the Land Titles Office.

It was interesting to discover William Degraves's connection with north Queensland, and to find the names and locations of his stations. This made it possible to speculate on Jessie's visit there, a visit deduced from information contained in her lectures, which had proved difficult to place.

What was missing from the story of her relationship with Charles Fraser in the early years of their marriage was any direct evidence of the reason for the break between them. Are there clues in how she handled similar situations in her novels?

Had Jessie during her honeymoon thought as Pauline Drafton of *In Her Earliest Youth* does, that 'the much dreaded future' could have 'put on quite a new aspect' if her husband had 'shown a little more power of adaptability to her tastes'? If, 'in this early stage of their married life, he had told her to put on her hat and come with him to see the shop windows in town, and if on their reaching Melbourne he had turned in . . . anywhere, to the public library, the picture gallery—a music-shop even, and there shown himself not utterly estranged to all the interests she had moved among from her childhood, part of the blank would at least have been filled up'.[47]

Perhaps the event which precipitated her leaving of Charles Fraser was similar to the scene of *In Her Earliest Youth* after George Drafton wins the Melbourne Cup with his horse, Victory. While drinking to celebrate, he muses as his wife Pauline reads a book, on 'what would satisfy her' if winning such a race did not. When she does not reply, he grabs her book and throws it violently on the sofa, exclaiming 'That's to teach you manners, madam!' She replies 'I don't want to learn manners from a drunkard, thank you.'[48]

Perhaps, like Pauline Drafton, Jessie thought of divorce. Unlike Pauline, however, tempted by a wealthy and compatible lover to leave her husband, the temptation for Jessie was the richness of her family's life, and the unusually close ties between herself, her sisters and brothers and, particularly, her mother.

4

What a change this year has brought

Windward, London, 1873

A little over two months after leaving Charles Fraser in Kyneton, Jessie
sailed away from Australia to London and Europe on the *Windward*. As she
sailed east from Hobart through the mountainous seas of the Southern
Ocean, her identity as Fraser's wife slipped from her and she became again
Charlotte Huybers's eldest daughter, responsible for the education of the
younger members of the family. Her novels suggest that her early married
life had affected her to such an extent that she recreated the incompatibility and unhappiness of those years over and over again. This was an
experience etched into her being. For the moment, however, her feelings
were deeply submerged. When reading the diary she kept on the *Windward*,
it is as if the previous five-and-a-half years of her life hardly existed.

Apart from the letter to her husband in 1868, and her poem published
in the *Australian Journal* in 1869, Jessie's *Windward* diary is the first of her
writing known to survive. It was an exciting moment when I was handed
this diary by her sister's grand-daughter. It is important not only as her first
substantial writing to survive but because of the self-portrait that emerges
from it. It also played a role as training for her later career as a writer.
Writing it provided discipline in observing and recording events. Jessie, by
then twenty-four, portrays herself in the diary as the older sister, happy to
be back among the companions of her childhood and youth, and educating
the younger children. From reading her diary, it would not be possible to
know she had been married for over five years, or had lived a life away
from her family during that time. The only mention she makes of this
period of her life is the comment, 'No one could imagine how different my
life was this time last year.'

The diary is also interesting in providing evidence of Jessie's use of her
own experiences in writing fiction. The description of the voyage from

Hobart to London made on the sailing ship, the *Queen of the South*, by the Clare family in *Not Counting the Cost*, is based very closely on Jessie's diary of her own voyage on the *Windward*. Like the Huybers family, the Clares had the stern cabins, and the first day out dead-lights were put in place to cover the portholes of their cabins, converting them into 'dark dungeons'. Like the Huybers, the Clare family at the start of the voyage lay sick, as the small ship tumbled and staggered in the mighty Antarctic waves. Their heavy trunks, not yet lashed to posts, slid over the floors, colliding with each other. The timbers creaked and groaned and shivered when giant waves crashed on the vessel's stern. The Clare family, like the Huybers, found the experience at first 'a terrific and crushing surprise'. They felt they were 'caught in a trap from which there was no escape'. In *Not Counting the Cost*, Eila goes on deck in a gale, as Jessie did, is enveloped by a huge wave and drenched from head to foot. Like the Huybers, after the first few weeks, the Clare family were 'dancing up and down the slippery decks in the chill, ice-laden air of the desolate Southern Ocean', 'such is the elasticity of youth'.[1]

When she left Kyneton late in December 1872, it is not certain whether Jessie knew that Charlotte and the children would be sailing for Europe within a few months. However, once it was decided that they would go, apart from her own desire to accompany them and experience the cultures of Europe of which she had heard and read so much, Jessie would have known that the trip could hardly proceed without her. It is doubtful whether Charlotte at fifty-five would have been capable of taking responsibility for the care and safety of her children Koozee (nineteen), Frank (fourteen), John (thirteen) and Edith (eleven), in addition to arranging the family's travel and accommodation and the teaching of the younger children. From family records and her own diary, it is obvious that Jessie's role on the voyage was to teach her sisters and brothers.

Although long planned in theory, the actual sailing seems to have been arranged very hurriedly possibly because of the availability of accommodation on the sailing ship the *Windward*. By 1873 it was much more usual for passengers to travel by steamship sailing from Melbourne. Alfred Huybers, with his contacts as an importer, may have been able to arrange more favourable terms on the *Windward* than would have been available for a party of six on a steamship. The younger Huybers children were not told they were leaving for Europe until a week before they sailed. When they heard the news, Edith wrote excitedly to her brother Willie in Melbourne:

> You cannot imagine how sorry we all are that we will not be able to say 'Good bye' to you, before we go to England. Frank, Johnny and I never knew that we were going 'home', till last night. You can imagine how astonished we were! First, we cried (rather yelled) then we were in rap-

tures, and we are in the same state still, but of course we are awfully sorry to leave Papa, and Eddie, and you.

Frank also wrote to Willie hoping that he would be able to follow them. 'Are you not delighted with the Brussels move,' he wrote:

> It seems like a wild dream that we are actually going to England, and when I first heard it, I was more startled than I ever was in my life. Papa took us to town today in order to show us over our future maritime destination, and I was bedazed when I walked mechanically about the deck. We have the two stern cabins; in fact they can hardly be called cabins, for they are rooms. A beautiful bath lies between them six feet long which is entered by means of a door on each side, one opening into Mamma's room, and the other into Jessie's. Edith's little pet cow is going in order to supply the ship with milk . . .[2]

Only three of the Huybers family remained in Australia. Alfred Huybers continued to run the family business in Hobart. William, at twenty-five, was employed in the merchant's business run by his father's former partner, Alfred Wilkins, in Melbourne. Edward, who was seventeen, after finishing his schooling at Hutchins School at the end of 1870, and coming first in the top class, had joined the Huybers firm in Hobart. 'It was very hard to part with so many,' Eddie wrote of the departure of six of the family, 'but it was a splendid thing for them, and a change of some sort in the house had to come.'[3] Highfield was let for three years to prominent Hobart tailor, Joseph Bidencope.

The *Windward*, a barque of 621 tons which sailed regularly between Hobart and London carrying cargo and a few passengers, usually arrived in Hobart towards the end of December with a cargo of general merchandise, and sailed early in March to catch the June wool sales in London.[4] When it left Hobart on 4 March 1873, the Huybers family, sailing away on their high adventure to absorb the culture of Europe that Charlotte had never ceased to extol, made up the bulk of the passengers.[5] The others were Marie Crowther, a member of a pioneering Tasmanian medical family, whose father William Lodewyk Crowther was a member of the Legislative Council and later, briefly, Premier.[6] Harry Walch was a member of the prominent Hobart bookselling, publishing and literary family. Freddie Des Voeux, from an aristocratic Irish family, was to remain a lifelong friend. The last was the elderly Mr Horne.

Freddie, the heir of Charles Champagne Des Voeux (later baronet),[7] who turned sixteen a few days before the *Windward* sailed, was being sent to school in England preparatory to taking up an army career. Harry (James William Henry) Walch was a son of James Henry Brett Walch, who with his father ran J. Walch and Son, booksellers and publishers.[8] This connection with the Walch family was to be important to Jessie at the start of her writing career. Harry's uncle Garnet Walch was to publish her first short story, 'Barren Love', in 1877. Since Harry was young, like Fred Des Voeux he was apparently under the informal care of the Huybers family.

Jessie decorated her cabin on the *Windward* with portraits of her father and brother. 'Dear Eddie . . . smiles at me night and morning', she wrote, while her father looked 'seriously across me at the great waste of water beyond'.[9] Apparently no portrait of her husband adorned her cabin. He is mentioned only once in her diary, when she reflects on the changes in her life as the *Windward* crossed the Equator. She wrote:

> What a change this year has brought in one's interests, and mode of life!
> When I think of this month spent last year in Kyneton,—of small mining
> speculations, and all my questions to Charlie in the evening about
> 'Glengomeers' and 'Frosty Morns', and so on, and think how they are
> exchanged now for questions about latitude and longitude, and variation of
> the Compass, the number of knots we are going every time they 'heave
> the log', and a hundred other minor details of the sort, it makes me
> wonder—granted I am alive this time next year—what new or old interests
> will take up my mind . . . [10]

The violent motion of the small ship as it sailed east through the icy gales of the Southern Ocean towards New Zealand made all the passengers seasick. Their cabins were cold and damp, and above was a grey, gloomy sky. Nothing else was visible except the slate-coloured expanse of tossing waves. Although she had intended to keep a shipboard diary, it was not until just over a month out of Hobart that Jessie was well enough to begin her record.

She began her diary on 6 April 'with the vessel in a calm', 'the atmosphere in a freezing condition' and the Captain laid up in his cabin. Recalling the early part of the voyage she described 'a confused picture of some prostrate wretches, alive to nothing but a sense of their own misery, dead to all the decencies of civilized life, feebly writhing on their shelves like overgrown silkworms in a flabby condition, too impotent to wish themselves back, or better, or any thing but unconscious of sickness and suffering'.[11]

As the passengers gradually recovered, the pattern of the long sailing voyage became established. After a morning spent in bed or resting, the group met at dinner at two o'clock, indulging in the monotonous and repetitive conversation inevitable among such a small group. This is conveyed in Jessie's diary through her descriptions of some of her fellow travellers. Old Mr Horne, the 'trumpeter, toady and chorus in general to the Captain', told doleful stories about Napoleon and Waterloo to anyone who would listen. Captain G. Lulham was a melancholy man, not at all the 'jolly skipper' the Huybers had expected, but more inclined to tell the passengers, frightened by the ferocity of the gales, of vessels that had been lost in the vicinity rather than reassuring them with a joke, as Jessie believed a typical skipper would. Sometimes they managed a laugh at the

Captain's expense, particularly when the great green sea swept over the deck and streamed down, drenching him. After dinner, if it was not too freezing, the passengers would tramp the deck. If it was too cold or wet, Charlotte, Jessie, the Huybers children, Fred Des Voeux and Harry Walch would gather round the cuddy table and read Robertson's *History* turn about, trying to find 'impossible jokes' in its 'rather prosy pages'. Later in the day some passengers played draughts, some cards, others read and the Huybers children played bezique. Then the younger ones, led by Jessie, would romp on deck 'tearing . . . dancing, tumbling, running, laughing—any thing to get warm'.[12] In the evening, there were comb and paper concerts or the singing of Christy minstrels, and after the younger children had gone to bed following grog and ship's biscuits at 10 o'clock, there was more dancing on deck.

With the rigging glowing in the moonlight and the deck and sails reflected 'in a bleached, weird semi-real appearance', they chased each other about until they had to stop for breath. Then Marie Crowther would produce a comb and paper while the rest danced—'downright dancing, I mean', Jessie wrote, 'the ship is so buoyant, that granted you keep your legs at all, which is quite a toss-up to begin with, you have to dance like . . . Wodenblock, on his patent peg . . .'[13]

In the earlier part of the voyage Koozee was often missing. She kept to her bunk during the bad weather, emerging only occasionally, once in scarlet wraps with her hair flying in the breeze, to glimpse a passing ship. 'In heavy weather Koozee tucks away her work, and herself, and like the vessel lays-to until it is over,' Jessie wrote.[14] Charlotte Huybers was also often in bed, hiding her terrified fears for her own and her children's safety. One night during a wild storm, Jessie went up the companion steps to observe the scene: 'wild blasts rushing through the bare rigging and screaming against the close reefed top-sails,—great black moving hills with white ridges glimmering in the darkness—bearing down on the ship—carrying her over them, and casting her on to others—battering her on one side, and banging her on the other, all in a few seconds'. She left the scene awe-struck. Down below she joined other passengers in laughing her fears away, but Charlotte Huybers lay in her bed listening with rising fear to the wind. 'She & it', Jessie wrote, 'reached their climax together'.[15] Listening to the 'sweet and true' voices of the sailors as they sang their sea songs was the only thing that calmed Charlotte. 'Mama has often stood for a long time in this way forgetting for the hour her uneasiness and her old apprehensions absorbed in the sounds which reached her ears', Jessie wrote.[16] Jessie was to recall her mother's fears and thought 'with infinite pity' of 'all she went through' when she made another wild voyage through the Bay of Biscay, nearly twenty years later.[17]

One night there was an alarm when a fire, the event most dreaded on board ship, broke out. The steward, 'with a face of consternation' told the passengers to search their cabins. The fire was traced quickly to the cabin of Mr Daniels, the second mate, who had allowed a waistcoat to catch alight. It did no damage but Jessie was to remember this incident. She used a fire on board a sailing ship as the climax of her first published short story, 'Barren Love'.

During the long, cold, desolate voyage across the Antarctic seas east from New Zealand, Cape Horn constantly dominated the thoughts of the passengers. 'That wretched Horn!' Jessie wrote. 'How I have learnt to loathe its very name! How it has been harped upon,—and argued about,—and hurled at one,—and thrown into one's teeth, at every hour and minute of every monotonous day and night. When we are past the Horn—When we round the Horn—As soon as we tackle the Horn—*if* we get safely round the Horn'. When she asked the first mate, Mr Matthews, in exasperation, 'But shall we *ever* round the Horn?' he replied 'Well Mrs Fraser we don't intend to be jammed here until the Day of Judgement, I suppose'. At his reply, Jessie subsided into her 'accustomed phase of philosophic apathy'. The memory of sailing around Cape Horn remained vivid all her life; many years later she was to give a dramatic lecture on the perils of the voyage.[18]

After the fearful anticipations of the passengers the ship rounded the Horn with relative ease, as a cold fresh breeze blowing against the sails carried them through the water. With their cabins in the stern, however, the Huybers family felt, more than the rest, the terrifying 'bumps' that came as a climax to the pitching and rocking. As the ship gathered her energy for the supreme moment, Jessie wrote, 'she would settle down with a thud which shook us and herself and everything on board, out of place and shape and time . . .'[19]

There was more dismal weather after Cape Horn—one day was 'dreary, cheerless, dark, dismal, wretched, suicidal'[20]—and there was a final frightening storm. The ship rolled violently and the cuddy was swamped by a monster wave, but the Captain ran before the wind, making good time as the ship 'ploughed her way among the great waves,—rising and falling hills such as no description can properly portray'.[21] The ship's carpenter put up stanchions at the stern windows to stop the ports stoving in under the weight of the crashing waves. When they became mountainous, the Captain had to hove to for nearly a day. But this desperate gale and the speed the ship achieved carried them 'clear out of the snow and ice and freezing regions into mild, warm latitudes'. The worst of the journey was over. Before long they passed the mouth of the La Plata River, on the east coast of South America.

Then shipboard life changed. The carpenter removed one of the deadlights which had been in place in the Huybers's cabins since the day after their departure from Hobart, keeping them for nearly seven weeks in 'a sort of semi-light'. They were shocked at the scene of disorder, dirt and mess— 'old reminiscences of our early miseries and souvenirs of long gone by meals in beds and tag-rags and wretchedness'—that the sunlight revealed. The whole family set to work to restore order to the cabins, until finally Jessie could write, 'Fancy exchanging two dens of horror, two sloughs of despond, two dismal, dark, abysses of trunks and dirt, for two clean, bright-carpeted, snugly furnished little apartments'.[22]

She resumed teaching her charges. 'Fred and Harry go in for no end of lessons with us. We all make flourishing beginnings, but somehow we very often stop at the beginning. Next week we are going in for hard work.' She spent many hours teaching these two French as the three sat on deck on a huge opossum skin. Fred and Harry said their sentences, showed an exercise, or read. But they were easily diverted.[23] Jessie and the younger children began a series of Shakespeare readings every afternoon. When reading matter ran short, Koozee and Jessie turned to French novels, 'with the Iliad and Odyssey as the most improving stuff in the way of heavy reading we can find'.[24]

Soon they were sailing through calm seas in warm, lazy weather and soft moonlight nights. The heightened sensations of the fearful storms were gone, and with them some of their boisterous merriment. There was one final storm as they approached the tropics, a gale that blew for three days. Charlotte Huybers sat apprehensively in her cabin. Jessie, Jack and Edith grabbed the top of the companionway as they watched the ship dig down into the waves like a scoop then toss herself up again. Edith burst into tears of apprehension as suddenly a great gust shrieked across the sails, unreefing one, and shaking the mizzen mast to its foundations. The crew rushed to the deck and suddenly the rigging was alive with clambering men, swarming along the yards to repair the damage.

Once they were beyond the northern tropics, the passengers grew impatient. Jessie wrote, 'If this were a journal of emotions instead of events, I might speak of the growing impatience with which we watch the progress of the voyage, now that we hope it is drawing towards its close'.[25] But then they struck a week of 'dreary calms or dreary contrary winds'. When a great ocean steamer steamed past barely acknowledging the existence of the *Windward*, the passengers remarked on what 'great awkward-looking hulks' steamers were. Jessie wrote, however, 'There is not one of us who would not give something to be on a steamer now. We are sick of having nothing to say, nothing to hear, nothing to do—sick of sea-sights—and sea-sounds—sick of porpoises, and whales, and floating monsters & rubbish of all descriptions'.[26] To while away the time, Fred Des Voeux organised a sweep for their date of arrival, and within a day or so they sighted the most northerly island of the Azores, 'the first cry of "Land-Ho" . . . for three long dragged out dawdling months'.[27]

As a diversion, they made a point of celebrating birthdays. Frank's and Marie Crowther's were in March. They even celebrated those of absent family members. Willie's was on 6 April, and Alfred Huybers's on 23 April.

On 9 June they celebrated Edith's twelfth birthday with a 'grand fancy Ball' on deck, with all the passengers joining in and ransacking their trunks to dress for the occasion. The crew cheered as 'four couples paired off on deck, a motley group of scarlet, and blue, and white and yellow, green and purple, a jockey and a vivandière, a grand Duchess, a Queen of the Revels, a Queen of the Ball, Capt. McGregor, Lord Grim-Doodle, Lieutenant Camberoni, Macaroni, any-thing you like'. They paraded around the deck, and passengers and crew drank grog provided by Charlotte. 'Fred made a splendid officer, and Harry was not to be recognized in uniform and cork moustaches. Jack came out in the heavy-villain style to perfection and Frank as usual as the slimmest and horsiest of dapper little jockeys.' But, Jessie wrote, 'This may sound jolly, but, I think, there is no amount of this sort of jollity we would not forgo for one breath of land air—one sight of trees and flowers'.[28]

Finally the ship began to run before the wind and within a week they were within sight of England. But they were to be becalmed in the English Channel. At last Dover appeared, an old castle, rows of handsome buildings, then, best of all, smooth fields of yellow and green, sparkling with brightness. 'A sight for eyes, sore with gazing out for three months and more upon one monotonous watery waste!'[29] When they finally sailed up the Channel, it was a gala day. The Channel fleet was out in force to greet the Shah of Persia, who was arriving that day for a state visit.

Jessie finished her diary on the *Windward* with the ironic touch which was to become a feature of her novels. She was 'winding up', she wrote 'like the Author of a 3-volume novel, with heaping on us all every imaginable and unimaginable benefit'.[30] Although apparently announcing the end of her diary with the completion of the voyage, Jessie continued with a description of their arrival in London and was later to record their first weeks in the city.

This voyage was an important turning point in Jessie's life. Not only had she escaped—at least for a time—from her marriage, to resume the life of the older sister in the family, one to which she was to revert many times in her life, but she had also begun to write. As she did not use her diary as a confidante we learn nothing of her inner thoughts, her views on her marriage or her husband. Nevertheless, it was her first disciplined attempt at writing over a long period, and so had great benefits.

The voyage itself was to provide material for her fiction. Her earliest published story, 'Barren Love',[31] a novella of four chapters, is a love story set on a ship similar to the *Windward*. There are echoes of the *Windward's* passengers, and of Captain Lulham. The climax of the story comes with a fire aboard ship, reminiscent of that aboard the *Windward*. In the story, the fire catches hold and cannot be put out. The heroine is saved from the fire by a fellow passenger who ensures she escapes in a lifeboat, pressing a box containing his money into her hands and expressing great love, which he recognises is hopeless since he faces death in a flame-enshrouded ship a hundred miles from land.

The story has the philosophical approach that was to characterise much of Jessie's later writing. In this case the question is what constitutes a barren life. Had the formerly cynical fellow passenger fulfilled a higher destiny by giving everything to the one love of his life? Whose fate was preferable, the cynic's or the girl's? Which was better, to die at the high point of a romance, or live on for what would be in all probability a prosaic life, with a husband who might prefer 'modern cooking' to 'Greek art'.

Ship travel does not have a significant role in most of the other stories or novels Jessie wrote. There is the journey of the Clare family in *Not Counting the Cost*, which is closely based on Jessie's *Windward* voyage, the journey to Melbourne by the English Cavendish family to join Mr Piper in *Uncle Piper of Piper's Hill*, and the journey of Englishman John Grantley to Adelaide in 'John Grantley's Conversion'. By the time she wrote *Uncle Piper of Piper's Hill*, Jessie had travelled on several steamships, including the *Sobraon*, 'one of the smart passenger liners of the day'. The journey by the Cavendish family is made on a much larger ship than the *Windward*. The trip made by John Grantley is by a French ship similar to the Messageries Maritimes ships Jessie favoured on later voyages.

London, after the Huybers's enormous expectations, was both wonderful and disappointing. To their colonial eyes it was crowded, dirty and expensive—but its cultural treasures lived up to their expectations. Jessie's London diary is that of a tourist, containing little of her impressions of English life apart from a comment on the rows of dingy houses they saw as they travelled from the dock by train to central London. Of the cost of living, she wrote: 'London, with heaps of money must be a paradise, since the world brings all her fairest goods there and lays them at the feet of the wealthy'. 'For the poor it must be like the river in which the Tautalus was sunk up to his chin, and I am afraid there are many poor.'[32] Both themes are repeated in *Not Counting the Cost*. The Clare family expresses disappointment at London with its 'forest of houses with red roofs . . . such miserable houses!' and the 'enormous dark railway-station, with crowds and crowds of people. The air smelt so funny, and everything looked huge and dingy'. The cost of living in London is a shock to Mrs Clare: 'London is all changed since I knew it; it is not the London I remember; and rooms are horribly dear . . .'[33]

The Huybers family was met on board by Mr Tobin, a clerk in the office of Mr Henry Hawley, Alfred Huybers's London agent, who brought letters from home and an offer of assistance in finding lodgings. The next day the family moved to an apartment in Bayswater, where they found they were living near friends from Australia. The Kings were in the next street, the T.J. Knights not much further off, the Henry Cope Smiths and Sir Francis and Lady Smith and family, as well as some of Charlotte Huybers's friends from her London days, were all there.

They were soon tourists, and within a week had walked along Regent and Oxford Streets, seen St Paul's—to Jessie a grimy disappointment, 'like a giant pepper-caster asserting itself by towering above all the other bottles in the cruet'—visited the Zoological Gardens, walked in Hyde Park and Kensington Gardens, gazed in amazement at the Albert Memorial—'a glorious work of art'—and seen Madame Tussaud's waxworks.

One day Charlotte took her children by train from Kings Cross station to Highgate, Jessie's birthplace, to the home of an old friend. From Jessie's description of the house they visited, 'a veritable fairy land of verdure and flowers', it may have been her birthplace, Southwood Lodge. There, she wrote:

> we realised all that has been said about the green lanes and hedges, the fields and gardens of cultivated England. You saw as far as the eye could ups and downs of park and meadowland, gentlemen's estates and country houses smothered up in flowers and surrounded by their own velvety grounds. It is all soft & smiling and picturesque, not bold and rocky and imposing as in Tasmania.[34]

There is no mention of Charlotte Huybers visiting or contacting the Simeon family during this visit to London. Like Mrs Clare, in *Not Counting the Cost*, whose purpose in taking her children to Europe is to search for a long-lost wealthy relative and who then promptly forgets about her search, Charlotte seems also to have ignored her Simeon connection once it was within reach.

The family's most interesting cultural visits were made in the company of Willie Knight, a son of their father's friend, T.J. Knight QC. After serving briefly as Tasmanian Attorney-General, he had moved to Melbourne to practise law. One day, Willie, 'the most amiable of guides', took them to see paintings by modern artists on show at the Royal Academy, Jessie's first visit to a major art gallery.[35] (She was to describe a similar visit in the development of the friendship between Portia James and Harry Tolhurst in *The Penance of Portia James*.)

In the afternoon they went with Willie Knight—surely at Jessie's suggestion—to Willis's Rooms to hear speeches on 'The Female Education Question'. Jessie was not impressed. 'The Rooms were grand. The speeches poor', she wrote. Described in the London *Times*[36] as 'a large and influential meeting in support of the National Union for Improving the Education of Women of all classes', the main speakers were the Marquis of Lorne, whom Jessie described as 'a mild looking young man,' and Member of Parliament, Sir Stafford Northcote. Jessie was critical of the Marquis because he read his short speech while trying to pretend he was not reading from notes. Sir Stafford Northcote, she wrote, 'spent a great deal of superfluous time, in trying to prove to his own satisfaction that women were worth educating'. Then having

> condescendingly settled this point, in the affirmative, on the ground of their relations with men he next considered how best to enable them to fulfil those relations to the greatest advantage to men. So on, till we were nearly asleep.—Then a few others got-up, but there was nothing very original said by any one. Indeed the prime object of the meeting seemed to be the collection of funds for the establishment of a Public School for girls . . .[37]

Jessie and her mother had held, since their birth, far more radical views on the education of women than those of this very distinguished English group.

Jessie's other encounter with feminist thought occurred at a dinner at the home of their Australian friend, Mrs King, attended by Emily Faithfull, public lecturer, editor and founder of an all-female printing press. Faithful, who was in the forefront of many organisations for the employment of women, had just returned from a lecture tour of America. She had been involved in a sensational divorce case in 1864.[38] Jessie wrote that she 'drank pretty fairly and smoked after dinner', was 'extra fat and red' yet 'notwithstanding all these combined disadvantages & advantages', she left 'a very pleasing impression . . . of a clever genial woman'.[39]

Their London visit, so long and eagerly awaited, was soon to end. Jessie wrote, 'It seems absurd to complain of the enormous extent of the places we go to see when the real grievance of which I have to complain is our lack of time and opportunity for taking in the details of these places'.[40] One of their last visits was to the International Exhibition at South Kensington, again in the company of the Knights. Like a subsequent visit to the Crystal Palace, they were left with crowded impressions of displays that they had little time to explore in depth, although the opera orchestra which played at the exhibition realised all their 'ambitious expectations'. They were to leave for Brussels the next week, 'having left undone many things we ought to have done'.[41]

Jessie's sister Edith expressed the family's disappointment with London in a summary to a diary she began in Brussels:

> . . . an immense, dingy, busy, crowded city with miles and miles of never-ending smoky terraces, no brightness or beauty, but a good deal of solidity. On the whole our stay was not pleasant, and we were glad at the end of a month's time to find ourselves approaching the old town of Antwerp in a steamer in which we had left St Katherine's Dock the day before.[42]

Despite her initial impressions, however, Jessie was to return to London many times, and to spend many months living there.

5

Are we the same people I wonder?

Brussels, Paris, 1873–75

If Jessie continued to keep a diary when she left London for Brussels, it has now disappeared. For glimpses of her life in the ancient city of Brussels, there are only a few fleeting references in her youngest sister's summary of the family's life there, and an important reminiscence in the diary Jessie kept from 1889 to 1891.

In Brussels, Charlotte Huybers planned to give her children the education in European culture denied them in Hobart. She probably chose the city in preference to Paris because of Alfred Huybers's family associations and because, while French-speaking, it would be cheaper to live in than the French capital. At Antwerp they were met by Alfred Huybers's sister, Adèle Morian, and drove through the old town with 'its turreted housetops' that had been the birthplace of their father, and his forebears, for generations. On the way to the railway station, they glimpsed the old cathedral, and thought the town romantic and picturesque.[1]

Their first accommodation in Brussels was in unsatisfactory rooms in the petit rue Malibran, a small street full of taverns. But Jessie, with her gift for creating make-believe surroundings, was able to convince the others (according to Edith) that it was 'the most lovely place right in the country' on the strength of 'a few sandhills' nearby.[2] Edith, through her curious twelve-year-old's eyes, saw their landlord, M. Muller, a commissaire of police, as 'a greasy important personage . . . with a very large paunch and a very small pair of eyes', and his wife as 'a thin little woman with a shrill voice'. Two elder sons, Charles and Adolphus, 'a ferrety daughter' Josephine, and a 'deceitful little boy', Oscar, made up the family. Going downstairs in the morning the Huybers were likely to meet members of the Muller family still in their dirty nightclothes on their way to dress in the warm kitchen that the two families shared. This was the Huybers family's first warning of the poorer living conditions they were to experience in Europe. 'Having lived differently at home', Edith wrote, 'we soon found the style of life was not so pleasant as we had imagined'.[3]

Soon the petit rue Malibran became unbearable, and Charlotte Huybers engaged an immense cart to carry away their furniture. The Mullers tried to seize their 'beautiful buffet', claiming damages must be paid for abandoning the lease, but Charlotte engaged a lawyer and the Mullers gave up. They moved to a house in the nearby rue les Broussart running off the avenue Louise, the magnificent boulevard that was the pride of Brussels.

Jessie's task in Brussels was to teach the younger children. 'Jessie taught Frank, Johnnie & me', Edith wrote, 'and we got on very well, especially in our Arithmetic, for we passed "Vulgar Fractions", Decimals, and got on to Practice'.[4] But, of course, it was Charlotte who taught them French. When Edith and Johnnie wanted to earn money to buy feed for their rapidly growing family of pet guinea pigs, they earned fifty cents a week by agreeing to converse in the language, and Frank was disciplined by being prevented from making a planned trip to Waterloo, because he did not know his French lessons. Supplementing Charlotte's lessons was their practice of speaking French with relatives and neighbours, and while shopping and travelling about the city. John and Edith, inseparable since childhood and sharing the same hobbies, bargained constantly with shopkeepers over the spending of their small allowances, particularly in buying their guinea pigs and providing them with food. They also bargained in stamps when a bundle of letters from Australia provided them with supplies of these exotic commodities. In her account of her life in Brussels, Edith recorded in French one of the conversations they had with a hard-headed female stamp-dealer in the rue de la Madeleine. 'They always tried to cheat at first', Edith wrote, 'but it was no use, for we knew how our stamps were valued in Belgium where few people knew the difference between Australia and America'. With the money gained they would buy either 'a large stock of hay to lay down in our guinea pigs' yards and a quantity of carrots, or smuggle in a couple of strangers to our large family'.[5]

With Charlotte in charge, who could doubt that the family absorbed much of the culture and historical knowledge that Brussels had to offer? They visited all the galleries, their favourite being the Musée moderne, and the Hôtel de Ville, the Town Hall in the Grand' Place, one of the great sights of Brussels. From the top the whole city lay before them, and they could pick out prominent buildings and monuments. They were conducted over the chambers, shown the paintings, saw the two massive keys of the town and the room where, in 1555, Emperor Charles V of France ceded his Belgian provinces to Spain.

Edith, for whom Charlotte saw a future as a ballet dancer, was taken to see Meyerbeer's opera, *Robert le Diable*, at the Théâtre de la Monnaie, expressly to see Madame Lamy, the first dancer. Charlotte arranged for the second dancer to give Edith lessons. They were held in a large room on the second floor of the Maison du Roi, the residence during the sixteenth century of the Spanish Duke of Alva when Spain ruled the Netherlands, including what later became Belgium. Through the old-fashioned windows Edith looked down on the centuries-old ornate Italian Baroque buildings lining the Grand' Place, the women selling flowers in the square, and to the monument commemorating Counts D'Egmont and de Hornes, Flemish soldiers and nationalists, 'victims of the despotism and intolerance of Philippe II'[6] beheaded on 5 June 1568, following an uprising against Spanish rule.

In winter when the snow lay on the ground for as long as three weeks at a time, the children skated up the avenue Louise and past Rond Point to the Bois de la Cambre, sometimes passing a sledge drawn by horses with velvet trappings and tinkling bells, 'looking so lovely in the dazzling snow, that one wished winter would last for ever'.[7] At Christmas, they walked passed the confectioners' shops, their windows filled with little boxes of bonbons and sugar cakes moulded in the shape of men, women and horses. Their Aunt Adèle 'although . . . far from rich' brought them enormous cake men and horses, sugar slippers, and little ships filled with bonbons, as well as knitted socks and stockings and the traditional present of an enormous piece of pain d'épice de Breda (Breda gingerbread). Their uncle, David Morian, knelt at the feet of Edith, being the youngest, and offered her the customary piece of gingerbread.[8]

In the spring they went to the park, which became green almost overnight. In the summer they listened to the bands playing in the afternoon and to the opera orchestra in the evenings. They watched the processions marking the great religious events of the Catholic year, and walked up the steep narrow rue Montagne de la Cour and rue de la Madeleine, in single file on the narrow pavement, two abreast at the widest sections. They watched the horse-drawn omnibuses driven carefully up the narrow roadway to avoid slipping on the steep incline. They also played cricket. The Australian youth Jessie describes in *In Her Earliest Youth* who, while playing cricket one November day in the Bois de la Cambre is challenged about his nationality, may well have been based on Frank. In the novel, he proves he is an Australian by naming the winner of the Melbourne Cup, run the day before: '. . . twelve thousand miles from the scene of action, the Cup has the power to set patriotic Australian hearts beating', Jessie wrote.[9]

Just before the family left Brussels, they decided to visit Waterloo, the site of the famous battle that nearly sixty years before had ended the Napoleonic Wars. The 'John-Bulls' raved about it, Edith wrote, but Charlotte, with her French blood, had an ambivalent attitude to this monument to the British defeat of Napoleon; she took no interest in the excursion. Jessie, Koozee, John and Edith walked to the Gare du Midi, about three kilometres from their house, for the train journey south to Braine d'Alleud, the nearest station to the battlefield. At Waterloo they walked to the British Lion on top of a mound, saw two Prussian monuments and explored the museum, which they found consisted of 'one wretched room with a few fusty old souvenirs'. By the time they reached the station for the return journey to Brussels, the younger children were worn out. 'The agony was piled up to its utmost height', Edith wrote, 'on hearing that the train for Brussels only left at four o'clock and it was not then two'. When they reached the Gare du Midi, it was raining hard, and the biting wind nearly cut them in two.[10]

The most important event we know of affecting Jessie during her stay in Brussels was her meeting with 'the Commandant'. They went riding together in the Bois, and a strong physical and mental attraction developed between them. It was, however, an impossible romance from the start, the only reminder of it an entry in Jessie's diary fifteen years later. One day in Brussels in 1890, travelling on a tram, Jessie was startled to see 'the Commandant' enter. She had not spoken to him 'since our dramatic parting from one another for *ever*', when she had left Brussels in 1875. She wrote in her diary:

> He looked so little altered that for an instant the fifteen intervening years seemed blotted out. I had some ado to refrain from showing my emotion, turning from white to crimson and crimson to white in the space of a few seconds. But he bowed so naturally that I recovered my sang froid, and a moment later found myself answering a string of questions that he managed to ask me all in a few seconds.

She recorded the questions in French as they came tumbling from him as her replies did from her. 'Est-ce que votre premier mari est mort? . . . Comment? Divorcée? Et vous ne vouliez pas—non—vous ne vouliez pas—dans le temps . . . Vous vous rappelez? Et vous avez-eu des enfants? Non? Et votre soeur? Elle est mariée? Et Madame votre mère? Et votre frère? celui qui a eu les doigts coupés?' [Is your first husband dead? . . . What? Divorced? And you didn't want it—no—you didn't want it—at the time . . . You remember? And you have children? No? And your sister? She is married? And Madame your mother? And your brother? the one who had the cut fingers?] The Commandant told Jessie that the horse she had ridden so long ago had died only six months before—'and so on—and so on!'

'Are we the same people I wonder?' Jessie wrote, 'or have our minds and hearts undergone the same transformation as our bodies? He is married—has been for ten months, and lives in a beautiful house opposite the Goblets. Perhaps he has made un mariage d'argent for his declining years—for he was not rich in that far away time, and his present pay as Colonel would not suffice for the actual train de vie'.[11]

Jessie's personal life was a problem. Separated from an incompatible husband, she was bound by marriage ties that seemed unbreakable. Young and vibrant, she played a static, ambiguous role, a married woman living a celibate life without male companionship. She broke temporarily from this during her relationship with the Commandant. But although the mutual attraction was real enough, its doomed outcome gave it an aura of unreality, similar to some scenes and characters Jessie was to include in her novels.

Faint echoes of the elusive almost magical spell of her romance are present in her short story 'Malus Oculus' ('Evil Eye'), published in *The 'Vagabond' Annual* in 1877, only a few years after she left Brussels.[12] In 'Malus Oculus' she tells the story of the mesmeric influence exercised by a mysterious stranger on a young recently married Englishwoman, Grace Lovatt, while she is visiting Brussels with her husband. At a masked ball at the Théâtre de la Monnaie, the Brussels Opera House, the stranger, dressed as Mephistopheles, exerts his power, and Grace follows him from the theatre. After her husband and his friend find and attack the stranger, they realise they need his help to withdraw the spell from Grace.

The next morning Grace and her husband leave for Germany and Grace reverts to being 'a demure little woman', her memory of that carnival night uncertain and confused. In the final scene some years later Grace admits to her husband that the incident in Brussels had happened because her vanity, in wanting to attract attention, had led her into the clutches of 'a devil'. Her husband unctuously agrees—'a passion for personal admiration is at the bottom of half the shipwrecks of women's lives that we see'. But Grace reasserts her independence with her final comment: 'for all that, I don't think I'll make our little Grace a Quakeress'.

The stranger in 'Malus Oculus' could exert his influence over Grace only through mesmerism, but it is clear she was seeking an unusual experience. Throughout her life Jessie, too, sought and welcomed relationships that defied convention and 'Mrs Grundy'.

During the years of her first marriage, constrained from forming long-lasting emotional links, Jessie welcomed the appearance of a mysterious stranger, someone apart from the mundane world in which she was a separated wife, and a teacher of her younger brothers and sister. In her Brussels diary of 1889–90, she recorded several instances of the reappearance of 'shadows' from former days.

Her experiences in Brussels began the process that was finally to separate her from both her husband and Australia. For the present, however, she was tied inexorably to returning to Charles Fraser. Divorce was not only almost unattainable legally, but carried a social stigma few dared incur.

Early in March 1875, the time came to pack up and leave Brussels for Paris. The children disposed of their beloved guinea pigs, the furniture was sold, and a cart arrived to carry off their trunks to a hotel near the station. Koozee stayed behind in Brussels for a further three weeks to console their Aunt Adèle, and she and Adèle and their servant Christie farewelled the family as they left. 'As the train set off [Aunt Adèle's] face was convulsed with sobs, and it was pitiful to think how much she loved us', Edith wrote. 'I wonder if I will ever see pretty Brussels again. I hope so, as it would be to see the place where I spent such happy days'.[13]

This period of nineteen months was to have an effect lasting a lifetime on the Huybers family. Some of them were to return to Brussels over and over again, some were to live there for long periods; and two were to die there. For almost none was Australia ever to have their undivided loyalty again. European life and culture had begun to cast an insidious, long-lasting spell, from which some escaped with difficulty, and others never.

After their arrival in Paris on 4 March 1875, the family took six small rooms on the third floor of an apartment building in the Champs Elysées.[14] Despite this superior location, their lifestyle was frugal, and their accommodation and food far inferior to what they had been accustomed in Australia. There were no lush strawberries and rich cream as there had been at Highfield, and they ate little meat. They saved money by walking immense distances instead of paying for transport, and by eating sparingly. But they threw themselves enthusiastically into sightseeing in this city that less than five years before had been under siege in the Franco-Prussian War and had seen the overthrow of Napoleon III and the establishment of the Third Republic.

Nothing had prepared them for the 'dazzling splendour' of the Paris boulevards and the 'grandeur and beauty' of the Champs Elysées, with its continually playing fountains, its velvety green lawns, and the freshness and cleanliness of the road and gutters. The day after their arrival they walked up the Champs Elysées to the Madeleine, where they ate. Then they continued up the boulevards de la Madeleine, and des Capucines, des Italiens and Montmartre, returning home by the rue de Rivoli and place de la Concorde.

Soon they had established the pattern of life for their five months in Paris. Though money was short, they ate their main meal at a restaurant each day, often paying a franc each. When money became scarcer, two in turn would stay home and eat boiled eggs, bread and butter. Those who ate out changed eating places as the food or the service became bad, or the expense too great. Their first eating place was Duval's at the Madeleine, then they favoured the Henri IV restaurant at the Palais Royale—but this was half as dear again. Then they deserted the Henri IV (they found the food 'dirty and distasteful') and started patronising the Bouillon in the rue Verinne.

On their second day in Paris, they paid the first of what were to be many visits to the Louvre. Jessie organised many of these, and those to other galleries, including the Musée de la marine. One day she took John and Edith to the Louvre to see the Flemish masters. Edith found the paintings of Rubens and Teniers oppressive but with each succeeding visit she liked the Louvre more. At the Galerie d'Apollon, with its gilded ceiling, she admired the statues, particularly the Venus de Milo, more than the paintings. Another day Jessie took John and Edith to the Louvre to see the gallery of modern sculpture, where Edith admired the statues of Cupid and Psyche.[15]

They also visited the church of St Adeleine, then the 'most beautiful modern church' in Paris, and toiled up the steps of Notre Dame to the cloche de Sebastapol. They moved on past the gargoyles to the top, where they scrambled up on the roof, to the iron pole that extended upwards. There they held on while the wind blew. When they came down, they went inside the cathedral, admiring the paintings, but generally finding it too dark and solemn. Later that morning they visited the Pantheon on the Left Bank, the eighteenth century church secularised during the Revolution. Edith found the four paintings of Death, Justice, Glory and Peace splendid and altogether preferred the 'bright & beautiful' Pantheon to Notre Dame.[16]

They chose the one day in the month that the grand fountains played to visit Versailles. After a two-hour drive through the country, they ate in the beautiful gardens, then looked at the battle scene paintings in the Salon du palais. But when the fountains played at five, they were a great disappointment. They returned by train, to Edith's dismay being held up in a tunnel, where she imagined a dreadful railway accident might occur.

In the warmer weather, they attended outdoor concerts. One evening Jessie, Koozee and Edith went to hear the Champs Elysées concert, but found they had to remain in the garden, since women were not allowed to enter unaccompanied by men. Edith followed every note of *The Merry Wives of Windsor* that she was learning on the piano Charlotte had hired so that she could continue to give lessons to her children.

Jessie took every opportunity to absorb the culture and the sights of Paris. But she also found time to read French novels she borrowed from a circulating library in the rue de Mehul. Ever after she was to be critical of the standard of contemporary French fiction.

One day soon after their arrival Charlotte visited Neuilly about five kilometres east to look for the old house where she had lived as a child more than fifty years ago. After searching unsuccessfully for some time she decided that the fortifications erected during the Franco-Prussian War had cut through the house and was disappointed at finding no trace of it.

Although they lived in Paris during spring and summer, and did not experience the severity of a Paris winter, various members of the family had a succession of illnesses—Frank suffered from neuralgia, and John had a toothache and later a bad throat which required medical treatment with caustic. When Jessie had an infected throat she preferred treatment with a mustard plaster, purchased nearby. Charlotte's finances were strained when she had to spend a great deal on treatment for her own teeth, from which she suffered constant pain.[17]

The Huybers had friends in Paris with the tantalising name of Deakin, who are never explained in Edith's diary. In the first entry in which they are mentioned she writes merely, 'Mamma, Jessie & I went to the Hotel du Prince Albert to see Mrs Deakin'.[18] Subsequently Mrs Deakin accompanied them on several outings, and her husband, a doctor, 'costicqued' John's bad throat.[19] Dr and Mrs Deakin are the only visitors to the Huybers's apartment mentioned in Edith's diary. It remains an intriguing question whether they were related to William and Sarah Deakin of Melbourne, and their children who included Alfred, later Prime Minister of Australia.

Mrs Deakin accompanied the family on many of their outings. She went with Jessie, Frank and Edith to the Jardin d'acclimation, where they admired the flowers and the monkeys, listened to the band music, and where Edith had her first ride on an elephant. When it was time to go home they found all the omnibuses crowded and unconventionally hitched a ride with a stranger driving a one-horse waggon.[20] One evening in May she joined Jessie, Koozee, Frank, John and Edith for a visit to the very popular circus which performed in a stone building near the Arc de l'Etoile. They were amazed at an acrobat dancing and doing somersaults on a tightrope, and at the 'dancing' and 'singing' horses.[21]

Apart from absorbing knowledge through visits to the Louvre and other galleries and museums, Charlotte had a more formal cultural education in mind for her children. One day apparently to get advice on art training for John, whose talent she regarded as exceptional, she took him and Edith on an omnibus to Passy, on the outskirts of the city, to visit the celebrated French painter, M. Yvon. Though they had a long walk along the rue de la Tour to find his studio near the fortifications, Charlotte returned again the following day, this time with Jessie as well as John. Then she enrolled her son at the atelier of M. Julian, at the Galerie des panoramas on the boulevard Montmartre, for drawing and painting lessons. Julian was a famous teacher, later awarded the Cross of the Legion of Honour for services to French art. After John had been attending for some time, Edith joined him at Julian's atelier, but she was not allowed to join the male students for life drawing, and had to sit in a small room adjoining the main studio. After a month, Charlotte was forced to withdraw Edith because the fees were too high. Instead she was enrolled in a free school in the rue de Seine which Jessie and Koozee were already attending.

Jessie described this school, the Ecole professionelle pour jeunes filles, in her first newspaper article, published in 1877.[22] To enter the school, Jessie must have cheated a little in giving her age, since it was open to women under twenty-five, and she was twenty-six. They learnt to draw from busts and live models, as well as engraving on steel, etching, wood cutting, fan painting, and faïence and porcelain painting. At first sight these lessons appear to be in ladylike accomplishments rather than serious art, but to Jessie this was important training because it taught skills that could lead to lucrative employment. In her article, written after her return to Melbourne, she advocated the establishment of a similar school in Victoria, to teach women skills they could use in earning money.

Edith continued with dancing lessons begun in Brussels. One day Charlotte took her to the Conservatoire de danse where dancers in the opera practised. Charlotte also took her youngest daughter, for whom she held the greatest expectations regarding a dancing career, to the 'nouvel opéra' to see *Hamlet* performed as an opera, with dances performed by Mademoiselle Beaugrand and Madame Lamy. Edith was enchanted. She thought 'that perhaps it was the last time in our lives that we should see *such* dancing'.[23]

Jessie's movements in Paris are known only through the eyes of her young sister. We can surmise that her imagination was stimulated by life in this great city. She probably began writing, and certainly began storing memories which were to surface in her factual and fictional writing. In *Not Counting the Cost,* she recounts the life of the Clare family in Paris, in a poorer quarter of the city than the Champs Elysées where the Huybers lived—and even shorter of money. *The Penance of Portia James* is set mainly in Paris, although it draws more on Jessie's experiences during subsequent stays, when she lived on the Left Bank. The cultural knowledge and acquaintance with philosophical theories she acquired during this stay in Paris were to inform her writing for the rest of her life. She had gained the breadth of knowledge that was to enable her to write about trends in art and philosophy as easily as she did of literature.

Reluctant, if not panic-stricken, about returning to her life in country Australia as Charles Fraser's wife, she probably dreamt of staying in Paris, supporting herself by earning her own living. Did she, like Eila in *Not Counting the Cost,* consider the possibility of sewing, drawing, singing or playing the piano to earn money, but decide her talents were insufficient? Did she consider, like Eila, looking after young children or giving English lessons, only to decide both were too poorly paid to make them worthwhile? In *Not Counting the Cost* Eila decides on the unlikely idea of entering a beauty contest at the Folies fantassin in an effort to win a prize of five thousand francs (£200). Was Jessie similarly tempted during the hot carnival days of that Paris summer? Did she contemplate auditioning for the stage, or writing articles for the press? If she did, the evidence is lost. Perhaps she accepted that she had no alternative but to return to her unhappy marriage.

In Paris, Jessie was ready for romance yet extremely wary of any commitment. She may have fallen in love in Paris as she had in Brussels, but as she was to write many years later, 'what [F]rench novelist, or indeed what person of any nationality would believe that the final step had never been taken?'[24]

In the middle of August an omnibus carried Jessie, the rest of the family and their luggage, to the railway station. They took 'a last look at dear old Paris' and boarded a train for Boulogne, from where Charlotte took Edith and John on a nostalgic return to Calais, where she had stayed with her mother as a child. From Boulogne they made an overnight Channel crossing, then drove to Mrs King's house in Bayswater, where they were to stay until the *Sobraon* sailed to Melbourne.

6

Her whole being was in a state of revolt

Malmsbury, Melbourne, 1876–79

There is no record of the meeting of Jessie and Charles Fraser after a separation of three years. Jessie, her head full of the stimulating experiences of European life, may well have felt dismayed at the prospect of returning to her former life as a country housewife. But to outward appearances, at least in the eyes of Jessie's young brother, husband and wife appeared reconciled. Eddie, aged twenty-one, wrote of Jessie's marriage that 'the most "troublous times" seem to have passed over and Jessie has the disposition to be happy anywhere. Charlie is always very good to her, and though of course she would have been much better had she not married so young, things might have been much worse . . .'[1]

Eddie was an optimistic rather than an astute observer. He may have seen not happiness but the polite tension before the storm. Or perhaps Jessie had decided, as she had once before, to try to conform, by leading a 'better life'.

Jessie, Charlotte, Koozee, Frank, John and Edith steamed into Melbourne from London aboard the *Sobraon* on 27 December 1875. The voyage had been very different from their experience on the *Windward*. The *Sobraon* was a fine ship, which carried many passengers. Its route was around the Cape of Good Hope, not the hazardous Cape Horn. Alfred Huybers had come over early from Hobart to Melbourne to meet his family and together with Willie and Eddie, both working in Melbourne, had spent some days at Pemberley, the property Charles Fraser had moved to near Malmsbury, a town just ten kilometres north-west of Kyneton. The day after Christmas they received a telegram that the *Sobraon* was off Cape Otway and they left Pemberley to travel to Melbourne.[2]

The younger members of the family were overcome at being reunited. For Edith words could not convey 'the idea of such a happy record in one's

55

life'.[3] To Eddie, meeting his mother, sisters and brothers was 'better remembered than written—We were all changed more or less, and had plenty to talk about our adventures in each others absence'.[4]

Jessie went to Pemberley with Charles, but seemed wary of an intimate reunion, and took with her Koozee and Frank. Koozee had been ill, so it was thought she would benefit from the country air. Frank, who had knelt and kissed the earth in an exuberance of happiness at being back in Australia, wanted 'to train for a station'. Nearly eighteen, he had spent the years in Europe homesick for the Australian bush, undermining his mother's efforts to have him trained as an artist. According to his brother, Frank had 'a heaven-sent gift, in the delineation of animal life' but he had 'spurned European art schools'.[5] He was soon 'busy thistle-cutting, sheep-shearing and fence-mending' at Pemberley.[6]

The homestead there had nothing of the stateliness of Montpellier. It was a simple timber structure with a detached kitchen, probably not even equalling the rough standard of the accommodation on the Degraves station on the Murray or at Oakville where Jessie had briefly lived. But, though small and rudimentary, it was beautifully situated on a high point overlooking a lagoon on the Coliban River, recently dammed to form the Coliban Water Supply Reservoir.

While Jessie was living in Brussels, Charles Fraser had, in March 1874, leased Pemberley from Mrs Henry Orr,[7] following the sale of Degraves's Montpellier estate. He was probably attracted to the property not only because of its closeness to Kyneton, the district that had been his home since his youth, but for its potential as a horseracing stud. Soon he had laid out a race track in one of the paddocks, begun a breeding program, and was winning races again. In September 1875, the *Kyneton Guardian* reported the great success of the progeny of his mare, Lady Kirk.[8] Even as late as November 1876, when his financial problems were escalating, Fraser paid 210 guineas for the thoroughbred stallion Impudence.[9]

Pemberley was on the outskirts of Malmsbury, like Kyneton a horseracing centre. In 1873 at least 2500 people, double the population of the town, attended the New Year's Day meeting, many travelling from Kyneton by horse cart.[10] The town, which had developed as a stop on the way to the Bendigo goldfields, was dotted with solid and distinctive buildings constructed from the famous Malmsbury bluestone, quarried north-east of the town.[11] Gold had been discovered in the district in 1858 by a Frenchman, and there were still people searching for it in the 1870s, many of them the Chinese mentioned several times in Jessie's writing. Malmsbury, with its seventeen hotels, and many others outside the town area, may have been the source of Jessie's description in her novel *In Her Earliest Youth* of a town in which practically every second building in the main street was a hotel.

The social life of Malmsbury was initially attractive. Edith wrote, following a visit to Melbourne by Jessie and Koozee, that they must have

The barque *Windward* on which Jessie, her mother and the younger Huybers children sailed from Hobart to London in 1873. Their journey through wild and freezing gales around Cape Horn took over three months. (State Library of Tasmania)

A nineteenth century illustration of the Grand' Place in the centre of Brussels. It is lined with centuries-old ornate buildings built as the headquarters of medieval guilds. The Hotel de Ville (Town Hall) is at left. When Edith Huybers had dancing lessons at the Maison du Roi she looked down from the second floor window on women selling flowers in the square, the old buildings, and the statues of patriots.

Left: Charlotte Huybers, photographed in Paris. She had an invincible belief in the extraordinary artistic talents of her children. In Paris she arranged painting lessons for John, dancing and painting lessons for Edith, and Jessie and Koozee attended a drawing and painting school. (Renée Erdos)   Right: After three years' absence, Jessie returned to Victoria at the end of 1875 to resume her life with Charles Fraser. Omens for their happiness together were not good, but divorce was almost unattainable, particularly for women. (Renée Erdos)

Frank Huybers had great talent as a painter of horses, but preferred life in the Australian bush to the art schools of Europe. Several of his paintings are held by the Huybers family. (Renée Erdos)

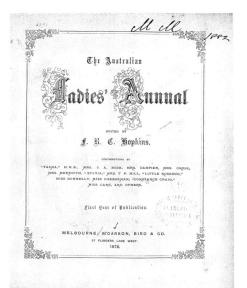

Left: Jessie had two stories published in *The Australian Ladies' Annual* in 1878. 'The Rubria Ghost', set on a station on the Murray, was the lead story. Her second contribution, 'Concerning the Forthcoming Melbourne Cup', featured a horseracing enthusiast, a character based on Charles Fraser. Right: French author Juliette Adam, began the influential fortnightly *La nouvelle revue* in 1879. Jessie's novella, 'L'amour aux Antipodes' was published in it the following year. The widow of Senator Edmond Adam and a powerful figure in politics, Adam continued to edit *La nouvelle revue* until 1899. She died in 1936 at the age of 100. (*La Grande Francaise*)

A present-day view of part of the apartment building at 1 place de l'Observatoire near the Luxembourg Gardens on the Left Bank where Jessie lived when she rejoined her family in Paris in 1879.

After a brilliant career as an art student in Paris, Arthur Loureiro moved to Melbourne with his wife Koozee in 1884, where he sold several paintings he had brought with him. He had a painting studio on the upper floor of Cabana, a house he and his wife Koozee built in Stawell Street, Kew. (*Illustrated Sydney News*, 1 August 1891)

Left: Soon after his marriage to Julia Ord in London in 1881, Edward Huybers returned to Hobart to work in his father's business. (Renée Erdos) Right: A painting of Koozee (Maria Theresa Huybers) by her husband Arthur Loureiro, whom she met while he was a student of Alexandre Cabanel at the Ecole des beaux arts in Paris. (Oil on canvas laid down on board, 40.6 × 29 cm, 1884—Renée Erdos)

found the city dull as 'they seemed to have been so festive' at Pemberley.[12] Apart from race meetings, there were fêtes at St John's Anglican Church,[13] which was to feature in *Uncle Piper of Piper's Hill* as the church to which the clergyman the Reverend Francis Lydiat was posted at Barnesbury, a town similar to Malmsbury.

If the meeting of Jessie and Charles Fraser was at least outwardly happy, their relationship did not remain so. After a period of wary reunion, Jessie learnt from Fraser himself that during her absence, he had had an affair with a servant, and fathered a child.[14] Her immediate reaction is unknown. Although she may have realised it would have been unrealistic for her to expect a robust man in his mid-thirties to remain without female companionship and sex during her three years' absence, Charles Fraser's news appears to have affected her deeply, and to have rankled all her life.

It may be instructive to look at Jessie's novels to see how similar situations were handled. In most of them, husbands exhibit Charles Fraser's faults: his recklessness with money, his gambling, his obsession with horseracing, his deeply philistine attitude to anything cultural. Some of the husbands are violent or mad. But in only one case is the husband a philanderer. When the heroine in *The Penance of Portia James* discovers on her wedding day that her husband, during their engagement, has a mistress and an illegitimate child, she avoids consummating the marriage, and escapes from London to Paris.

In a similar situation Jessie found no easy escape. She may have found Fraser's sexual advances repugnant, as did Portia in *The Penance of Portia James*. Portia resisted John Morrisson's 'hungry, devouring kisses, upon forehead, lips and neck', and felt 'an inexplicable physical shrinking in his presence, as though he were literally hungering to devour her bodily, and were whetting his lips in anticipation of the feast'.[15]

Judged by her subsequent actions, it seems that hearing of Fraser's affair reawakened in Jessie all her old feelings of resentment towards him. They were living at Pemberley when she heard the news, and it was to darken her view of this property for life.

It is impossible to visit the site of the Pemberley homestead, to find the remains of the rough path that connected the house with the kitchen, to look down on the trees edging the dam, and out over the paddocks, without directly experiencing its resemblance to Tarooma, the home of Ruth and James Fenton, in Jessie's last novel, *A Fiery Ordeal*. The Fentons live in a small, run-down, ill-furnished house with a detached kitchen, built of rough wooden slabs and with an earth floor. In summer the sun heats 'the mean dwelling to the pitch of a baker's oven'. Ruth escapes from the heat and the dissatisfactions of her life by swimming in the water-hole at the bottom of the garden while James Fenton is busy squandering what money he has on cards and hoping to make good his losses by a big win backing his horses.[16]

Despite the intervening years and the changes in her life, when Jessie came to write *A Fiery Ordeal* so many years later, she appears to express some of her resentment about her life at Pemberley through her character Ruth Fenton. Did she feel, as Ruth did:

> Her whole being was in a state of revolt against the conditions under which she lived and moved and breathed . . . the surroundings, like the air of Baynton, were hateful to her for the good reason that, hating her existence there, she hated everything connected with it.[17]

Did she, like Ruth, find exhilaration only in diving into the lagoon in the early morning, and striking out for the reedy shore opposite, or in racing over the solitary plains on her brown cob?

Jessie was probably not as devoid of hope as the fictional Ruth. She saw the key to escape from her marriage not, at this stage, in divorce—the laws of Victoria did not allow a wife to divorce her husband for adultery—but in becoming independent, in being able to keep herself. She began to plan for a future in which she would support herself by writing. While she remained at Pemberley, she had only limited access to publishers. But after hearing Charles Fraser's news she would have felt no obligation to spend all her time with him. Conveniently, her mother, her brothers and sisters were living in Melbourne, only a few hours away, by train. As she had done during the earlier years of her marriage when she was particularly unhappy, she found both a retreat and a stimulus with her mother and family. In Melbourne, both through her family's and her own Tasmanian connections, through the friends her brothers had made in the city, and through her own efforts, she built up a circle of acquaintances in the literary world that was to lead to an avalanche of publishing opportunities.

Charlotte Huybers had set up house at Blairgowrie, an historic house in South Yarra. The break with her husband had been a *fait accompli* before she sailed for Europe and although she visited him in Hobart for a few weeks with John and Edith soon after returning to Australia,[18] it was never intended they would resume life together. Alfred Huybers put his family at first into a furnished apartment at 8 Royal Terrace, Melbourne, then, from February 1876, they leased Blairgowrie from Mrs Helen Forbes, widow of the Presbyterian Minister, the Reverend James Forbes, who had baptised Charles Forbes Fraser.

Blairgowrie was situated on the south bank of the Yarra on land originally sold at auction only six years after the founding of Melbourne, and later bought by George Augustus Robinson, protector of Aborigines in Van Diemen's Land and Port Phillip District. On two lots totalling twenty-eight acres on a high ridge sloping down to the Yarra River, he built three substantial houses, Blairgowrie, Rosemount and Tivoli. A cutting was later made through the ridge to form Chapel Street, Prahran connecting over a bridge across the Yarra with Church Street, Richmond and the city of

Melbourne. Blairgowrie was a large home built of stone, said to have been carried up from the banks of the Yarra by Aboriginal people under Robinson's direction. From the house there was a wide view of the surrounding countryside and in the acres of gardens and orchards there was room for Edith to keep a cow and pet pigeons.[19]

At first Charlotte had Koozee, John and Edith living with her at Blairgowrie. Then they were joined by Willie and Eddie, both working in the stockbroking business that Willie had begun in Melbourne in 1874. John and Edith began studying for their matriculation, and later were joined by Frank, since it was considered he, too, should matriculate before pursuing his dream of becoming a station manager. John and Edith also attended the Gallery School of Painting[20] under Austrian-born landscape painter, Eugene von Guérard.

I discovered the Huybers family's residence at Blairgowrie only through its being written as an address on the diary Edward Huybers began there in 1877, with his reminiscences of the family's early life. Searching in street directories and then in local histories for information about the house and its occupants, I came to realise how important it was in Jessie's life and her writing. Not only was it a convenient base, close to the city, it was also the centre of a district from which Jessie was to draw inspiration for her writing. Across the paddocks was Como, one of the most beautiful homes in Victoria, situated overlooking Como Park, the Yarra and Richmond to the north. This is a house with resemblances to Tom Piper's mansion in *Uncle Piper of Piper's Hill*. In addition to Como, there were other houses nearby to provide the inspiration for Tom Piper's mansion, and the way of life of their *nouveau riche* occupants.

All the information I discovered about Blairgowrie itself (which does not now exist), points to its being similar to the Fullertons' home, Riverview, in *A Knight of the White Feather*, a novel which includes scenes describing characters travelling from their riverside home across to the city.

Melbourne itself was also a source of inspiration and information for the novels. A city made rich by gold, with a rapidly growing population of more than 200,000, it had extensive cultural assets including its Public Library, National Gallery and Museum, regarded as highlights by visitors.

Divorce was so difficult for a woman to initiate and so infrequently granted, that Jessie maintained a façade of marriage. She seems to have taken any opportunity, however, to visit Blairgowrie, and it is unlikely that Charles Fraser would have done anything to keep her at Pemberley.

From Blairgowrie, she could venture into publishing offices and in this way her writing career began. During the last few months of 1877, 'Tasma', the name she adopted for her writing, became widely known in Victoria. She adopted this pseudonym to honour the colony where she grew up nine years before Helen Mitchell honoured Melbourne by adopting the name of Nellie Melba for her first recital in Brussels, late in 1886 and for her public debut in 1887. Thereafter Jessie was to use the name Tasma for all her writing and from 1880 she used the name Jessie Tasma for her lectures in Europe.

From the beginning, she was regarded as a bright new talent. In the annuals and collections in which her stories appeared, her contributions always took first place. Her first published story, 'Barren Love', which drew on her experiences on the *Windward*, appeared as the first story in *'Hash.' A Mixed Dish for Christmas*, edited by Garnet Walch for release for Christmas 1877. This was a great honour, since among the contributors were much better known authors, including Marcus Clarke, author of the classic convict novel *For the Term of His Natural Life*; 'The Vagabond', then at the height of his fame as an investigative journalist; Arthur Patchett Martin, editor of the intellectual quarterly *Melbourne Review*; and Francis Rawdon Chesney Hopkins, a grazier, playwright and editor.

Jessie knew Garnet Walch's family in Hobart, had travelled on the *Windward* with his nephew, and Walch himself was a friend of her brother's. He was a well-known writer and publisher of Christmas annuals, and also a theatrical producer specialising in pantomimes and extravaganzas, many of which he wrote himself. In 1873 he had been appointed secretary to the Melbourne Athenaeum, the leading literary institute in Australia.[21]

Another of Jessie's stories, 'Malus Oculus', her sensational and exotic story set in Brussels dealing with the topical subject of mesmerism, had the leading place in *The 'Vagabond' Annual* also released for Christmas 1877. 'The Vagabond', editor of this collection, which included contributions from Marcus Clarke, Arthur Patchett Martin, Francis Hopkins and many other writers well known at the time, was a sensational figure in Melbourne, following publication in the *Argus* of his series of articles on life among the outcasts behind the façade of the respectable city. 'The Vagabond's' first-hand accounts of what it was like to be 'inside' Pentridge Gaol, the Kew Lunatic Asylum, the Immigrants' Home, or to sleep and eat in the cheap lodging houses and cafés frequented by the city's poor and homeless precipitated many official inquiries into the appalling conditions he revealed. Intense public interest in the identity of 'The Vagabond' added to the notoriety of his articles. Though he remained a mysterious figure to most of Melbourne, 'The Vagabond' was a friend of the Huybers family and a frequent visitor at Blairgowrie.[22] They probably knew him as Julian Thomas, the name he claimed at the time, but he is now known to have been born John Stanley James.[23] 'The Vagabond's' journalistic methods and his sympathy for the outcasts of society were to influence Jessie's subsequent career as a writer.

While in Melbourne Jessie also met Gowen Evans, a barrister and journalist who had arrived from London about ten years earlier. Evans[24] was twenty-two years older than Jessie, a sophisticated, well-connected man of the world, a type who was to appear in her novels, and to whom she was often attracted. After studying at the Inner Temple, Evans had in 1864 been called to the Bar, but turned to journalism and began writing for the London *Spectator*, a weekly in the forefront of English liberalism. Then one of the proprietors of the Melbourne *Argus*, Edward Wilson, chose him to represent the Wilson interests in the management of that paper. From his arrival in Melbourne in 1867, apart from practising as a barrister, Evans took a prominent part in the direction of both the *Argus* and its associated weekly publication, the *Australasian*, particularly from 1878 when he was appointed managing partner representing the Wilson interests, a position he held until his death in 1897.[25] It was said that he had a special regard for the *Australasian*: his 'spirit infused all its counsels'. He also became a well-known figure in Melbourne society. 'Wherever club-life brought states-men, judges, and professional or social stars together, he was in the midst of them, boldly discussing the problems of the day, and ventilating and maintaining the views which a high-minded, cultured man of the world could freely express.'[26] Apart from providing Jessie with influential support as a contributor to the *Australasian*, the two were strongly attracted. Many years later, Jessie was to refer to her relationship with Gowen Evans as what 'might have been'. He may have been a suitor dissuaded from the possibility of pursuing her by her ambiguous position as a woman partly separated from her husband but unable to contemplate freedom from him. When Jessie met Evans in Paris many years later, after her life had taken other turns, she wrote that she had 'spent the last week in dissipations of all kinds thanks chiefly to the presence of Mr Gowen Evans'.

'Difficult to help pondering occasionally upon the "might have been", though not, I hope and trust, to the detriment of what is—though the wise saw "whatever is, is right" is certainly not proven', she wrote in her diary.[27] Eight months later, when she met him again in Paris, she was again nostalgic about what might have been:

> For two days an old memory was revived—and wonderful to say 'the new wine—the new wine' tasted 'better than the old'. I met a friend of former days and the time I spent with him (just as in the past) leaves a strong sense of happiness without the sting of remorse. The tie seems indeed closer than ever, and the memory of his words that he cared for me for *myself*—and the manner in which he has proved it lie warm at my heart. But what [F]rench novelist, or indeed what person of any nationality would believe that the final step had never been taken! The drive to the Bois at night and halt before the Tour Eiffel with its garland of glittering lights remain two bright spots in my memory. He came to see me off at the Gare du Nord, and is now on his way to Australia, and I think or try to think as little as possible of the 'might have been'.[28]

Like some other men to whom Jessie was attracted, Evans remained a bachelor all his life. With her wariness about close involvement, it appears she may have encouraged, consciously or unconsciously, admiration from men who were sexually unthreatening.

I discovered Jessie's connection with Gowen Evans through the mention of his name in her 1889–90 diary. The more information I discovered about him the more it seemed some of his characteristics had appeared in at least one of Jessie's fictional creations: Sir Francis Segrave, the sophisticated English visitor who pursues Pauline Drafton of *In Her Earliest Youth*. He temporarily captivates her by appealing to the intellectual side of her nature, and is the antithesis of Pauline's colonial husband, who thinks of nothing but horses and betting. Segrave talks to Pauline about books, arousing 'a bright interested light in her eyes', and delights her with presents of the latest novel, a copy of Matthew Arnold's poems, and 'an almost new' French novel.[29] Then he organises a visit to the National Gallery where she listens as he talks about 'The Pilgrim Fathers' and 'Sunset at Rotterdam', the pride of the collection, and about 'Rachel at the Well', 'Moses Descending from the Mountain' and 'The Brigands'.[30] He talks about the significance of the *plein air* school of painting, the latest art topic in Paris. Afterwards they take a picnic hamper to Royal Park where Pauline, in an exuberance of pride in her native land, delights him by imitating the laugh of the kookaburra, the chirp of the minah, the double note of the wattle-bird, and the croak of the mopoke.

Jessie's acquaintance with Gowen Evans may have facilitated her entry into the columns of the *Australasian*. Under editor Henry Gullett, the paper had been among the earliest in Australia to introduce a column specifically for women readers. Gullett's wife, Lucinda (Lucy), one of Australia's pioneer women journalists, wrote many of the columns under the name of 'Humming Bee'.[31] The first of Jessie's many articles and stories to be published in the *Australasian*, 'A Hint to the Paris Commissioners', appeared in 'The Lady's Column' on 24 November 1877. Written in an essay style, with a discursive beginning that gradually led to the main topic, the article had many of the characteristics of her later work. Its theme was very close to her heart: the employment of women in meaningful tasks. She wrote with sympathy of the growing number of women in Victoria who, unable to find paid employment, frittered their time away debating 'the particular depth of shade which must edge a flounce, or in the laborious execution of a piece of lace-work in No. 200 thread—if such a number exist—to the detriment of their eyes and their spinal marrows'. Instead of plodding through 'piles of superfluous anti-macassars' and toiling over 'lengthy and unrepaying strips of embroidery', she believed they could be more profitably employed.

Jessie advised the commissioners in charge of Victoria's exhibit at the

Exposition universelle, then being staged in Paris, to slip away from it and visit the Ecole professionelle pour jeunes filles, the school that Jessie, Koozee and Edith had attended. She advocated that a professor should be encouraged to come to Victoria to set up a school of porcelain painting, believing this tuition would be welcomed not only by those who wanted to possess luxury items but, more importantly, by those looking for lucrative employment. Despite the 'Mrs Somervilles, George Eliots, Harriet Martineaus' it was to 'finger work not brain work' that the mass of women looked for employment, Jessie wrote.

Once having breached the barrier, in having her article published in the *Australasian*, Jessie followed with many other articles and short stories. Some were based on her life in Victoria and Tasmania, while others drew on her European experiences. Two were tales of human relationships in bush settings: 'How a Claim was Nearly Jumped in Gum-tree Gully',[32] set on a tributary of the Coliban River in the country around Pemberley in the period following the passing of the 1860s Free Selection Acts, and 'A Philanthropist's Experiment',[33] set in a decayed Victorian mining town, Burrumberie, the unrelenting boredom of which is rejected by the main female character in favour of returning to a much harder but more exciting existence in the crowded tenements of Paris.

These early stories remained favourites. Jessie chose 'How a Claim was Nearly Jumped in Gum-tree Gully' and 'The Philanthropist's Experiment', as well as her first two stories, 'Barren Love' and 'Malus Oculus' to include in her collection, *A Sydney Sovereign and Other Tales*. This was published in 1890 when her reputation as a writer was at its height.

Apart from stories, Jessie wrote articles on diverse subjects. One was a lengthy review of the great French novelist Emile Zola's new novel, *La faute de l'Abbé Mouret*, a study of French provincial life. The review is said to have caused controversy.[34]

Another article was on disposal of the dead, an important subject to Jessie, just as it was to her mother. In 'About Burial', published in the *Melbourne Review* in July 1878, she took an avant-garde view of this subject. It had first been raised in Victoria in 1873, when the City Coroner, Dr James Edward Nield, in a talk to the Royal Society of Victoria advocated the legalisation of cremation. Nield, who viewed many human bodies in the course of his work, believed that much illness was caused by the poisonous gases emanating from graves.[35]

Cremation was opposed by most Christian religions. It was associated with radical thought, and those advocating it were regarded as anti-religious. Both Jessie and her mother would have been happy being classed among the radicals. But Jessie's attitude, which she had absorbed from her mother, was based on two aspects of burial in coffins, which both abhorred. Both had an obsessional fear of being buried alive. Charlotte had probably developed this by reading of well-documented cases in history, and perhaps by reading Edgar Allan Poe's horror story 'The Premature Burial', first published in 1844.[36] With his particular gift for horror and suspense, Poe related cases of burial of living persons in several countries and his own experience in imagining he had been buried alive. Apart from this fear, both Charlotte and Jessie believed that if bodies must be confined to the earth they should be allowed to disintegrate as quickly as possible. The wicker coffin which Charlotte had brought with her to Australia was a second best effort to defeat current burial practices; cremation remained beyond the law.

Like her mother, Jessie wanted 'coffins consigned to museums, with racks and thumbscrews'. She argued in her *Melbourne Review* article that burial in oak and leaden coffins forced bodies 'through hideous stages of revolting decay', since they were closed up tightly with the poison they generated. If burial were practised, it at least should be unhindered by 'corruption-preserving boards and bolts'. Then she raised the culminating horror to all who argued against burial in coffins: 'the possibility of being buried alive'. She advocated freedom for individuals to decide on their method of burial, providing means for 'burial in wicker, for cremation, or for immersion'. She concluded by favouring cremation, which should be so simple that it would be looked upon 'as the shortest and best method' of disposal. The paraphernalia of funerals could be retained by those who wanted this, 'only the corpse might be a heap of ashes, or the coffin might be the lightest wicker, charcoal-lined and airy'.

Both Charlotte and Jessie were eventually to ensure that their bodies were not consigned to graves.

In February 1878, Jessie and Charles Fraser travelled together to Tasmania, for the end of the summer racing carnival. This may have been a last attempt by Fraser to recoup his racing losses and he probably also rode in some races. Jessie may have used the opportunity to attempt to win her father's support for travel to Europe with Charlotte, who was determined to leave Australia once again.

They arrived by the *Derwent* in the Tamar on 6 February, in time for the race meeting in Launceston, then travelled by train to Hobart for the summer meeting of the Tasmanian Racing Club, on 13, 14 and 15 February. This was a major social event under the patronage of the Governor.

As she was to do many times in the years ahead, Jessie used her experiences on this trip to write an article, 'Holiday Impressions of Tasmania',[37] for publication. She wrote about the train trip, the Theatre Royal where she saw Mrs Scott-Siddins play Pauline in the comedy *The Lady of Lyons* by Bulwer Lytton, and a visit to the warship HMS *Sappho*. She included a section on 'Rat's Castle', the decrepit building that had been a ghoulish source of interest in her childhood.

Jessie and Charles returned from Launceston to Melbourne on the

Derwent on 22 February, accompanied by Alfred Huybers. They arrived only a few days before Charlotte Huybers was to leave for Europe after only two years back in Melbourne. This time she took Koozee, who was twenty-four, John, eighteen and Edith, who was sixteen. Eddie, by then twenty-two, left his post at the Commercial Bank[38] to join the family at the last moment on the *Sobraon*. Although they expected Jessie to join them quickly it was to be over a year before she was to do so.

Although Jessie and Charles appear to have accommodated to each other at intervals following her return from her first trip to Europe, their interests continued to diverge. She did, however, accompany Charles on his trips to race meetings. After the trip to Tasmania they attended the St Patrick's Day races at Kyneton in March. In November the previous year, she had been with him in Melbourne for the Melbourne Cup, as she had been on many other occasions. Probably at these race meetings Fraser tried to wager himself out of his financial problems, as did many of the male characters in Jessie's novels. There is every indication he was just as unsuccessful. In particular the trip to the Tasmanian races, followed by the St Patrick's Day races, a major event on the Victorian racing calendar, seems to have precipitated a crisis in Fraser's financial affairs. Soon after, on 3 April 1878, his entire racing stud at Pemberley was sold, including the thoroughbred sire Impudence, and the imported mare Lady Kirk. The latter brought £200, the amount Fraser had paid for her. Altogether, thirty-eight horses and thirty head of cattle realised £800.[39] The sale appears to have been caused by a pressing need to pay off his gambling debts. Fraser was declared insolvent that year.

Jessie and her family apparently had hoped the sale would raise sufficient money to provide her with her fare to Europe, but it is unlikely she received anything. Eddie wrote sanguinely, 'Charlie is likely to do very well now with Pemberley'.[40] But the proceeds of the sale seem to have gone entirely towards paying Fraser's debts. Though left without stock, he retained the lease of Pemberley, and was later to rebuild his stable of racers.

With her base at Blairgowrie gone following the departure of the Huybers family, it is uncertain where Jessie stayed when visiting Melbourne. Although in later years two of her sisters and, more briefly, two of her brothers were to return to the city to live, this was a time when, apart from William, no Huybers lived there. William also left, following his marriage on 4 September 1878 at All Saints' Church, St Kilda, to Emily Maria Gregory, daughter of the late Dr William Gregory and Mrs Gregory, who had taken over the lease of Blairgowrie. William's business as a broker, once so flourishing, had collapsed, and he and his wife began their married life in Launceston, where he took charge of the northern branch of his father's merchant business.

Although Jessie continued to live at Pemberley, a complete break with Charles Fraser seems to date from the time of his insolvency. It coincides with a change in her writing, with the inclusion for the first time of a character clearly based on someone associated with her husband. In 'Monsieur Caloche', the most popular and reprinted of Jessie's short stories,[41] published in the *Australasian* in two parts, on 27 April and 4 May 1878, one of the major characters is Sir Matthew Bogg. He must have appeared to Victorian readers to have many resemblances to Fraser's brother-in-law, William Degraves. Degraves in 1878 was living in retirement in Tasmania, being supported by his still wealthy brothers after the failure of his own vast empire of warehouses, flour mills and station properties. He was still remembered in Victoria as one of the flamboyant capitalists of the 1860s and 70s.

Jessie depicts Bogg as a man who bullies his staff, a man without education and refinement who reads only 'with the plentiful assistance of the tip of his broad forefinger', and drops 'h's' when he speaks. She was to develop the self-made Sir Matthew Bogg further, into Josiah Carp, in her second novel, *In Her Earliest Youth*.

Towards the end of 1878, Jessie had stories published in two further collections. 'What an Artist Discovered in Tasmania', a story of Van Diemen's Land in convict days, appeared in Garnet Walch's 1878 Christmas annual, *Australasia. An Intercolonial Christmas Annual*. Again, Jessie's story was placed ahead of the other contributors', including poet and novelist J. Brunton Stephens, journalist, theatrical manager and bohemian Richmond Thatcher, and Garnet Walch himself.

Apart from this story, Jessie's last appearance in print before she left Victoria consisted of two stories published in *The Australian Ladies' Annual*, edited by F.R.C. Hopkins and released to coincide with the Melbourne Cup in November 1878. Jessie probably knew Francis Hopkins through his association with Tooringabby, the former Degraves station on the Murray portrayed as Rubria in Jessie's fiction. After Degraves lost the station, Hopkins took over as manager, later managing Perricoota, with which Tooringabby was merged. Jessie's story 'The Rubria Ghost', with its setting at Tooringabby, was the first item in his collection.

Ada Cambridge and Louisa Meredith were the other well-known contributors to *The Australian Ladies' Annual*. Ada Cambridge contributed 'By the Camp Fire', taken from her latest book of verse, and Louisa Meredith two poems, 'To my husband' and 'The Cockatoo', the latter reprinted from her *Grandmama's Australian Verse-Book*.[42]

Jessie's other story published in the *Annual*, 'Concerning the Forthcoming Melbourne Cup', contains an explicit representation of Charles Fraser as the racegoer Edwin, a character she was later to develop into George Drafton of *In Her Earliest Youth*. She describes Edwin, dressed for the races in close-fitting trousers and cut-away coat, as 'the sporting-man, with a dash of the gentleman' who could run through the pedigree of horses that had won in Melbourne and Sydney for years back, give times to a second, and all the names of the jockeys. As George Drafton does, Edwin, when back at his station, studies the racing pages of the *Australasian*. Like Drafton, Edwin, after each betting disappointment, clings 'the closer to his golden dream', his 'whole soul . . . absorbed in contemplation of his card, or of the black board . . . inscribed with the cruel white numbers that have so often dispelled his golden dream'. In Jessie's story, Edwin's companion, Angelina, imagines Edwin is thinking of her. But Jessie knew better: 'figures ride rampant under Edwin's waistcoat . . . gloomy forebodings of horses to be scratched, and impossible hedging, with a dreary settling-day in the background, fill her Edwin's breast'.

In a critical review of the *The Australian Ladies' Annual*, published in the *Melbourne Review*, Tasma's 'The Rubria Ghost' received the only praise. It was described as being 'as usual, clever and well-written', although the story was described as 'not very pleasing'. This was an apparent reference to its defiance of moral convention in providing the heroine with an easy way of carrying out her intention of joining her young lover (the 'ghost' of the title), following the opportune death of her aged husband. The reviewer preferred Tasma as an essayist. Remarkably, he did not think she had 'the story-telling faculty in a high degree', but did possess many of the qualities of a first-rate essayist. 'The thoughtfulness and frequent originality of her remarks and the elaboration of her style are peculiarly suited to the essay', the reviewer wrote, in a misjudgment of the potential of the acclaimed novelist she was to become.[43]

Jessie sailed from Melbourne on the *Sobraon* on 28 February 1879 to rejoin her mother and the rest of the family in Europe. By then, according to editor Philip Mennell, Jessie had become 'a universal favourite' with her essays and tales published in Australian periodicals.[44] In a very short time she had achieved great success in writing both short stories and articles and this had given her great confidence in her ability to earn her own living. The break with Charles Fraser was final. He promised to send her £100 a year but she was never to receive this.[45]

Jessie 'intends to extend her literary connexion', her brother Eddie wrote in Europe. '. . . She has already written a good deal in Victoria, and ought soon to make a name for herself here.'[46] Her transformation from an unhappy wife to writer was well under way.

7

She has come out as a conférencière with much success

London, Paris, Brussels, 1879–82

When Jessie sailed from Australia her only apparent prospect of keeping herself was by earning her living through writing. In Europe, she was also to find another, more unusual career. Within eighteen months she had become a celebrity lecturer, a career for which there were few female models. Very occasionally reports appeared in the press of the time of women such as Emily Faithfull giving public lectures, but women's appearance in this role was largely a curiosity. Jessie expressed the unusual nature of the role through a character in *A Knight of the White Feather*. When the heroine, the Paris-educated Linda Robley, addresses a public meeting on Positivism in the local schoolhouse near the family property in Victoria, her suitor Jack Fullerton is shocked, not only by the subject of her lecture, but by her 'having the face to do it'.[1]

Jessie may herself have given lectures in small country halls in Victoria, but no record of her doing so has been discovered. She was, however, an inveterate attender of them. She reported on many she attended in Paris and London for the *Australasian*.[2] No doubt she had attended many in Melbourne, a city where a visitor of the 1860s, Clara Aspinall, discovered a wealth of 'lectures on every conceivable subject', always with a preponderance of women in the audience.[3]

Women had begun lecturing in public in the United States in the 1850s. Almost invariably they spoke as advocates of women's rights, or against slavery, or on one of the other great issues of the day. When Jessie began her public speaking career, she may have wanted to speak on women's rights or women's education, on literature, art, or Positivism, the philosophical theory developed by Auguste Comte on which modern sociology is based—all subjects in which she was interested and knowledgeable. Instead, in the heyday of colonialism when most European countries looked to colonial conquests and markets, she tailored her talks to the market, finding enthusiastic audiences for talks on the geography, history, industries, culture and social progress of Australia.

Her success was so great and so unusual for a woman that she became in a very short time a highly regarded public figure. In Paris she was honoured with a high decoration, and in Brussels, King Leopold invited her to an audience at the Palace. The transformation from her role as country housewife was complete—but at some cost. Even after she had been lecturing for ten years, she was still to suffer agonies of nervous apprehension before beginning a talk.[4]

Before these public triumphs, however, Jessie continued to earn money to keep herself as she had done for the previous two years in Victoria, by writing articles for the *Australasian*. She began with three articles from Cape Town during her voyage to England.[5] In these she showed her usual adeptness at interweaving a great deal of information about a new place with references to Melbourne and Victorian topics designed to arouse or maintain the interest of readers back home. She advised them not to go to Cape Town expecting an equivalent of the Melbourne Cup—'an up-country racing committee in Victoria would smile at the Cape Town notion of a day's sport'—or an academy of music. Instead they should look to 'untamed Nature of savage majesty'.

She found Cape Town backward and cut off from the rest of the world. There was no later Australian news than that brought by the *Sobraon*, so the passengers got no answers to their questions 'What of Berry's mission?' and 'Have the Kellys been caught?'[6] 'Neither the names of "Berry" [n]or "Ned Kelly" were "household words" at the Cape', Jessie wrote. From these topical comments, she glided easily into informing her readers of the Zulu wars, and travelled outside Cape Town to report on ostrich farms at Wynberg, and vineyards at Constantia.

Sitting near her in the dining room at the Royal Hotel, where she stayed while the *Sobraon* was in port, was an Australian, the Reverend Charles Clark, who told her he had made £10,000 from lecturing. Perhaps it was from this chance meeting, and learning of the money to be made, that Jessie began to think of becoming a lecturer herself.

When she arrived in England in June 1879, Jessie was met by her brother Edward Huybers, who for the past year had been working in London for Alfred Hawley, his father's agent. She stayed for a few months in London with old family friends, the Kings at Bayswater, while she wrote about London in two articles for the *Australasian*.[7] As usual, her articles were about the serious, intellectual aspects of life rather than the superficial or frivolous. She reported on a sermon preached at Westminster Abbey by the Bishop of Manchester, the most liberal bishop of the day; a stage performance of *Drink*, an adaptation of Zola's novel *L'Assommoir*; a visit to a women's prison at Woking; and a crematorium chimney near Woking unable to be used because the House of Commons had voted against cremation. The Bishop spoke on 'How humanity is to get on when it has discarded all belief in a personal God'. Jessie thought his sermon was a 'good fight in a losing cause'.

Her plan from the time she left Australia was to live in Paris, and a few months after arriving from Australia she joined the rest of the family at I place de l'Observatoire, on the Left Bank in the 6th arrondissement. Charlotte, John and Edith had been living there for nearly a year, after staying at the Des Voeux's home in South Kensington. Koozee had joined them after suffering from pleurisy in London, preventing her enrolling in the nursing training school at St Thomas's Hospital.

The life of Jessie and the Huybers family in Paris at 1 place de l'Observatoire[8] and later nearby, at 29 rue des Feuillautines, was similar in frugality to the life of the Clare family Jessie described in *Not Counting the Cost*. Their accommodation at first was in an identical situation, in an apartment building overlooking the Observatoire gardens, a long narrow offshoot of the magnificent and extensive Luxembourg Gardens. Their social milieu, however, resembled life in the artists' colony which Jessie was to describe in *The Penance of Portia James*. They were within walking distance of Montparnasse and the streets favoured by artists, including the rue de Montparnasse where Edith was later to live, and the rue de Vaugirard which Jessie used as a locale in *The Penance of Portia James*.

Charlotte's main role, as always, was the advancement of her children's talents. John resumed his art studies under M. Julian, and Frank, making another attempt to break away from the bush and become an artist, joined him after he arrived from Australia in 1880.[9] Edith and probably Koozee, both of whom were to become accomplished art critics, studied under Alexandre Cabanel, one of three celebrated artists who had studios at the Ecole des beaux arts in the rue Bonaparte. Cabanel was renowned as the teacher of 'many of the finest painters of the day, representative of the most varied styles in art'.[10]

The Huybers became part of the colourful bohemian world of Parisian art students, joining in the high spirited groups that descended on the nearby wine shops to eat, drink and talk. Among these, Koozee met Arthur Loureiro, one of Cabanel's most brilliant students. Born in Oporto, Portugal on 11 February 1853, son of physician Francisco Loureiro, Arthur José de Souza Loureiro studied art in Oporto and at the Academia portuense de bellas artes in Lisbon before being sponsored by the Count d'Amedina to study in Madrid, Florence and Rome. In 1879 he won a Portuguese government travelling scholarship for landscape painters to study in Paris for three years, and in 1880 entered the Ecole des beaux arts in the atelier of Alexandre Cabanel, where his work was so outstanding his paintings were exhibited at the Paris salons of 1880, 1881 and 1882.[11] Within a short time of meeting, Koozee and Arthur Loureiro fell in love.

Jessie's world extended beyond art circles to the wider intellectual and cultural life of the capital. From Paris she wrote on the theatre (the Comédie Française tour in England),[12] on art (the annual art exhibition at the Paris Salon, including a discussion of a painting of Joan of Arc by Bastien Lepage),[13] and literature (the latest novel by Alexandre Dumas, *La Princesse de Baghdad*, then being performed by the Comédie Française).[14] She also reported some of the many lectures she attended, including one on a divorce reform bill then before the French Assembly.[15] Another article described a gathering of Communists addressed by French anarchist and author, Louise Michel, recently released from prison in New Caledonia, and by an early feminist, Madame Rourzade, author of a pamphlet 'L'union des femmes', who spoke on the superiority of the female sex.[16] Jessie also described two talks given to the Commercial Geographical Society of Paris, one by a Frenchman who had visited Victoria,[17] and another by Finnish-born Swedish explorer Professor Nils Adolf Nordenskiold, the first person to navigate the north-east passage through the Arctic Ocean from Europe to Asia.[18] Nordenskiold's lecture, which drew a huge crowd of 3000 to 4000 people, took place in June 1880, only a month before Jessie herself was to give a talk to the Society of which she had become a member.[19]

Interspersed with accounts of lectures and other events, Jessie included in her articles her views on divisive elements in French life, including the divorce bill proposed by M. Naquet, which promised 'bitter strife', and the recently passed decree against the Jesuits. Although she sometimes expressed criticism of the Catholic Church and religion in general, Jessie with her regard for freedom found the law against the Jesuits disturbing 'amounting, in its prohibition of their teaching in France, and its sudden destruction of their office and means of livelihood, to something very like persecution'.[20]

During the summer of 1880, Jessie made a trip north by train through St Quentin to Guise, to see for herself the experimental collectivist group established there by the French socialist, Jean Baptiste Andre Godin. After making a fortune from an ironworks, Godin had introduced profitsharing into his business, which he transferred to Guise. There he built dwellings, called familistères, as accommodation for his workers. Jessie described the huge three-storey buildings in which the thousand inhabitants were cared for in all aspects of their lives, including the education of their children from nursery age. Although enthusiastic about the socialist principles on which the familistère was based, Jessie did not see as much need for such organisations in Australia, 'where eight-hour champions carry broidered banners along the public streets' as in a country 'where violence follows oppression, and strike succeeds strike'.[21]

Later she wrote of a different type of industrial enterprise, following a visit to Belgium in September 1880, for the Brussels Exhibition. In the industrial city of Liége she described a zinc factory on the banks of the

Meuse.[22] As usual, she excited interest in her subject by including an Australian comparison. Belgium, she wrote, 'does not cover much more space than a Queensland cattle-run'. She found the director of the foundry, a man with a long lineage and aristocratic name, living in a mansion full of tapestries and antiques, heedless of how his workers lived, in contrast to the director of the familistère. Despite these unfavourable comparisons Jessie found the zinc foundry a happier place than the familistère of Guise. She reflected on 'whether a dead level may not have a more depressing effect than the prospect of a beautiful hill-top, even to those who live in the valley, without hope of reaching the summit'.

Jessie's remarkable success as a lecturer is documented in a collection of cuttings from French, Belgian and other newspapers, apparently collected by Jessie herself, and after her death kept by her brother, Edward Huybers. The collection was given to the Fryer Library, University of Queensland, by a descendant. I was able to supplement this collection by seeking reports of Jessie's speeches in the bulletins of the Commercial Geographical Society of Paris and the Royal Belgian Geographical Society, and in *l'Indépendance belge*, *La nouvelle revue* and other publications during visits to libraries in Brussels and Paris. It was through a short statement in a report of one of her lectures, published in March 1881, that I discovered Jessie had had a very popular serial story 'L'amour aux Antipodes' published in *l'Indépendance belge* 'some months' previously. I searched *l'Indépendance belge* in the files of the Bibliothèque Royale in Brussels, fortunately persevering a little more than 'some' months back, until I discovered this hitherto unknown story published in eight episodes in September 1880—on the front page of the paper. Subsequently I discovered a slightly earlier publication of the same story in the files of *La nouvelle revue* in the Bibliothèque Nationale in Paris.

The reports of her lectures together with the appearance of her articles in the *Australasian* are, apart from summaries of family movements in her brother's diary, the only evidence of Jessie's life in Europe during the period 1879–83. They provide a record of her public life and the acclaim that followed her success as a lecturer. It is possible only to speculate on her personal life during this period. She was constantly under the strain of her uncertain financial position requiring her to keep up her supply of articles to the press, and to accept public appearances at lectures in order to secure enough income to support herself. There was also the strain of her ambiguous position as a separated wife. There are hints in her later diary that she had many opportunities for liaisons with distinguished men, but there is no record, except her own statement that 'the final step has never been taken', of the outcome of these relationships.

Jessie had been noticed in geographical circles through the publication of an article on the prospects of emigration to the fruit-growing districts of

Tasmania.[23] In a surprising move for a conservative organisation whose speakers were almost invariably male, she received an invitation to address the Société de géographie commerciale de Paris. Her first public lecture on 'L'Australie et les avantages qu'elle offre a l'émigration française', given on 20 July 1880, was an enormous success. As she was always to do, she had learnt her speech by heart, and did not need to consult notes. For the occasion she discarded both her maiden and married names, and was known, as in all her subsequent public appearances, as Madame Jessie Tasma.

She spoke about the discovery of Australia, the explorers and the convict settlements, then described the great affluence of the capital cities where life compared with that in Europe: the same luxury, the same shop window displays, public buildings and parks, churches and theatres. Where forty years before the indigenous race had roamed, there were now beautiful streets and shops, she told her audience, and contrasted this with the life of the squatters in the interior. Continuing the traditions of the heroic pioneers, they tended millions of sheep and cattle grazing on land as extensive as the ancient provinces of France. She appealed for the emigration of artists, something she was often to repeat, assuring her audience that there were fortunes to be made, careers to be followed, and a future for their children. At the same time, they would enrich Australia with their artistic industry.[24]

The Secretary-General of the Society, M. Gauthiot, described her ninety-minute speech as a triumph, and the president, M. Meurand, thanked her for imparting so much knowledge of 'this fifth continent of the world'. M. Gauthiot said Australia had appeared to the French to have nothing to offer—a land of Aborigines who lived in the Stone Age, of convicts, of starving and brutal goldseekers, and of innumerable sheep, all without poetry or soul. Jessie in her talk had changed these perceptions, and proved to the audience that there was poetry in Australian life. So much so that, M. Gauthiot said, if more French people could hear 'cette charmeuse' they would rush to Australia in great numbers where they would contribute to raising the level of civilisation and come back with well-filled purses. M. Meurand also commented on 'les projections a la lumiere oxhydrique' (a magic lantern show of photographs) which, he said, had contributed to the success of Jessie's talk.[25] A newspaper report described Jessie as 'a young and gracious Australian' who spoke to a packed room 'in strong and gripping images'.[26]

Following the immense success of this lecture Jessie received invitations to speak from many towns in France and Belgium.[27] Everywhere she spoke the halls were crowded. She wrote about her new career in two articles published in the *Australasian*,[28] following a visit to Bordeaux in February 1881 to address the annual meeting of the society. During the event she was presented with a silver medal specially struck by the Society to honour her as a speaker.[29] Jessie noted that the Geographical Society in Bordeaux was 'established upon the model of the British Association, with the little difference that it pays its lecturers handsomely, [as did other European societies] which the British Association does not', a very important difference to Jessie, who on this trip, apart from her talk to the Bordeaux society, also earned money for her two articles in the *Australasian*.

Soon after her triumph at Bordeaux, accompanied by Koozee, she left on a speaking tour of Belgium. As reports of her speeches in the provinces, at Ghent, Marchiennes and Bruges, appeared in the press, interest developed to a crescendo. When, on 16 March 1881, she spoke in Antwerp to the Artistic, Literary, and Scientific Circle a crowd of 1200, including a large number of women, gathered to listen. A report said she presented a very interesting picture of Australian trade, flora, fauna, geography, the indigenous race, political institutions, society and 'the gigantic and rapid progress' made in forty years. Her speech was described by the President as remarkable, one of the best ever given in the annals of the Circle. He extended Jessie's success in her role as a public speaker to Australian women in general, referring to 'the intrepidity of Australian women' and 'the merits of the civilisation of your country'.[30]

Almost all reports of Jessie's speeches referred to her appearance, accent and charm. One newspaper described the reason for the great crowd at Antwerp simply as 'Mme Tasma'.[31] Another remarked on her 'limpid clearness', and 'honest British humour'.[32] Another, describing her as a daughter of Antwerp, said she spoke French fluently 'with a pronounced accent but there is none more charming'.[33] It is obvious from some of the comments that part of Jessie's attraction was that she was a beautiful woman taking an unusual role. Some comments had a patronising, sexist tone and Jessie recognised them as such, on one occasion remarking on the 'sugarly amiable' comments made in a newspaper article.

Jessie's lectures, culminating at Antwerp, created such a sensation that she received a telegram inviting her to a private audience with King Leopold at his Palace at Laeken, Brussels.[34] When the visit took place, on 20 March 1881, it was widely reported in the Belgium press. One newspaper, describing her as 'Mme Tasma, the eminent Australian lecturer', said Jessie made a plea for the establishment of a direct shipping link between Belgium and Australia similar to that she had recommended between France and Australia, something that would be eminently useful for the industries of both countries, which had need of new outlets.[35]

Another short report, typical of many, referred to Jessie as 'l'éminente conférencière' [the eminent lecturer] whose lectures at Antwerp, Ghent and Bruges had been 'a remarkable success'.[36] Another reported that the King spoke for a long time with 'l'éminente conférencière' about the usefulness of direct communication between Belgium and Australia. He encouraged her 'to continue her propaganda' towards this goal.[37]

Jessie's own report of her visit to the Palace appeared in the *Australasian* on 16 July 1881. She described how, accompanied by M. Pecher, president of the Artistic, Literary and Scientific Circle of Antwerp and head of the Liberal Party in Belgium, she drove to the great, plain, bare-looking palace. After passing through an arched doorway under a covered gallery, they were conducted up a long marble corridor to an antechamber, then to the King's study, a lofty, spacious, octagonal room, through the windows of which she glimpsed the green glades of the park.

Portraits of King Leopold had led Jessie to believe that he was a sparsely built man with a long, fair beard, a long, refined nose, and much dignity and gentleness of expression. Nothing, however, had prepared her for his great height. The King, dressed in a plain dark uniform, advanced from behind his table, and invited her to sit. He spoke mainly of Australia, particularly the need for a shipping link between the two countries. M. Pecher told the King he thought Jessie might become 'a medium of propaganda' in that direction. This surprised Jessie, she told *Australasian* readers, 'having never had anything more ambitious in view than the familiarising of the colonies to the minds of my hearers, within the limited and quite unofficial range of a woman's experience'. The King asked her to say wherever she spoke that he 'encouraged the useful and practical mission to which I had devoted myself'. She concluded 'It is a great drawback that royalty cannot be argued with. Otherwise I might have pleaded that I was innocent of any mission'.[38]

Jessie made a lasting impression on King Leopold. When she met him on other occasions, he talked of their meeting. Nearly twenty years later, when her brother Edward was received by the King, he remarked, 'I remember her well; she told me many interesting things about Australia. In fact [pointing to a chair] that was the very seat she occupied during our conversation'.[39]

After giving talks in Verviers and Liége, Jessie returned to Antwerp to address the Commercial Geographical Society, drawing another huge crowd which included most of the notable people of the city as well as a great many members of the society and teachers. Flanked by the joint chairmen, the Burgomaster (Lord Mayor) of Antwerp, M. de Wael, and the president of the Artistic, Literary and Scientific Circle, and accompanied by the president of the Commercial Geographical Society, Colonel Wauvermans, Jessie walked to the stage carrying a large bouquet presented by the society. On either side of the platform were large wall maps of Australia and Asia by Captain Ghesquiere, destined to be hung in the Stock Exchange, and portraits of Mercator and d'Ortelius.

Jessie's speech followed her usual pattern. She pointed out the enormous size of Australia compared with European countries, its small population of three million, and its need for more people. She drew attention to its potential as a trading partner, and the principal sources of its riches. As she usually did, she stressed Australia's need not so much for manufactured products as for 'artistic industry'. She mentioned her talk with King Leopold a few days before. 'Dites bien partout', me disait-il, 'que j'appelle de tout mes voeux l'extension du service d'exchange regulier entre la Belgique et l'Australie, que je l'appuierai de tout mon pouvoir'. '[Spread it everywhere', he told me, 'that I give my support to the extension of regular exchange between Belgium and Australia, which I support with all my power'.]

At the end of her speech, given 'with charming simplicity full of humour', the assembly applauded enthusiastically, and the society made Jessie a member correspondent in honour of the brilliant success of her lectures in Belgium. At a private reception afterwards guests applauded the reading of a congratulatory telegram from the Paris Society asking them to drink to the health of the lecturer and her continuing success.[40]

With her fame well established, Jessie was invited to speak to several organisations in Brussels, including the Soirées populaires,[41] the Cercle artistique et littéraire and the Cercle des anciens normalistes. Her address to the Cercle artistique was a prestigious affair. King Leopold often attended meetings and the society had a membership of over 1000, including authors, journalists and artists. Meetings were held at the headquarters in a park in the centre of the city. Amenities included a huge library, a salon for exhibitions and an annexe for concerts and social gatherings in summer. Jessie's speech to this organisation was again a widely reported success, and her speech to the Cercle des anciens normalistes was described as 'one of the most remarkable' ever given to this group. In this talk, apart from her usual themes, Jessie described the three principal Australian cities—Melbourne, Sydney and Adelaide—with their public buildings, churches and theatres. She donated her payment for this lecture to the work for poor children in communal schools.[42]

When she returned to Paris from Belgium, she was immediately on the lecture circuit again. At the end of March she lectured at one of the oldest suburban institutions for the education of adults, the Philotechnique Association, at Boulogne-sur-Seine.[43]

In the winter of 1881–82, Jessie returned to Belgium to give another series of talks. Again she spoke to large audiences at towns around the country, as well as in Brussels and Antwerp. This time her subject was New Zealand. It is not clear whether Jessie had visited the country, though perhaps the *Windward* had stopped there, but she spoke knowledgeably about it. Again, newspapers reported on her accent—usually described as charming—her graciousness and her rapport with her audiences, as well as the content of her speeches.[44]

Fame in another field followed the publication, in August 1880, of her novella 'L'amour aux Antipodes', a love story with the same exotic appeal as her lectures, in the highly regarded French fortnightly *La nouvelle revue*. It was published the following month in *l'Indépendance belge*.[45]

'L'amour aux Antipodes' is a story concerning an English cavalry officer,

Arthur Lascelles Saint-Jean, who migrates to Australia, where he becomes tutor to Robert, the son of a widow Mrs Murray, who has a vast, 50,000 acre station, Tamburroona, reminiscent of Degraves's stations in the Riverina. Saint-Jean, in a scene which has similarities to the climax of Jessie's later novel, *A Knight of the White Feather*, dramatically saves Robert after he appears to have drowned in the flooded Murrumbidgee. He and Robert's mother eventually marry. The story is told against a background of information, similar to that which Jessie conveyed in her lectures. It was interesting and surprising to her listeners. She writes of the cultivated life of Australian cities, the vastness of the country, the isolated station homesteads, small townships in themselves, and the intensity of seasonal changes. There is the Melbourne she described in her lectures with its impressive stone buildings, wide streets and public gardens. She describes the isolated station in the Riverina, with its huge luxurious homestead where incongruous banquets included imported French champagne and Australian wines served in crystal glasses, to accompany curried kangaroo and wild duck. She describes the devastation of drought and, finally, the floods that come with its breaking.

As a result of appearing in *La nouvelle revue*, Jessie was one of a distinguished group of contributors who attended a banquet held late in 1880 in Paris in honour of the founder and editor of the *Revue*, Madame Juliette Adam. Among them were such famous people as General Pittie, ADC to the French president; the doyen of the Paris press, Emile de Girardin; and engineer and diplomat Viscount Ferdinand de Lesseps, builder of the Suez Canal. Launched in October 1879, the *Revue* had been an immediate success, Adam being inundated with articles on literature, art, politics, science, history, mythology, military arts, fiction and poetry, from all over Europe. Born Juliette Lamber in 1836, Adam was the leading woman writer in France for over fifty years, and a powerful public figure. She was the founder of an influential salon referred to as 'the birthplace of the Republic',[46] but Jessie was a little sceptical of her reputed influence. 'Politics are her hobby,' Jessie wrote, 'though the supposition that several of [President] Gambetta's measures are to be ascribed to her influence is probably as groundless as many others.'

Among the contributors at the banquet, Jessie noticed only one woman apart from herself, and remarked on the extraordinary dearth of female writers in France. In England there were women novelists 'without end', but France had hardly six—'not authoresses of repute, but of any kind at all'. The woman author present, who wrote under the name of 'Henri Greville', some of whose serials were published in *La nouvelle revue*, was regarded as the 'first of female novelists'. But, wrote Jessie, 'she is not a Georges Sand, and it is singular to reflect that she should hold so exceptional a place among a nation which could produce one'. By contrast,

France had many male novelists, their serial stories being in every newspaper 'by the ream'.[47]

From her base in Paris, Jessie continued writing articles for the *Australasian*. In June 1881 she sent an article on 'The "Actualités" [topical
events] of Paris'[48] which ranged over politics, the theatre and painting. It
included a description of the French statesman, M. Leon Gambetta, then
president of the Chamber of Deputies; an account of a very popular new
play at the Comédie Français, *Le monde ou l'on s'ennui*, by Edouard Paille-
ron, and a description of Minkacsky's vast painting of 'Christ before Pilate',
to which 'all Paris flocked'.

For another article, on 'Autumn in Paris',[49] she followed the example of
'The Vagabond' in Melbourne by visiting a night shelter for destitute men
run by the Catholic Church. She watched as the men were admitted and
given a bed for three nights. She found that, since it had opened three
years previously, the institution had admitted 26,000 men, including a small
number of professionals—civil engineers, officers and lawyers, teachers and
professors. Only six had been Australians. 'It is through works like these
that the clerical party maintains its influence in France', Jessie wrote, ' "les
cléricaux" has almost turned into a term of contempt, but charity appeals
to every shade of feeling'.

From about the middle of 1881 Jessie had been living alone in Paris in
a hotel in the Latin Quarter. The rest of the family had moved to London,
where it was hoped twenty-three-year-old John would earn a living as an
artist, and where Edith began singing lessons. They all, including Jessie,
had spent a summer holiday at Ryde on the Isle of Wight, a nostalgic return
for Charlotte to visits of her childhood with the Simeon family.

While they were holidaying Eddie, on 30 July 1881, married Julia Ord,
the elder daughter of his landlady at Mildmay Park, north London. The
marriage was at St Mary's Church, Islington. Julia was regarded by the
Huybers family, always critical of in-laws, as unacceptable socially and
financially, and was never more than grudgingly accepted. Later that year,
Eddie and Julia sailed on the *Lusitania* for Australia, where Eddie rejoined
his father in the family firm in Hobart, taking up residence at Hillside, the
cottage in the grounds of Highfield which had been let to the Reverend
Francis Hudspeth.

By the autumn, when the family moved to Brixton in south London,
Frank, now aged twenty-four, also had left for Australia. Once again, he
felt the call of the Australian bush. Although his father offered him work
clearing a 320-acre property he had bought at Ringarooma, near
Branxholme in the north-east of Tasmania, Frank went north to Bulloo
Downs, beyond Thargomindah in the far west of Queensland, where he
became a boundary rider and jockey.

On 5 September 1881, Koozee married Arthur Loureiro, at the Registry
Office, Lambeth, Surrey. They were both twenty-eight. Jessie, John and

Edith were witnesses. Arthur Loureiro was apparently unaware that marriage would terminate his scholarship from the Portuguese government. Without this income, he and Koozee spent the next few years intermittently living in Paris where at times they took a studio near Jessie's hotel. At other times they lived in a cottage at Brolles in the forest of Fontainebleu, where Arthur did *plein air* paintings, or at Brixton where they stayed with Charlotte, or at Milford, Surrey, where Arthur taught painting.[50] They were in Brixton when their first child, Vasco, a name famous in Loureiro's home city as the name of the Oporto's famous son, Vasco da Gama, was born on 27 October 1882.

A few years later, partly because of Arthur Loureiro's poor health and partly because it seemed to offer better opportunities, Koozee, Arthur and their son, accompanied by John Huybers, moved from Europe to Australia. They arrived on the *South Australian* on 15 September 1884. Loureiro's intention was to set up a school of art in Hobart,[51] but he was persuaded by Alfred Huybers that Melbourne, then enjoying the long-lasting boom that gave it the name of 'marvellous Melbourne', was a much better prospect. He soon had a following of art buyers in the studio in Collins Street which he shared with Italian artists Ugo Catani and G.P. Nerli and where both John and Frank Huybers joined him briefly as artists. His painting 'The Forest of Fontainebleu' which he brought with him was bought by Sir William Clarke. Later he moved to Cabana, a two-storeyed Queen Anne style house and studio in Kew, which he and Koozee built with financial help from Alfred Huybers. The opening of Cabana in 1888 was a spectacular social event, with the Governor of Victoria one of the notable guests. Loureiro was by then a leading painter in the *plein air* style, although some of his paintings were influenced by the Symbolist painters he had known in Paris.[52] He painted several religious pictures, including 'Vision of St Stanislaus' and a major work on that quintessential Australian subject the death of explorer Robert O'Hara Burke. His painting of his son, Vasco, 'Boy with Apple', is in the National Gallery of Victoria.

Jessie's future was regarded by the family as very bright. 'She has since come out as a "conférencière" with much success', her brother Eddie wrote. Her success had been 'beyond all expectation . . . her name being now established she ought to find the path to fame clear & easy'. She moved backwards and forwards between London and Paris 'as her literary engagements require'.[53] She was in London in the winter of 1881–82, reporting a lecture on molecules given in February 1882 by the brilliant British physicist, Professor John Tyndall, at the Royal Institution in Albemarle Street.[54]

During this or a visit a few months later, Jessie heard that Charles Fraser was in London, having travelled from Australia with 'the Degraves party'— his sister Robina and his brother-in-law William Degraves. After years of living quietly in Hobart, following the collapse of his pastoral, manufacturing and financial empire in the early 1870s, William Degraves had been left an annuity of £500 on the death of his wealthy surviving brother, John Degraves, on 19 June 1880. With their financial position improved, William and Robina Degraves decided to visit England and Europe in 1882, and Fraser accompanied them.[55]

Jessie met him in London. Her brother Eddie believed that at the meeting they arrived at 'a definite settlement'[56] of their matrimonial impasse. According to Jessie's evidence, given at their subsequent divorce case, she offered to return to Fraser as his wife, but 'he treated her with the utmost coolness, and told her that he had formed a connexion with a Miss Seal, in Melbourne, which he thought would be lasting'.[57] Jessie's offer to return to Fraser appears to have been made in the context of obtaining evidence of desertion for the subsequent divorce hearing. At the meeting, Jessie and Fraser having long since realised that their marriage was finished, apparently decided on a plan of action that would make it possible for them to obtain a divorce under the stringent requirements of the 1864 Act in the colony of Victoria. In this they risked the penalties against collusion.

The 1864 Act consolidated the marriage laws first adopted in 1859, and amended in 1861, under which civil divorce was allowed for the first time in Victoria.[58] Previously divorce had been an ecclesiastical matter, as it had been in England. The only method of breaking a marriage civilly was through individual acts of Parliament, in effect confining divorce to the very wealthy. (During the two centuries to 1850, there had been only 250 divorces in England.)[59] In 1857, the English Parliament passed an Act which made divorce possible through the civil courts, and the Australian colonies followed with similar legislation.

The 1864 Victorian Divorce Act, like the law in England, applied a very blatant double standard. A man could obtain a divorce from his wife on the grounds of adultery but a wife could only seek dissolution of a marriage if her husband had been guilty of adultery combined with other conduct specified as 'incestuous adultery, or of bigamy with adultery or of rape or of sodomy or bestiality or of adultery coupled with desertion without reasonable excuse for two years or upwards'. The Victorian Parliament had attempted in 1861 to insert a clause allowing divorce following desertion by either husband or wife for four years without reasonable cause. This was vetoed however, by the English Secretary of State for Colonies, the Duke of Newcastle, on the grounds that it would allow divorce in Victoria which would not be allowed in England or other colonies.[60]

The restrictions of the law, and the need for an expensive Supreme Court action, meant that very few people sued for divorce in Victoria from 1861 until the law was liberalised in the late 1880s. The number of divorces granted each year from 1862 to 1882 often totalled only single figures. In 1877, 11 were successful out of 27 petitions; in 1878, 8 of 17; in 1879, 3 of 10; in 1880, 11 of 16; in 1881, 9 of 18; and in 1882, 9 of 29.[61] These were not encouraging statistics. Jessie's knowledge of them was probably limited to the general idea that divorce was almost unknown in the colony of Victoria, and the chances of successfully suing for it not good.

She provided no apparent grounds for Charles Fraser to obtain a divorce on the grounds of adultery. Although there had been romantic interludes in her life away from Fraser—notably 'the Commandant' in Brussels and Gowen Evans in Melbourne, with hints of many others—there is no evidence that these resulted in sexual relations. Either could have made a case against the other for desertion, but Jessie, feeling the more wronged, probably insisted that divorce proceed on her petition. While Fraser bore the brunt of accusations in the subsequent divorce case, he had a monetary advantage in that he engaged no lawyer, leaving the case undefended. Jessie, on the other hand, had to pay her fares to and from Australia [62] and spend six months there, in all being away from Europe, her main source of income, for nearly a year. She also had to pay fees to the prominent lawyer she engaged, Dr (later Sir John) Madden.

She had more reason to hope for the success of the divorce action than at any other period of her marriage. During 1881, while visiting Venice to give a lecture, she had met Auguste Couvreur,[63] the epitome of the older, distinguished, sophisticated man to whom she had always been attracted.

8

She goes home unfettered by any tie

Paris, Central Europe, Melbourne, Florence, London, 1882–85

When Jessie met Auguste Couvreur, he was one of the most distinguished, highly decorated and best-known political figures in Europe. He had been a member of the Belgian Chamber of Representatives since 1864, and in 1881 had become its vice-president. By profession a journalist and economist, he was an advocate of free trade and European federalism. In Belgium he worked indefatigably for universal education, the improvement of conditions for the working class, and expanded educational opportunities for women. It was said that his 'conversational ability and his distinction of manner gave him a rapport with the élite of contemporary society',[1] and that his actions were 'graced by vast culture and sagacity of judgment'.[2]

Auguste Couvreur had recently lost his first wife, Hélène Charlotte Henriette Corr, daughter of Delphine Marie Hélène van der Maeren and Michel Corr, an Irishman who had become a naturalised Belgian and, like Couvreur, was an ardent free trader. After some twenty-five years of childless marriage, Hélène Couvreur died in 1880, at the age of forty-six years.[3]

Auguste Pierre Louis Couvreur was born at Ghent on 24 October 1827, the son and grandson of well-to-do Flemish industrialists. His mother was Jeanne Charlotte van Maldeghem and his father Louis Joseph Couvreur, who had a flourishing fabric mill in the dependencies of the ancient Château of the Counts of Flanders. The mill was destroyed by fire in 1828, and his father was further ruined by the 1830 Revolution, which led to the establishment of Belgium as an independent country. Louis Couvreur remained faithful to the King of Holland and was exiled from newly formed Belgium for ten years. In 1835, he became director of a cotton mill at Haarlem, and his son Auguste was enrolled in the Realschule d'Elberfeld, from which he graduated with the prize of honour. In 1844, Auguste went to the University of Ghent to study philosophy, and then attended the College of France at the Sorbonne in Paris. On the day following the 1848 Revolution, in which French King Louis Philippe was overthrown and the Second Republic established, Auguste Couvreur, aged twenty, took the position of secretary to the prefect of l'Herault, a family friend. After about a year in this post he returned to Belgium, where he worked on various journals including *l'Observateur*, for which he was a journalist and translator of English and German serials. In 1857, he joined the leading Brussels daily, *l'Indépendance belge*, soon establishing his career as a political journalist. He was put in charge of the foreign section of the paper, a position he held for many years, and he remained a contributor even after retirement.

A committed free trader, in 1854 he founded, with Corr-van der Maeren, the Association for the Reform of Customs. In 1856 he organised a major congress aimed at revising the protectionist system practised by many European states. A friend of English free traders, Richard Cobden and John Bright, and of Europeans Jules Simon and Saint-Hilaire, he became a member of the Cobden Club, set up in London to honour the pioneer of the free trade debate in Britain. Couvreur believed that free trade would have benefits beyond the economic sphere, that it would eliminate the principal cause of friction between nations, and that its introduction would be followed by an era of universal peace. Like Cobden, Couvreur worked for international arbitration and the reduction of armaments.

His political career began in 1864. After a political crisis following the election by a small majority of an anti-clerical government led by the founder of the Liberal Party, Frère-Orban, another election was called. Standing as a Liberal for a Brussels electorate, Couvreur won by a big majority. One of his major political aims was the extension of education, particularly the provision of compulsory education run by the state. This was opposed by the Catholic Church and the clerical party.

Couvreur at various times held official positions in the Association for the Advancement of Social Sciences, the League of Education, the Association for the Professional Education of Young Women, the Royal Belgian Geographic Society, the Archaeological Society, and the Society for Colonial Studies. He was also a prominent Freemason, serving for some years as Belgian Grandmaster. In the course of his public life he was awarded the decorations of Officer of the Order of Leopold (for his work in supporting King Leopold in his purchase of the Congo, and in international negotiations to decide its borders), Commander of the Royal Order of Charles III of Spain; Commander of the Order of Saviour of Greece; Chevalier of the Order of Lion of the Netherlands; Chevalier of the Order of Saints Maurice and Lazare (Italy), and Officer of the Academy of France.[4] The awards from Italy and the Netherlands followed his success in organising, as secretary-general, conferences of the Association for the Advancement of Social Sciences in 1862 and 1864.

To Jessie, Auguste Couvreur was not only a distinguished and sophisticated man of the world, but also had interests and ideals compatible with her own, if less radical ones. His anti-clericalism was not dissimilar to her own views on religion. In her articles she was critical of clerical authority, although she often praised the charitable works of the church. She had the same enthusiasm for education, particularly the improvement of educational opportunities for women, and at least as much sympathy with the plight of the working class. She even had an interest in promoting free trade. There was no protection for the agricultural and pastoral products whose export she advocated from Australia. On her lecture tours of Belgium, she had met many of the officials Couvreur knew, and was used to mixing with people who were his friends and associates. She enjoyed the company of intellectuals and the challenge of discussing philosophical ideas and theories with stimulating people. Both she and Couvreur earned their living by writing for the press.

Whatever mental and physical attraction Jessie felt towards Auguste Couvreur, however, she could not contemplate marriage until her marriage to Charles Fraser had been dissolved. Even then, as subsequent events showed, she was in no hurry to tie herself again to a husband.

Having decided to travel to Melbourne to try to obtain a divorce from Charles Fraser, Jessie made a concerted effort to earn as much money as possible, sending articles to the *Australasian* from Paris and several Central European countries. From her base in a hotel in the Latin Quarter, she reported as she had done since 1879 on the cultural life of France. Probably neither before nor since have readers in Australia had the opportunity to read so consistently and in such depth about the intellectual life of Europe. Although on the surface many of her subjects were of limited interest to readers in far-off Australia, she managed to make them acceptable to a popular paper, largely targeted to country people, sportsmen and followers of racing, by using her gift for making the erudite interesting. She gilded and rationed her extensive knowledge of contemporary European political and philosophical thought. In 'Literary Notes from Paris',[5] for instance, she made an election to the Académie Française interesting by including descriptions conveying the atmosphere of the building of the Institut de France where the election was held, the excitement among the crowds queued outside for hours, the distinguished audience and the stirring of interest as the Academicians filed in and the judges took their seats. Without ignoring the erudite subjects of the speeches, she interspersed these accounts with physical descriptions of the speakers and their speaking styles. For instance, she described the unusual physical features of Joseph Ernest Renan, one of the three judges, presenting him as an interesting character to those unaware that he was a famous French philospher. Jessie wrote:

> It is contended that M. Renan's mysticism often leaves his readers in
> doubt as to his exact meaning . . . But even though we should be driven

to embodying our faith in what someone has called 'a point of interrogation upon the universe', the discussion of its various phases in such language as M. Renan employs is a glory to a nation that would otherwise stand low in the literary age in which we live.

In another article for a different audience, [6] Jessie was to write about Renan's philosophical ideas; *Australasian* readers, while not being overburdened with philosophy, could feel through her dispatches that they were part of the exciting intellectual world of Europe.

Towards the end of 1882 Jessie began a two month tour through Central Europe, perhaps accompanied by Auguste Couvreur.[7] This resulted in six articles, on Hamburg, Berlin, Dresden and Prague, Vienna and Budapest. As usual, she described the cultural, social and religious life of the cities she visited, as well as the day-to-day life in the streets. Her comments were always informed by her strong social conscience, her concern for the plight of the poor and for the working classes, and her understanding of the oppressiveness of dictatorships. Whenever possible, she increased the interest of her articles by making comparisons with Australian life. In Hamburg and Berlin, she noted the enjoyment of outdoor entertainment, and pleaded for this continental custom to be adopted in Australia. She wrote of Berlin:

> For all its protestantism and its propriety—and it is strong in both—on Sundays, as on week-days, the gardens of Flora and of Krolle are crowded with happy families. Long lines of lamps glitter in the leafy alleys, hundreds of little tables are set out, there are always bands playing, and the people dine, sup, smoke, laugh, and flirt as though there were no conscription and no Bismarck behind it in the world.

She thought it 'an infinite pity that the Anglo-Saxon should represent almost the only type of unsociability among the European races in its national amusements'. It would be 'a greater pity still if the influence of Australian sunshine does not work a change some day in this respect at the antipodes, and if the colonists should never know the innocent radiance that is shed around the work-a-day world by the pleasant customs it would be so easy to borrow from any continental city'.[8]

Jessie's visit to Dresden coincided with a visit by the Emperor of Germany, the Crown Prince, 'and a string of Royal Highnesses'. She was not so much interested, however, in the royal progress as in the early morning procession over the old bridge across the Elbe of 'market-carts, drawn for the most part by women and dogs'. When a dog was beyond financial reach, women carried their goods to market on their backs. 'There is something that jars upon the Australian sense of the "fitness of things" in the evidence that the poorer class of women of all ages in Germany are regarded very much as beasts of burden', Jessie wrote.[9]

In the first of two articles on Vienna, she commented on the large numbers of businesses owned by Jews. In the second, she remarked on the anti-Semitism common in Austria and Germany. She wrote on Vienna: 'There is another disturbing element in the constant outbreaks against the Jews. If the same trouble did not occur in Protestant Germany, one might be tempted to attribute it solely to an excess of catholic fanaticism on the part of the populace'.[10]

In each article, she commented on the state of culture—painting, music, literature, collections in museums, religion—as well as on other aspects of life which impressed her observant eye. In Vienna, she was astonished to see worshippers throw themselves into attitudes of 'self-abasement' in their excesses of piety, and others kissing the glass in which a statue of the Virgin was encased. She was also interested in the frank sexual advertisements in Viennese newspapers, adding a light touch to the information packed into the preceding sections of her article. She quoted advertisements by students offering their hearts to rich ladies willing to pay their fees and another by a pathetically vulnerable young orphan, who advertised that she would live with an old gentleman and 'would marry him later if there was harmony of disposition between them'.

In her article on Budapest, she wrote of the plight of the Hungarian peasants freed from serfdom but still living in crowded and primitive conditions on the estates of wealthy landowners. Comparing Hungary and Australia, she wrote, 'all the material well-being, the personal freedom, and the real equality of rights are on the Australian side, and all the poetry and colour, the stirring tales, and the crying needs on that of Hungary'.[11]

Returning to Paris, just before she left for Australia she gave a major lecture to the Société de géographie commerciale de Paris on 'Queensland. The last of the Australian colonies, her livestock, her cotton, her sugar'.[12] In previous talks, she told her large audience, she had 'painted a picture of my country, of its beautiful cities, its vast space, of its strange animals and its material and moral welfare'; in this lecture, she would speak about development. She emphasised the trade ties between France and Australia, with France importing Australian wool and the 'elegant people of Melbourne' paying 'their weight in gold for the hat confections of Paris, to appear at the racecourses'. Apart from wool, she urged France to import Australian wine, which had recently been awarded a medal at the Bordeaux Exposition. She also urged imports of meat, assuring her audience that frozen meat arrived 'as juicy as at the moment of departure', despite its long journey.

As usual, she introduced some diversionary humour with stories of ignorance about Australia in Europe. She related the story of a merchant who, when it was suggested that he visit Australia to sell his clothing fabrics, exclaimed in surprise, 'one dresses over there!'. Another was of an English family plunged into despair on receiving news that their son in Brisbane was about to marry a local girl. The family expected she would be 'a savage and in addition a cannibal'. General hilarity greeted these anecdotes, according to the report of the speech.

Jessie described Queensland, with its vast stations, its 'life of abundance and gaiety' where everyone rode horses and its squatters who were 'as hospitable as the ancient patriarchs'. It was, she said, the colony preferred by the sons of English families who wanted to establish 'a new territorial aristocracy'. She explained that the huge properties had the appearance of feudal domains, with their own supply depots, butcheries and schools. 'I have seen that region', she said, a reference to her trip to the Degraves stations. Then she quoted the comment of a English traveller who claimed that the standard of living and housing was dictated by the size of the owner's flocks: the owner of 100,000 sheep has a butler and a great house; with 40,000, a piano is essential [hilarity]; with 20,000 one does not have a serviette during the meal; with 10,000 it is permitted to serve a small meal'.

Her description of the great stations was balanced by her account of the laws enacted by 'the very democratic colonial government' which did not 'wish for the ancient territorial system of England to be recreated in Australia'. Emigrants brought to the colony at the expense of the government were given the opportunity to become farmers, and the right to select small acreages 'on the land of the capitalist', she said, for which they paid a small amount per acre. They could become proprietors after some years.

She ended with an account of the cultivation of sugar and the development of the industry, from the first planting near Brisbane in 1846 by Louis Hope. She then outlined the problems of getting labour to harvest sugar cane, and the resultant introduction of Kanak labourers. At the end of her lecture, she gave a magic lantern show of photographs.

Probably as a result of the success of this and previous lectures, moves began in the Paris Commercial Geographical Society to have Jessie's outstanding achievements honoured.

Within a few days of this occasion, on 7 June 1883, she boarded the Messageries Maritimes steamer, *Melbourne*, in Marseilles to travel to Victoria to arrange her divorce hearing. Charles Fraser also made sure he was back in Melbourne in preparation. He arrived on 21 June 1883, on the *Siam*, which he had joined in Bombay. On her voyage, Jessie landed at Port Said, which she described as a malodorous hole of flies and sand, at Aden, at Mahe in the Seychelles Islands, at St Denis, capital of Réunion, then at Mauritius, where she was the guest of the Governor.

Jessie arrived in Melbourne on 18 July 1883. Although the following year several members of the Huybers family were to move from Europe to Melbourne, this was one period in which no member of the family lived there. Jessie probably stayed with friends. Her writing had made her a well-known personality: 'She was everywhere received with open arms' her brother Eddie wrote—in Melbourne, in Launceston, where she visited

Willie, his wife and two children, and in Hobart where she visited her father and Eddie, Julia and their two children. In Hobart she gave a private lecture to friends.[13]

Within a week of arriving in Australia, and probably at the suggestion of her solicitors, Mallesons and Co., she wrote on 23 July to her husband at Pemberley, asking him to take her back as his wife. There was no chance that he would agree, and doubtless Jessie would have been dismayed if he had. His negative reply was written on 27 July.[14] Such stratagems were necessary to prove that Charles Fraser had deserted her.

Meanwhile, she continued her work. In Melbourne, Jessie apparently renewed her friendship with Gowen Evans, still a director of the *Argus* and the *Australasian*. She submitted two articles she had written about her voyage.[15] They were published as 'To Australia by a Messageries Steamer' soon after. She also had an article on Renan to offer Mortimer Franklyn, the editor of the monthly *Victorian Review*. Two years earlier, it had published her article on 'women who kill', a passionate feminist plea, still relevant today, supporting women forced by extreme cruelty into killing their husbands or lovers. Jessie's comments were made in the context of a review of Alexandre Dumas's book *Les femmes qui tuent et les femmes qui votent* [the women who kill and the women who vote],[16] which had been an immediate bestseller in France. Dumas argued that if women 'had been permitted to share in the framing of the laws by which they are governed, they would not have been, for so many centuries, the victims of the time-honoured injustice' exposed in his book. It was based on recent events in France where juries would not convict 'women who kill'—'women who shoot, stab, or poison those men who, after sacrificing them to caprice, outrage their instincts of maternity, and disown or cast off the children they have given them'. Jessie wrote: 'When public feeling thus manifests itself, legislation can do nothing; and the sooner that laws which have ceased to take effect are remodelled, the better for the dignity of government'. She agreed with Dumas that if women had the vote it was likely that 'their influence would inaugurate a reform in a matter so closely connected with themselves'. However, she was not nearly as sure as Dumas that women would win the vote within ten years. Although votes for women were less than twenty years away in Australia, it was to be much longer before women in England and most European countries were enfranchised.

Jessie's long article on Renan was published in the *Review* in December 1883.[17] In twenty-three pages she reviewed Renan's autobiography, *Souvenirs d'enfance et de jeunesse*, an account of his childhood, schooling and life in several seminaries before he came to the conclusion that 'no will superior to that of man acts in an appreciable fashion' in the universe. Jessie wrote, 'I cannot say that he found the ocean of doubt more navigable than the rest of us, but his evidence to the effect that his life has been so well worth the living negatives the supposition that without faith it must be intolerable'.

The case of *Fraser v. Fraser* came before the Chief Justice, Mr Justice Higinbotham, and Mr Justice Williams of the Victorian Supreme Court, on 13 December 1883. Ironically, while she waited in Melbourne for six months before her case began, Jessie would have read many reports of the attempt by lawyer William Shiels to reform the divorce laws of Victoria. The section of his Marriage and Matrimonial Statute Amendment Bill, which would have interested her most, allowed women to divorce their husbands on the grounds of adultery alone. This was soon abandoned, but Shiels was eventually successful with other relatively minor amendments, including allowing women some custody rights over their children. It was the start of a process of reform, culminating in 1889 in changes to the grounds on which women could obtain divorces in Victoria.[18] Jessie, however, faced the prospect of fighting for her divorce under the provisions of the 1864 Act. Her lawyer had probably warned her that in the previous year less than one-third of the petitions for divorce in the colony had been successful.[19]

In my research for this book I made the most exhaustive inquiries over a considerable time in an effort to locate the official papers of the *Fraser v. Fraser* divorce case. Initially I found it impossible to believe that the file would not be located, having previously, for research for another book, had great success in finding much older legal files in the New South Wales Archives Office. At various stages my hopes were raised, for instance, when it was found that *Fraser v. Fraser* was listed in the contemporaneous index of divorce cases before the Supreme Court of Victoria. The file should be located in the Victorian Public Records Office (at VPRS 283, Box 45, File 545), which now holds the Supreme Court records. However, a search of the files for 1883, and those for adjacent years in case of misfiling, revealed that the file I sought, as well as some others, were missing. In 1968 the files had been passed from the Supreme Court of Victoria to the Archives Division of the State Library, and later to the Victorian Public Records Office. According to the Records Office, the files arrived with no accompanying documentation, so 'it can never be known whether the file you seek was transferred'. On the other hand, the Prothonotary's Office of the Supreme Court wrote that 'The Supreme Court Records disclose that the file is held at the Public Record Office.' I had minor success in locating a preliminary reference in July 1883 in the Divorce and Matrimonial Court Book, and also the listing of the case in the Divorce Cause Book, both held by the Victorian Public Records Office. My efforts to locate any reference to the case in the papers of the instructing solicitor, Mallesons and Co. (through their successor firm Mallesons Stephen Jaques) or in the papers of Sir John Madden, Jessie's barrister, were also unsuccessful.[20]

It is still possible that the records of the case will be discovered wrongly filed, or they may have been in such decayed condition that at some stage they were discarded. Newspaper reports, therefore, provide the only source of the proceedings in *Fraser v. Fraser*. The reports in the *Argus* and *Age* are similar, consistent and, like all law reports in newspapers at the time, reasonably lengthy. It seems unlikely that significant evidence was omitted in these reports, but the official file, if it is ever located, would probably provide more intimate details. Its loss is frustrating.

The *Argus* reported that Dr Madden, appearing for Jessie, told the Court that Charles Fraser 'was a man somewhat given to horse racing and betting'. He had 'failed in pecuniary means', causing his wife on several occasions 'at his request' to go to live with her family, either in Tasmania or England. Madden said that after Fraser became insolvent, he suggested his wife should go to her mother in England, and said he would send her £100 a year maintenance. He had sent, however, only £10 in total. He said Jessie had written several letters to Fraser, but he had replied to only one, in which he said 'he did not want anything more to do with her'.

Regarding their meeting in London in 1882, Jessie testified that she had gone to see Fraser 'to see if they could rejoin each other, but he treated her with the utmost coolness, and told her he had formed a connexion with a Miss Seal, in Melbourne, which he thought would be lasting'. Jessie said she had supported herself by 'literary skill', since leaving Victoria. After arriving back in Melbourne, she had written to her husband 'asking if he intended to take her back as his wife, and put away the woman he was living with'. He replied that 'he did not intend to have anything to do with her or give her any maintenance whatever unless the law compelled him to do so'. Evidence was given that Fraser had lived with Miss Seal, and was still doing so and that in 1877 he had told Jessie he had had 'connexion with a servant girl', who had borne a child to him.[21]

Substantially the same report appeared in the *Age* with a slight variation in the response of Charles Fraser to letters from Jessie asking for support and the means to return to him. 'The only reply she received was a curt note stating that he did not care if she never came back to him.'[22]

Jessie's case was supported by statements from her father, from Gordon R. Stewart of Mallesons, Alfred Druce and Mary Ann and Louisa Stephens.[23] The identity of Druce and the two Stephens, and the significance of their evidence, is not known because of the unavailability of the divorce papers. Alfred Druce, an accountant, probably gave evidence concerning Charles Fraser's financial affairs, and the two Stephens may have testified to the association between Fraser and Miss Seal.

The divorce was granted immediately, one of a record number of twenty-five granted in Victoria in 1883.[24] There was obviously so much collusion between Charles Fraser and Jessie in presenting uncontested evidence that would ensure the success of the action that there is some doubt about what was fact and what was fiction. Jessie did not want to return to her husband, yet was obliged to offer to do so to reinforce the case of desertion against Fraser. It is possible, although unlikely, that Miss Seal may have been fictional. She may have been the single woman, Annie Myra Seal of Belmont, Geelong, to whom a son, Charles Henry (father, not stated) was born on 14 November 1880.[25]

Fraser's statement that he expected his association with Miss Seal to be lasting did not prove correct. She may have been suitable for a lengthy relationship but, in choosing another wife, Charles Fraser returned to the establishment world of Hobart. On 17 June 1884, less than six months after his divorce was granted, Fraser, describing himself as a bachelor, married Lucy Benson of Double Bay, Sydney at the fashionable church of St Mark's Church of England, Darling Point.[26] Lucy Benson was a daughter of Dr William Benson, a Master of the College of Surgeons, Edinburgh, who had been a surgeon in the convict service in Van Diemen's Land. On her mother's side Lucy was descended from John Lakeland, principal superintendent of convicts from 1820 to his death in 1828, and from Thomas Arndell, a member of the aristocratic Arundell family. Dr William Benson, after serving at various convict establishments as assistant surgeon, became colonial surgeon in Launceston in 1846 while Major Fraser and his wife Christina were in charge of the Female Factory. He was later in charge in Hobart, before moving to Sydney.

After their marriage, Charles and Lucy Fraser lived at Pemberley, where their three children were born. In 1891 Fraser was appointed stipendiary steward to the Victoria Racing Club, a position that must have fulfilled his most sanguine dreams. Lucy Fraser died on 5 July 1909 and Charles Fraser on 21 June 1913, both in Melbourne. One of their daughters, Dora, married as his second wife Ralph Sadleir Falkiner, a member of the celebrated pastoral family of Boonoke stud in the Riverina district of New South Wales. His son Charles White Fraser served as a sergeant in the Australian Provost Corps in World War I, then settled in England with his French wife.[27]

Jessie was not as anxious to remarry as her ex-husband. When she sailed from Melbourne on 2 February 1884 on the *Melbourne*, her brother Eddie wrote 'the principal event in connection with her visit was the successful outcome of her "case" in Melbourne, and now she goes home unfettered by any tie'.[28]

Jessie's eight months in Melbourne were valuable in renewing her knowledge of aspects of colonial life, which she was to use in her future fiction. Although she was to write some further factual articles from England and Europe, her major literary efforts from this time were to be fictional. It was probably during this time that she began to think about the characters and setting of her greatest novel, *Uncle Piper of Piper's Hill*, which she set among the parvenu upper class in the Melbourne of the post-goldrush era. Almost certainly while in the city she wrote her novella, 'Mr Schenck's Pupil', which contains some memorable vignettes of life there, including descriptions of the hot, searing north wind days of Christmas and January, the empty social life, dominated by dresses and balls, and the sharp-eyed 'Mrs Grundys' of the social scene. By far the longest story she had written to that time, it was published in nine chapters over five weekly episodes in the *Australasian*, early in 1885.[29]

With its many coincidences not a very credible story, 'Mr Schenck's Pupil' is the tale of Maggie Queen, formerly a music teacher at Gissaile Seminary, Collingwood. Left a wealthy widow after the death of her elderly husband, the continuance of her large annuity depends on her not remarrying. The story contains some revealing comments about love and marriage. Perhaps Jessie reveals a little of herself through Maggie, a woman who slowly awakens to a first experience of love and sex after an eight-year marriage, during which she has been untouched by any deep feelings. Perhaps some of the comments reflect Jessie's own situation, deprived for years of the opportunity of real marriage by her ties to Charles Fraser, and from affairs by her fastidious conscience and reluctance to bind herself to any man. In 'Mr Schenck's Pupil' she writes of Maggie:

> Many in Maggie's place would have consoled themselves by becoming queens of fashion. And others whose heart-wants Fashion could not satisfy, would have found outside of marriage what marriage could not give them. But to Maggie there seemed nothing but to bear as best she might the consequences of what she had done. Make-shifts of any kind would have seemed so poor a substitute. She told herself that because she had awakened too late to the comprehension of what love and marriage should signify, she would not then desecrate her own ideal of them.

Once she reached Europe, Jessie joined her mother who, with John and Edith, had spent the winter in Florence. Charlotte still entertained the highest hopes that further education and training would develop the talents of her gifted youngest children, although both were by then well into adulthood. In Florence they continued their extraordinarily deep and varied artistic and cultural education, studying painting and Italian.

Jessie sent back two articles about Florence to the *Australasian*.[30] Again she employed the investigative journalism techniques she had first encountered used by 'The Vagabond' in Melbourne. As a lead in to the story of a band of men engaged in charitable works, she commented: 'It is not by going around Florence, Baedaker in hand, and attending to the points at which you are to experience commas or full stops of emotion, that the most interesting spectacles are to be seen'. She first saw some of these men known as the Misericordia in the role of mourners at a funeral, but later discovered they cared for the sick, being particularly active during cholera epidemics. Jessie who was always impressed by evidence of practical Christianity, wrote, 'If the Catholic religion had never been responsible for other martyrs than these, what a hold she would still have upon our hearts long after our minds had rebelled against her dogmas'.

There are indications in her articles and her diary[31] that Auguste Couvreur joined her in Florence. He was certainly with her when she went to London, where both attended the highly successful International Health Exhibition, opened in South Kensington on 8 May 1884 by the Duke of Cambridge.[32] According to her brother, Jessie wrote articles about the Exhibition, but these have not been located.[33] Auguste Couvreur attended as President of the Committee appointed to represent Belgium at the Exhibition.[34] He also had an engagement to open a session of the annual conference of the Philosophical Society, held in Edinburgh in 1884 where he spoke on the history of popular education in Belgium.[35]

During June 1884, Jessie and a group of friends undertook a high-spirited adventure in the form of a walk to Canterbury modelled on traditional pilgrimages. She described the journey in a series of articles for the *Australasian* as 'A Latter-Day Pilgrimage'.[36] The five pilgrims, one apparently Auguste Couvreur, a man 'of sage appearance' dressed in a grey knicker-bocker suit with grey gaiters, a grey felt hat, red tie and carrying a red umbrella, met at Charing Cross railway station. 'None of us were English in the true sense of the word', Jessie wrote. 'We had all come from beyond the seas—some of us from a land where the habitual garb of Nature is dark and solemn, and the unchanging forests never put off their robe of sombre mourning'. After leaving the train at Blackheath, they set out on foot for Gravesend, arriving that night 'jaded and footsore'. Then they walked on through Cobham to Rochester, where they climbed the ruins of Rochester Castle, saw Rochester Cathedral, and continued on to Canterbury. There they were disappointed to find that St Thomas's shrine had been 'wholly destroyed, and his bones scattered to the winds'. They had, nevertheless, walked seventy miles 'and *that* was glory that nothing, not even another Reformation, could deprive us of'.

Despite the close relationship between Jessie and Auguste Couvreur in the summer of 1884, Jessie hesitated for a year before deciding to marry him. It could have been at this time that she was rumoured to have received a proposal of marriage from Cecil Rhodes, British imperialist and coloniser of Africa.[37] With more recent knowledge of Rhodes's homosexual interests, this may seem unlikely. It is also difficult to see that Jessie, with her radical political views, sympathy for the working class, and attraction to socialism, would have found a great deal in common with Rhodes's empire building, and exploitive views on colonial development. Nevertheless, Jessie more than once implied that she had had the opportunity to take decisions in her life which would have resulted in her being materially much better off. Such a proposal, if it occurred, is at least indicative of the level of society in which Jessie now felt at home. Despite their lack of financial resources and a settled home, the Huybers family always maintained links with important and aristocratic families, and Jessie's writing and lecturing made her welcome in the higher strata of society. Another of her close friends in London was Sir Charles Dilke,[38] famous as the author of *Greater Britain: a record of travel in English-speaking countries during 1866 and 1867*, and as a politician with radical views regarded by many as a possible future prime minister. His political career was to be shattered when he was involved in a spectacular divorce case in 1885–86. After another tour of British colonies, he wrote *Problems of Greater Britain* (1890) in which he praised Jessie's first novel, *Uncle Piper of Piper's Hill*, as 'a colonial novel of much merit'.[39]

Jessie was reluctant to marry, whether to Auguste Couvreur, Cecil Rhodes or any other man. Reinforcing her own doubts were her mother's implacable views. Charlotte believed Jessie had made a disastrous mistake in marrying Charles Fraser, and was strongly opposed to her linking herself to anyone else. She kept reminding her daughter, as she was to do after her remarriage, that she had ruined her life with her first marriage, and warning her not to risk another entanglement. Like the independent New Woman then appearing, the woman who refused to conform to traditional female roles and who rejected conventional ideas of marriage, Jessie had shown she could lead an independent life. Charlotte believed that was how she should continue.

After spending the summer in England, Jessie returned to Paris to resume the life she had left a year before, lecturing and writing. Only one article appeared in the *Australasian* from this period[40]—about the opening of the spring 1885 exhibition of paintings at the Paris Salon and the latest literary sensation. The absence of other articles in the *Australasian* suggests she had found another outlet for her writng, almost certainly in England but so far undiscovered. The need to make money would have made the continuation of her work imperative.

Jessie continued her lecturing. This was to provide her with an income until well into the next decade. Her lectures were so successful and universally admired, that at about this time she was accorded the extraordinary honour of being named an Officier d'Académie by the president of France, entitling her to wear the violet ribbon and silver laurel leaves of the order. This was a decoration awarded by decree of the president of the Republic to persons who had rendered 'exceptional services in the field of education or in influencing French culture'. It was an award 'at the time rarely given to foreigners and even more rarely to women'. Since 1955, the award of Officier d'Académie has become a national order ranked with the Legion d'Honneur or le Merité. The title l'Officier d'Académie now corresponds to the grade of Chevalier de l'Ordre des Palmes Académiques.[41]

After a year of indecision Jessie, perhaps with some misgivings, decided to marry Auguste Couvreur. Her ever-optimistic brother Eddie wrote in his diary, 'she bids fair to make a happy union as regards a sympathetic marriage, and a position in life to which she is well suited',[42] but he may have been the only member of the family to hold this view. Charlotte seems not to have attended the ceremony. She was ever after to express regret at Jessie's second marriage, as she did at her first.

The marriage between Auguste Pierre Louis Couvreur, aged fifty-seven, and thirty-six-year-old Jessie, took place at the Registry Office in Paddington, Co. Middlesex on 7 August 1885.[43] The witnesses, R. Murray Smith and A.M. Des Voeux, came from the official and aristocratic world in which Jessie had kept many friends. Robert Murray Smith was the Agent-General for Victoria in London and Alice Magdalen Des Voeux, a daughter of the Earl of Wilton, was married to Sir Henry Des Voeux, the fifth baronet, a member of the Des Voeux family with whom Jessie had been friendly in Tasmania.

After their marriage, Jessie and Auguste went on a tour of Germany. For the rest of her life Jessie was to live in Brussels, the city which had been her home for nearly two years in the 1870s and which she had often revisited.

9

I am not born with a wife's instincts

Brussels, Paris, Athens, Constantinople, 1885–90

Jessie returned to Brussels as the wife of a distinguished citizen. Her home soon became a centre of intellectual, political and social life.[1] Auguste Couvreur's relatives, and his friends in journalism, politics and diplomacy, became her friends. Auguste's brother-in-law, Adolphe de Vergnies, director of the Bank of Belgium, and his unmarried sisters, Delphine and Victorine Couvreur, were frequent visitors. So too were Liberal politicians Senator Montéfiore-Lévy, representatives M. Vanderkindere and Count Goblet d'Alviella and the Burgomaster of Brussels, Charles Buls; journalists Léon Berardi, director of *l'Indépendance belge*, Gaston Berardi and Gérard Harry; educationists associated with Couvreur's work in founding in 1888 the Ecole professionale des jeunes filles, together with many artists, sculptors, architects and archaeologists.[2] Their friends held similar liberal, often radical, views on social and educational policies, but Jessie was to find their ideas on manners and morals disturbingly restrictive. Used to leading an independent if not bohemian life during the six preceding years, and before that to the informality of her own family, she chafed at the restrictions of life in Brussels society, and found 'Mrs Grundys' even more active than they had been in Australia. She had little to do with the quite populous Anglo-Belgian community. She thought they were 'rather amusing' and anxious 'to air their aristocratic connections'.[3]

The Couvreurs mixed exclusively with people on the Liberal side of politics. In Belgian society, Catholics and Liberals formed two distinct cliques. They did not visit each other's homes or shop at each other's shops. 'The *noblesse* with rare exceptions', Jessie wrote, 'belonged entirely to the Clerical party. The Liberals were recruited from the ranks of university professors, journalists, the representatives of financial and commercial interests, and, generally speaking, from among the *bourgeoisie* of the principal towns'.[4]

Small by the standards of her friends' houses, the Couvreurs' home, a narrow three-storeyed house with basement and attic, had small balconies on the first floor, curved gables, twisted chimneys and mullioned windows with wrought iron decoration. It was at 230 chaussée de Vleurgat, a street running off the fashionable and elegant avenue Louise. The house had been exquisitely designed by Charle Albert, 'the apostle of the Flemish Renaissance', and decorated by Auguste Couvreur in a style that was greatly admired. Jessie ensured that the rooms were always bright with bowls of fresh flowers. Marble steps led from the square entrance foyer to the main rooms which, when undivided, stretched from the bay window at the front of the house to a lead-paned window at the back framing a birthwort (*aristolochia*) tree in the small garden. Creepers and wild roses covered the outside walls. The rooms contained many beautiful paintings by Flemish Renaissance artists, and 200-year old oak carvings, said to be among the best in Europe.

Jessie's contributions to the decoration of the house reflected her anti-establishment views. They included relics of the 1798 Irish rebellion which had come to her from Smith O'Brien, one of the Irish political prisoners sentenced to transportation to Van Diemen's Land, following the Young Ireland revolt in 1848, and a Flemish poem engraved on the diamond panes of the window nearest her desk. The poem, translated, read:

Dear liberty—joy of life
Should'st thou succumb I would have death;
But before thou fall'st many blows will be exchanged
There are still valiant men in the country.

The house was situated in an historic street. Long before the avenue Louise was formed, the steep and stony chaussée de Vleurgat stretched upwards from the eastern end of the Ixelles ponds to the junction of the road to Waterloo with the Forêt de Soignes. In 1815, residents of the street had helped wounded soldiers as they struggled back to Brussels after their defeat at the Battle of Waterloo. From the steps at the entrance to their house, Jessie could glimpse the high roofs and spires of the city of Brussels.[5]

Despite the expensive taste conveyed by the house, the Couvreurs had only the modest income Auguste earned from journalism and from investments. With the defeat of the Liberals in the 1884 election, he had lost his seat in the Chamber of Representatives, and retired from his full time position on the *Indépendance belge*. It was a constant problem for Jessie to juggle her housekeeping allowance to pay for the frequent entertainment of visitors, and she often complained in the diary she kept during 1889 and 1890 that she was poorly dressed compared with the people with whom she associated.

Even after her apparently favourable marriage, Jessie needed to make money as she had when she was keeping herself. Her life in Brussels, however, was not as suited to gathering material for articles for the *Australasian*[6] as it had been when she was free to move around Europe and England. There is an indication, in a letter she wrote to English lawyer and journalist Alexander Broadley,[7] that she had an outlet for political articles in English periodicals:

> The opening of the Chambers was a most uninspiring ceremony. Short of writing a treatise on the political situation of Belgium which is not 'de ma compétence' there is not much to be said about it. I have given my fugitive impressions and am relieved by your *assurance* that they shall remain anonymous.

One specific example mentioned in her diary of her freelance writing was an article about the fight by Mademoiselle Popelin, the first woman lawyer in Belgium to be admitted to the bar. Publication of this article has been traced to the *Pall Mall Gazette* of 6 December 1888, where it appeared anonymously.[8] After her marriage, however, she put her main literary effort into writing novels. They seem to have been waiting to be written during the time when she was too occupied earning a living to write them.

From the appearance of her first novel, *Uncle Piper of Piper's Hill*, late in 1888 Jessie's position changed. Its remarkable critical success and the public acclaim for its author made her an important literary figure overnight. She was no longer merely the wife of a well-known and respected European elder statesman. It is probably not a coincidence that it was at this time Jessie began to keep a diary.

There is no information available on her life between her marriage in 1885 and the end of 1888, when the novel was published. If she wrote articles or short stories during this time, only a handful have been found. If she gave lectures, reports of them have not surfaced. If she was involved with problems in her family, as she undoubtedly was, we know little of these. It is obvious she led an active, busy, demanding life in Brussels as the wife of Auguste Couvreur. But it seems that these three years, the first time since entering her first marriage when she had both time and a reasonably secure financial status, were devoted to writing full-length novels. What is recognised as her greatest novel, *Uncle Piper of Piper's Hill*, was a product of the relative serenity of these years. It seems likely, because of the speed with which she produced the books that followed, that parts of them were also written during this time. But it is *Uncle Piper of Piper's Hill* that was quintessentially a product of the early years of Jessie's marriage to Auguste Couvreur. She felt happy and secure before family problems and a certain disenchantment with her marriage began to crowd into her life.

The diary she kept in 1889 and 1890 is immensely important. It provides the most intimate view we have of Jessie's thoughts on herself, her family and her husband, on her life, her writing and her social obligations. Reading it is to enter the life of a complex woman, vaguely and at times acutely unhappy, weighed down with worry about family members long past the age when such worry and concern could be said to be usual. Not even the truly amazing success of her first novel was enough to raise her more than momentarily out of the ennui, the tiredness with life, that she often commented on in her diary.

There are various ways in which this important diary could be used in a biography. I have chosen to bring together entries dealing with themes in her life: for example, her overriding and quite unusual preoccupation with her family; her relationship with her husband and her dalliances with other men; the demands of her social position; her tours to foreign countries; and her writing and lecturing. Together, they present a more intimate picture of Jessie than any mere account of the facts of her life, or her literary and journalistic successes, could ever do.

Microfilm copies of her diary are available in several libraries. They are difficult to read, and even in the original, which I was privileged to have on loan, her diary requires concentrated attention, particularly the sections in French. There are references to people whose names are not easily decipherable, and which, when deciphered, need to be identified. It repays the time spent on it, however, since it is such a rich source of information on Jessie's attitudes, preoccupations and life at that time. It is something that is not available in any other material about her, or at any other time in her life.

When Jessie began her diary on 1 January 1889, it was with her translation of a deeply pessimistic extract from a poem by the German poet, Heinrich Heine:

Lay your head where my breast is, sweet
In this little chamber, & feel it beat.
There is a carpenter grim at work within
Making a coffin to bury me in.

He is hammering there by night and by day
It is long he has driven my sleep away.
Oh Master Carpenter, finish it fast,
And let me get to sleep at last.[9]

Thoughts of eternity haunted her, as they had in her childhood. When she talked to lawyer Paul Errera at a social gathering, she 'was surprised to find how free his and most minds are of the crushing conception of eternity—which has been and will be my nightmare as long as I can think at all'.[10]

Scattered through Jessie's diary are hints of the oppressive ennui which seized her, even at times when her own life seemed eminently successful. After failing to record any entries for some time, because there had been 'nothing "marquant" [outstanding] in our lives', she wrote 'The days follow and resemble each other'. On another occasion, she remarked on her 'curious lack of *deep* interest in things'.[11]

As always, Jessie's intense feeling for the well-being of her family overrode all else, including her attitude to her husband. 'I am not born with a wife's instincts I fancy', she wrote. 'The news about the others—brothers and sisters—always seems more exciting and interesting than any that affects *us*.'[12]

All members of the Huybers family were affected by the collapse of the family business in Hobart, in December 1884, with liabilities of £85,000. 'Father's position had been looked upon here for many years as that of a wealthy man, and the surprise was great', her brother wrote.[13] Though Alfred Huybers appears to have continued to provide limited support for Charlotte, younger family members overseas were thrown on to their own resources. The firm struggled on for a few more years, but finally went out of existence when it was merged with Ferguson and Co. in May 1887.[14] Subsequently, the contents of the Murray Street house, including the huge library of French and English works, were auctioned, and Highfield was sold to Lucy Mills Hudspeth.[15] Alfred Huybers stayed on in Hobart, but his son William, with his wife and five children, moved to Melbourne, where he joined the firm of Jules Renard, mercantile broker and importer of Melbourne, Sydney and Antwerp, and Belgian consul in Melbourne.

One after another Jessie agonised over her brothers and sisters. When her diary opened, Eddie's failure to be appointed to a position with the Victorian exhibit at the 1889 Paris Exhibition caused her such concern that progress on her writing stopped.[16] Edward Huybers had returned to London in 1885 with his wife and two children, after the failure of the Huybers firm in Hobart, but despite his command of eight languages, he had not succeeded in obtaining permanent employment. 'My first bitter bout of crying this year apropos of Eddie's letter', Jessie wrote. 'The idea that intrigue and jealousy should be successful in depriving him of the post he filled so well and upon which all his future seemed to depend is too hard to bear'.[17] Calling on past friendships, she wrote to Robert Murray Smith and Gowen Evans in Melbourne and the agent-general, Sir Graham Berry, in London on Eddie's behalf. Eddie's problems were temporarily solved by his appointment as secretary to the Victorian commissioner for the Paris Exhibition. Jessie, however, returned from a visit to London in March 1889, worried about other members of the family:

> Would have enjoyed myself very much had it not been for the constant oppression of the thought of mother in the dreary poverty-striken atmosphere of Lisle St—still eating her black bread for Jack's sake (she has done nothing else for the past five or six years) while Jack, with talent, mental ability and an apparently tender heart, actually allows this state of things to continue indefinitely, always expecting to 'percer' [make a name]. It is one of those pitiful cases one reads about in books, but never thought

of realising in one's own family. For the 10th time a new arrangement has been made. If Jack does not succeed in getting self supporting work by the end of March, he has promised to return to Australia, which he should *never* have left. Whatever may be his artistic feeling and power of giving it effect by lifelike drawings (which might and ought to gain him his bread and perhaps more) the fact remains that he has burdened mother's declining years for many a long day, and that it makes one sick at heart to see where she is now, and think of where she ought to be. I am afraid that these homeless wanderings of later years have distorted the points of view of both Mother and the younger members of the family.[18]

John Huybers was to remain of great concern to his family. In 1884, he had joined Koozee and Arthur Loureiro in Melbourne, intending to teach painting. He soon returned to Europe, however, where despite his unusual artistic talent and success in exhibiting in 1886 in the highly competitive Paris Salon and at the Marlborough Gallery, Pall Mall, was unable to support himself. His exhibit at the Marlborough Gallery, typically displaying his well-developed social conscience, was of a Paris soup kitchen. He exhibited again at several leading galleries in 1887, but 'like many who stand on the borderline of genius, he lacked certain qualities necessary to ensure the material benefits of his talent', as his brother Edward wrote. Although in his studio days in Paris his work had surpassed that of colleagues who later became famous, 'the egg was hopelessly addled: visionary ideals impossible of realisation, passions that ensnared reason, these and other stumbling-blocks barred the way to success'.[19] Unable to earn a living he existed precariously in London or Paris, sometimes with his mother, sometimes probably with male intimates, but always dependent on her.

Jessie continued her diary by expressing the 'keenest anxiety' about Edith, 'sacrificed willingly to and for Jack . . . She deserves an exceptional husband and what will be her fate as things are? No wonder one is frightened and anxious'.[20]

Edith, while working in Paris as literary and art critic for the London *Spectator*[21] and the *Universal Review* (begun on 16 May 1888 by English art critic Harry Quilter), had met the famous writer and art critic, Joris-Karl Huysmans. Huysmans was then at the height of his fame as the 'Supreme Decadent', following publication of his great decadent novel *A Rebours* (Against the Grain). It was to inspire many similar works, including Oscar Wilde's *The Picture of Dorian Gray* and *Salome*. Edith became part of the exciting intellectual coterie, including writer and propagandist Léon Bloy, Symbolist writer Villiers de l'Isle Adam, and Symbolist painter Odilon Redon, which revolved around Huysmans, joining the most controversial cultural group in contemporary French society. Huysmans had several long-lasting relationships with mistresses, including Anna Meunier, a former prostitute, Henriette Maillot, who encouraged his interest in occultism, and Berthe Courriere, who introduced him to satanism. He also fell in love with Edith, and they are believed to have become lovers.[22] She was to remain a friend of Huysmans for the rest of his life,[23] but the love relationship ended quickly after a 'momentous crisis', which brought her mother hurrying to Paris to support her daughter.[24]

Soon after, Edith met Jean Reverdy, a sculptor and woodcarver, son of Jean-Baptiste Reverdy, a painter who had won the Prix de Rome, and his wife, formerly Zoë Courbet. Although the nephew, on his mother's side, of the famous artist and revolutionary, Gustave Courbet,[25] a radical connection that appealed to the Huybers family, Reverdy's education, in the village of Ornans, apparently had been neglected,[26] and Edith's family considered him ignorant and ill-bred. On 1 May 1889 while Jessie was visiting Athens and Constantinople Edith, who was twenty-seven, married thirty-one-year-old Eugène Jean-Charles Reverdy, in Paris.

Reverdy had trained under the great French sculptor Chapu, and also under the woodcarver Lapierre,[27] but at the time of his marriage had no material prospects. He and Edith moved into her tiny room in the rue du Montparnasse, where Jessie later visited them. She was dismayed with their situation, as well as that of Charlotte and John, who had moved from London to Paris. She wrote in her diary: 'it is heart sickening to see him [John] with his fine brain and good heart unable to keep body and soul together by his own exertions living eternally upon poor Mother like an out door pensioner and darkening all the outset of Edith's married life as he spoiled her girl's life before'. Her views on Reverdy were frank. Although he had 'sterling qualities and real grit' and was 'full of artistic talent as a sculptor', he had 'such a rustic exterior—such an insignificant build—such utter ignorance of the subjects that every ordinarily well educated man, to say nothing of a man of the world, is supposed to be conversant with'. She continued:

> As for his means, though his talent and perseverance will doubtless bring him to the front some day—he and Edith have literally married upon nothing, and depend upon the workman's wages he earns as assistant in Graphus atelier. And Edith has refused steadfastly a really good offer, and turned her back upon a fairly good one—to end like this! But sympathies are too subtle? Ou l'amour va se nicher [there's no accounting for love] one may well say.[28]

When Jessie visited Paris again in November, John Huybers had a job doing illustrations on Paris life for the *Pall Mall Budget*. Jessie almost dared 'to hope he has his foot in the stirrup at last'. Edith, her husband and Charlotte had moved to the boulevard du Montparnasse, an improvement on the 'dreary Lisle St rooms', or 'the pauper precincts of the rue du Montparnasse'. Charlotte was recovered in health 'with her wondrous elasticity of yore' and Edith was pregnant, leading Jessie to express ambivalent comments on motherhood. 'To think that the great mystery should come upon her at last and that she is making for the strange sweet fearful heights of motherhood to which I cannot follow her', she wrote.[29] After the birth of Edith's son, she added: 'On principle Edith is against the bringing of children into the world—as who would not be, who gives an instant serious thought to the monstrousness of the mystery we call Life'.[30]

In May 1890 Jessie visited Paris again, staying in the small cramped rooms on the boulevard du Montparnasse with Charlotte, Edith, Jean and their baby son, Maurice, finding the experience sad and Edith's expression tragic:

> What would I give to transport them all into large cheerful rooms, with proper service, and the comforts and refinements of life. To think of Edith's powers. To remember her articles in the *Spectator* and to see her with her rustic un-intellectual husband who has all the qualities of heart possible, and artistic talents besides, but who is really in no way removed from a little ouvrier [labourer]! And to see Mother in her old age in such comfortless surroundings. Sweeping her room emptying the bath, washing up the dinner things, nursing the baby, performing all kinds of menial tasks when she is fitted by birth, education and association to take her place among such entirely different surroundings![31]

A temporary solution to Edith's situation came when she, Jean and the baby sailed for Australia on the SS *Tongariro*, in July 1890, to join Koozee and Arthur Loureiro in Melbourne. Before they sailed they spent a month with Jessie in Brussels, and she again wondered, 'What *was* it that made her marry him? What particular need of her nature does he supply? He has not intellect enough to be a companion—though he would lay down his life to please her'.[32] While in Brussels, Jean Reverdy did a bust of Jessie, and exhibited several sculptures in the 1890 Paris Salon.

Towards the end of April 1890 John Huybers arrived in Brussels to cover the triumphant arrival of explorer Henry Stanley returning from a mission in Africa for Leopold II, with orders to do sketches for the *Pall Mall Budget* and the *Illustrated London News*. 'It *did* seem as though this time his foot was fairly in the stirrup, and that he had nothing to do but mount & ride to victory', Jessie wrote. But within a few days, John was sick and unable to work. Jessie thought this was more than ill-luck: 'There is incapacity for the prompt rapid work required for illustrated weekly papers. He is capable of performing a good drawing under special conditions—but seems painfully at sea when there is necessity for "looking alive" '.[33] By June John was destitute in Paris, and Jessie sent him fifty francs as 'a stop-gap'. He was soon dependent on Charlotte again. When she moved to Brussels to live with Jessie, she fretted about him and Jessie continued to send him money.[34] Months later she was still concerned about her family:

> I could be so fairly contented with my very modest and almost niggardly programme of existence if only the others were no worse off than myself.

But to be seeing youth recede into the past, and one's brothers and sisters grown men and women, and to feel that each has married so inexplicably sadly, (excepting perhaps Willie) and gone out of the way to choose some absolutely penniless mate, when life is already so hard, is to feel desperate when one thinks seriously about it all.[35]

Socially, 1889 began for Jessie with the 'usual formal visits from sisters-in-law and de Vergnies' as well as from her husband's more distant relatives. 'I try to get up an interest in this one's rheumatism and that one's projects', Jessie wrote, 'and refuse to be condoled upon "mes neuralgies" '. Then return visits had to be made, one to Auguste's sisters. 'They have a very "cossu interieur",' Jessie wrote, 'and there is a kind of unexciting agreeableness in going to supper and whist playing with them'. Further duty calls on two days running brought the comment, 'Pas très divertissant' [not very amusing].[36]

At regular intervals she had to entertain more formally at dinner parties. 'What preparations it required to seat and *feast* a dozen people according to modern requirements', she wrote. 'It is a horrible nuisance to be without the proper means of keeping up an establishment like this. The Renaissance diningroom looked charming—but if the invités could only see me whisking the duster and house working every morning. Enfin!! . . . I have never known, and apparently never *shall* know what it is to have enough means, to be able to live *consistently*'.[37]

When Jessie and Auguste were invited out, she worried about her lack of suitable clothes. After attending a soirée dansante at the wealthy Goldschmidts, Jessie wrote: 'Unexpected gorgeousness of toilettes and displays of diamonds, making me feel almost Cinderellaiste before the transformation in my modest gauze . . . Came away about half past one in the morning with Auguste, reflecting as we drove back in the hired brougham, how "out of it" one feels in these splendid gatherings with such narrow means as *we* have'.[38] But meeting interesting people always diverted Jessie; at the dance she had met a young man who had visited Melbourne and Tasmania, with whom she could talk of old friends. The Couvreurs were at the Goldschmidts again the following month, and again in her diary Jessie contrasted these brilliant social events with the reality of her life, 'carpet shaking' with the maid in the morning, and in the evening 'coming out in the unexpected splendour of an old rose satin' while the other guests were 'bedecked in priceless jewels'.[39]

After a visit to the Montéfiores' chateau, she wrote, 'Never was a person called upon to undergo such wild changes of scene as I am. One week helping to wield the broom or duster at the rue du Montparnasse, or lending a helping hand to Rosalie to shake the carpets—the next staying in a princely residence surrounded by every imaginable luxury'.[40] One day she pondered with her mother 'upon the "contrariness" of the family destinies'

Mme TASMA   Gravé par Bescherer.

Left: Auguste Couvreur was a highly decorated man, a journalist and politician, known throughout European diplomatic circles for his work for free trade and the advancement of social progress, when Jessie met him in Venice in 1881. In Belgium he was a member of the Chamber of Representatives for over twenty years, and its vice-president from 1881–84. (Kenneth Huybers) Right: Under her public name of Mme Tasma, Jessie was immensely popular in Europe as a lecturer on Australia. In June 1883, just before leaving to return to Australia for her divorce hearing against Charles Fraser, she spoke to the Société de Géographie Commerciale de Paris on Queensland. Soon after, moves began in France to have her awarded the very high honour of Officier de l'Académie, an award rarely given to foreigners, and even more rarely to women.

A present-day photograph of 230 chaussée de Vleurgat, the address Jessie wrote at the beginning of the diary she started in 1889. Later, the Couvreurs' address was 254 chaussée de Vleurgat, but this may be explained by possible renumbering. The latter has been demolished and replaced by apartments.

Left: Edith Huybers, art and literary critic, was a member of the circle which gathered around Decadent writer, Joris-Karl Huysmans, in Paris in the late 1880s. In 1889, she married French sculptor and wood carver Jean Reverdy. In later life Edith was an art critic, writer and translator. Her *Au Réveil* (The Awakening) was published in Brussels under the auspices of Princess Clementine in 1905. (*Bruxelles philanthropique*, 15 October 1905) Right: This statue of Charles Buls, Burgomaster of Brussels 1881–99, is in a prominent position in a Brussels square. Jessie's horse rides with Buls, a bachelor, were frowned upon by the 'Mrs Grundys' of Brussels, and her husband insisted she abandon them.

Jessie's first novel, *Uncle Piper of Piper's Hill*, had an exuberant Australian title page, described in one English newspaper as 'a graceful little sketch of a gum-tree and other foreign growths', when it was first released late in 1888. Some English critics queried the sub-title, *An Australian Novel*, noting the absence of kangaroos, bushrangers and even coo-ees, and unable to recognise the portrayal of urban life as distinctively Australian. When the book was reprinted in 1892, 'Australian' was omitted from the sub-title.

During their visit to Constantinople, Auguste Couvreur arranged for Jessie to be photographed in Turkish costume, 'stayless—and in loose robe, broidered trousers and small cap—with hair hanging loose to the waist'. She was afraid the result would be 'caricatural', and was pleased when it was the 'reverse'. 'I think it would be wise to abstain from being photographed for the rest of my natural life—and to rest upon this Turkish presentment of myself, as one rests upon one's laurels', she wrote. 'I have never had—and it would be hard to have—a more satisfactory portrait taken.' (JC diary, 17 May 1889, National Library of Australia)

Left: Alfred Huybers, photographed in his eightieth year. Following the failure of his once very successful merchant's business in Hobart in the 1880s, he made two trips to Europe to see members of his family living there. He left Hobart to stay with his daughter Koozee in Melbourne in 1893, but died eight days later, at the age of eighty-two. (Kenneth Huybers)
Right: Jean Reverdy sculpted a bust of Tasma during the time he and Edith (née) Huybers and their son stayed with her in Brussels in 1890, before leaving for Melbourne. Jessie's portrait was painted by two painters in Brussels, also in 1890. Madame Franz Philippsons's oil painting is on the cover of this book; the other, a pastel portrait by Miss Bell, appears to have been lost. Auguste Couvreur liked the pastel portrait. (Kenneth Huybers)

Charlotte Huybers lived with Jessie for some years from 1890. She remained as highly individualistic as she had been in Hobart, but her range of coversation made her a welcome guest at the homes of Jessie's friends. Jessie dedicated her first novel, *Uncle Piper of Piper's Hill*, to 'my dear mother' in recognition of the encouragement she had received from her. (Renée Erdos)

until they 'increased each other's latent pessimism'.[41] At the beginning of 1890 she wrote in her diary:

> Curious! the chill of poverty that seems to rest upon every one connected with me . . . I myself with a thousand possibilities that seemed to point in a contrary direction have never been able to escape from it . . . In my own case I am in a home of which the appearance implies an income of a thousand a year at the very least. It is all the harder to have to get along on a quarter of that sum. I am going to begin housekeeping and clothing myself, and paying all but rent & Auguste's clothes upon two hundred pounds a year. It will be such a close shave that I fear I shall have to make a hole in my own poorly-filled stocking to keep things going.[42]

The affluent ease of her friends' lives provoked envious comments. Countess Goblet d'Alviella was a 'young, pretty, intelligent [A]merican, with children, husband, health, fortune, position' and seemed to have 'nothing on earth to wish for'; Madame Franz Philippson was 'young, rich, full of charm, gifted to an exceptional degree with husband, children and friends to surround her with adoration and love'. Jessie wrote, 'I so often meet now with people who seem to have come into the world with the traditional silver spoon. I doubt whether the members of our family can be said to have had an iron one amongst them'.[43] Among her friends only a fellow writer, Madame Poradofska, who had had stories published in the Paris *Revue des deux mondes*, was worse off, her 'house so dreary and small', the poverty 'so much more evident—than in my case'.[44]

In Jessie's diary, Auguste Couvreur except during an illness when she nursed him devotedly, is a figure in the background, in comparison with her obsessive preoccupation with her own family. He provided the social setting in which Jessie lived, the entrée to important social and political events, and the opportunity for friendships with prominent people. He appears, however, not to have satisfied her need for an intense relationship. Jessie enjoyed her beautiful home, always expressing pleasure on returning there. She also enjoyed many of the advantages of her social position. She was clearly less happy at their lack of money, and appears to have been uninterested in Auguste as a sexual partner. To Jessie, he was kindly but unromantic—she particularly noted when he gave her a present of a fan on two successive New Years' days. Though their marriage remained intact, it seems to have been too predictable, too rigid in social obligations, to satisfy Jessie. She often found other men more interesting and exciting, both those from her past and new acquaintances.

Before visiting Brussels late in 1991, I had read in Jessie's diary about her relationship with M. Buls. I had discovered he was the burgomaster of Brussels, that he was a Liberal associated with many of the same causes as Auguste Couvreur and that he was a bachelor. I hardly expected to come across him in the way I did while sitting one day on a bench in a square below the Grand' Place in Brussels. Facing a pleasant fountain with a sculpture of a man and his dog, around which a group of schoolgirls clustered taking notes, I idly looked at the inscription. To my great surprise and satisfaction, the sculpture was of Charles Buls—and I wondered again whether there had been more to their relationship than a mutual love of horse riding. Had he perhaps been her lover?

In the autumn of 1889 Jessie began a socially risky venture when she took up horse riding with Charles Buls. On 4 October, she recorded, 'Have just come in from a long ride with M. Buls. Had the first of a series with him the day before yesterday.' The next day she recorded her sensual pleasure during these rides: 'This morning's ride with M. Buls in the Bois very pleasant. A strong free wind blowing, and the autumn leaves whirling down upon us as we cantered through the deserted alleys'. She rode on Grau, a big chestnut horse Charles Buls had lent her. A few days later she wrote: 'I chronicle my rides because I enjoy them so much'. That morning they rode beyond the Bois de la Cambre to St Job. Just before Jessie left for a trip to Athens, they rode even further: 'Last ride yesterday morning through the beautiful Forêt de Soignes and back by Biotsfort'.[45]

The rides were interrupted for more than a month by Jessie and Auguste's visit to Athens, and their journey through Avignon, the Palais des Papes, Tarascon, Arles, Montpellier and other towns in southern France, then to Paris on the way home. They resumed when Jessie returned to Brussels. But gossip was soon at work, and Auguste's sisters, with whom Jessie maintained a polite but distant relationship,[46] were very ready to pass it on. She wrote in her diary:

> Disgusting! A feeble edition of Mrs Grundy—spiteful and stupid has
> turned up in Brussels. My delightful rides with M. Buls are knocked on the
> head. Delphine & Victorine came to Auguste the other evening—with mys-
> terious nods. C'est par affection qui nous le disons—Les gens commence-
> ment à faire des observations—M. Buls est très heureux &c—Il est dans
> les bonnes graces de Madame Couvreur et patati et patata as they say
> here. [We speak from affection—People have begun to make remarks—M.
> Buls is very happy etc. He is in the good graces of Madame Couvreur and
> so on and so forth] Auguste pulled a long face. I laughed at the whole con-
> cern, and declared that my innocent pastime should not be stopped
> because of the wagging of a few empty heads—audible tongues. But I have
> had to give in to Auguste's desires—sans conviction which makes it all the
> harder.[47]

Jessie argued about the rides with Auguste, but a week later acknowledged defeat. 'Mrs Grundy has had the best of it & the rides are tabooed for the present', she wrote.[48]

She continued to see Charles Buls, who was often a guest at her dinner parties. On one occasion she visited Antwerp with him and Madame

Philippson. There were also other men to whom she was attracted. Some were from the past such as Gowen Evans, 'the old wine that was better than the new', whom she twice met in Paris. 'The Commandant', her romantic interest during her previous residence in Brussels, she met on a tram and at an event at the Palace. General Türe was another ghost from far-off days in Venice, whom she re-met in Athens. She commented on the later meeting:

> A long-closed page in the book of my life was opened once more, and I seemed to hear the dead speak across the lapse of years. How many differ-ent experiences I have lived through already—each of which might suffice in itself for the romance of a life time. Small wonder if now the only things I feel very strongly are those which concern the welfare of the other members of the family.[49]

She also developed a friendship with an admirer in London, whom she met as a result of his interest in a story, 'The Lady of the Christmas Card', published in the *World*.[50]

Always in the background was her mother Charlotte, telling her how unwise she had been to marry Auguste Couvreur.[51] Jessie was with her mother when she met another man to whom she was strongly attracted. During the summer of 1890, she and Charlotte spent two weeks in a pension in Düsseldorf, where she met Rittmeister [Captain] von Wilucki, a man of noble birth of about her own age. Jessie was enthralled. 'He had all the exterior charm of a splendid physique, a thorough-bred manner, a sympa-thetic comprehension of every-thing that could be laughed at—a wonderful quickness in seizing the meaning of things, and the most musical voice and feeling in the world.' Leaving the Rittmeister's wife at the pension, they took long walks including 'a three-hours epic around the entire town'. 'How we came to understand each other as well I cannot say', she wrote, 'but it came to my telling him my past history, and to my listening to his, and our promising that we would be hold-fast friends for the rest of our natural lives'.[52]

When she returned to Brussels another man who had been a guest at the same pension, a young Australian, Mr McCarthy, descended on his mother's side from the pioneer a'Beckett family, became a centre of interest. He aroused 'a kind of elder sisterly—almost maternal instinct':

> We have a thousand tastes and associations in common, and I have the curious feeling of having known him, for un-numbered years . . . Among other strong points of sympathy there is the one of being able to laugh with him, as I have never been able to laugh for years. He sees the funny aspect in which our treatment of some of Mother's Carlylean remarks pres-ents itself occasionally, from a point of view that I thought no one out of the family could understand. I have the rare sensation of feeling entirely myself with him, just as I might with a brother with whom I am in intel-lectual and spiritual sympathy.[53]

After 'a day of vagabondage' with McCarthy, Jessie found a dinner at the Goblets brought 'a curious chill'. When McCarthy left Brussels to resume his medical studies at Edinburgh University, it left a 'dismal blank' in her life. He left wearing a silver chain ring Jessie had given him.[54] Auguste's sisters observed this new friendship and were 'rather puzzled'. But on this occasion, probably regarding McCarthy as no more than a passing threat, Auguste did not oppose Jessie's friendship with him as he had that with Charles Buls.

Jessie partly overcame her restlessness and dissatisfaction by throwing herself into physical activity. Never happy since childhood unless physically active, she walked all over Brussels even as far as Biotsfort. She learned to skate on the frozen lakes in the capital, and whenever possible she went swimming. She gained great physical well-being from these activities, a hangover from her active childhood in Hobart. In late nineteenth century Europe, such activities were unusual for a woman in her early forties.

One day when she was visiting Greece, while staying at a house over-looking the Bay at Phaelus, Jessie and a young Irish woman decided to go for a swim while the other guests watched from the roof-top terrace. 'I never had a more enjoyable dip', Jessie wrote. 'The sea was so warm and so limpid. We seemed to swim without effort, as in a delightful dream, and when we got out, we felt like well-oiled machines'.[55]

In the summer of 1890 she took up swimming in the Brussels baths, with Comtesse Goblet, Mme Philippson and Mme Prinis, remarking 'the dives, plunges, and jumps from the gallery into the deep water are a keen physical pleasure, only coming second to the rides of which I was deprived, to my everlasting regret, by Mrs Grundy'.[56]

Another opportunity for swimming of a different sort came when Jessie was invited to stay with Madame Franz Philippson, the rich and talented friend who was painting her portrait. When Madame Philippson heard that Charlotte was living with Jessie she, too, was invited to stay at the Philippsons' seaside villa at Middlekerke on the North Sea. As she had arrived in Hobart nearly forty years before, Charlotte arrived at Middlekerke in eccentric fashion. She alighted from the Brussels train at Ostende railway station during a violent thunderstorm, carrying 'nothing but a paper parcel for all her "swag" and in lieu of a waterproof a string of Australian shells round her neck'. But she was 'wonderfully fresh in feeling' and in no time despite 'a wild sky and tempestuous sea', seventy-two-year-old Charlotte was swimming with Jessie in the wild and freezing North Sea, 'rolling round in the waves and sand like a retriever'.[57] Jessie's friends must have met few women like Charlotte with her wide-ranging mind and remarkable conversation. Despite her eccentric dress and lack of anything approaching fashionable clothes, she was a welcome guest at Jessie's dinners, and at her friends' homes.

When winter came Jessie took up skating on the frozen lakes in the Bois or the Parc Leopold, sacrificing 'everything to the delight of learning'. At first she had a 'baptism of bumps'. She often skated in temperatures of fourteen below freezing before nine in the morning: 'I have the enthusiasm of a beginner for skating, and having just reached the point past which I can skate fearlessly alone, would like to be all day on the ice', she wrote.[58]

When she came close to the end of her diary Jessie's main concern, as always, was for her family, particularly her mother whom she wanted to make happy 'after the bitterly hard knockabout life she has led'. But Charlotte was a difficult case:

> To shed a quiet and restful influence around seems such an utter impossibil-
> ity to her nature. *Not* to long for the unattainable, *not* to try and make me
> discontented with my lot, by constant comments upon what she would
> have me look upon as my folly in marrying—that is all one would ask.
> The awful cold may make her restless though the atmosphere is always full
> of brightness and warmth in her room. But it is a fearful season for the
> poor, of whom there are so many alas! in Belgium.[59]

Jessie ceased to keep her diary with this entry in December 1890. In July the following year she added a more cheerful note, 'how changed is the aspect of things! Eddie has a good post and a salary of five hundred a year. Mother has found interest and occupation in zealously teaching English to two intelligent men . . . "Time and the Hour run through the roughest day" '.[60]

Ten years after her first lecture in Paris, Jessie continued to be in demand as a conférencière. Even with her years of experience, each lecture presented a challenge she would have liked to avoid. Before she started she suffered from increasing nervous tension. When she was asked to lecture to the Royal Geographical Society in Brussels, early in 1889, she started to write out 'certain disjointed reminiscences' about her Queensland experiences nearly twenty years before. She confided to her diary she was inclined to 'funk' the lecture.[61] When it was over she wrote:

> Like Europe when Napoleon died, I give a great sigh of relief. My lecture
> for the Geographical Society of Brussels on 'Melbourne et le Bush
> Australien' came off last night. The nervousness which reaches the climax
> as I mount the platform only gives away after the first few moments—but
> then comes the reward! The sense of expectancy with the audience is so
> delightful and then the wrapt attention, the early laugh at the mildest of
> jokes, and when all is over the crowding round of friends, the jubilant con-
> gratulations! Auguste's intense gratification! I spoke for an hour, and never
> consulted my notes. It was really a little effort of memory but it sounded
> like improvisation.[62]

Jessie was introduced by the president, Charles Ruelens, to a huge audience, predominantly female, gathered in a large hall. She was, he told them, an author who wrote 'with the pen of a Dickens'. In her speech she contrasted the hard life of the squatters in the vast hinterland of Australia, riding over their huge stations rounding up their cattle, a life which she had witnessed in Queensland, with the more luxurious life of Australian cities. They rivalled in comfort and splendour European ones, she said. As usual, the simplicity and elegance of her speech, its humorous anecdotes, her exotic accent, and her showing of photographs, was remarked on in newspaper reports. When Jessie read the hyperbolic account of her speech in the *Indépendance belge* she thought it 'so sugarly amiable' that it must have been 'dictated by the French instincts of the critic'.[63]

When she was invited to give a talk soon after for the Geographical Society of Antwerp she wrote, 'I don't want to appear in public again. I am too miserable beforehand'. But again the occasion was a great success. During the formal dinner preceding the lecture, Jessie 'felt the shadow of the conférence' hanging over her too acutely to enjoy herself. With the governor of Antwerp, the president of the society, General Wauvermans, and other dignitaries seated on the platform, Jessie stood to face the crowded Town Hall.

> A mighty effort at first. All was indistinct before my eyes. Then all smooth sailing, and for an hour, an audience as still (to use a worn expression) as waxwork. The trying part was the Governor's effusive speech at the close of my conférence. I was simply smothered—not covered only—with laurels! Then came the presentation of a superb bouquet. Then my views; then clapping, congratulations, and departure. I had carried the usual qualms to the Hall, but I carried away with me a warm glow of satisfaction and—my flowers! The supper which followed at the Wauvermans was crowded. Consuls general—and consuls, their wives and families in a large majority.[64]

Early in 1890 she gave a lecture on the status of women to a packed audience. Again it was a strain beforehand, but a great success once she started speaking. 'Spring is coming', she wrote, 'and I have got my conférence off my mind'.

> I had to speak in the presence of a full hall at the Palais des académies—subject 'les transformations dans l'état social de la femme'. As usual I had it off by heart so pat, that I never consulted a note the whole time, and spoke as though upon the spur of the moment. The awful entrance, and the awful beginning once over, I enjoy speaking in public—especially with such immense encouragement as I receive here. But Victorine says I was 'blême' [pale] as I entered. The after-felicitations are very gratifying. My address lasted exactly an hour.[65]

Jessie was again a speaker on 23 March 1892, when she addressed a session of the Société Royale Belge de Géographie. Auguste Couvreur had been elected president the previous year, Count Goblet d'Alviella was a vice-president, and Charles Buls a member of the Committee. Jessie's subject was 'Le Tasmanie, Voyage par le cap Horn'. She spoke about the history of Tasmania, from its colonisation by convicts, the destruction of the Aboriginal race, the exploits of the bushrangers and runaway convicts, to the late nineteenth century, with its peaceable population composed mainly of farmers. She also spoke of her voyage, nearly twenty years before on the *Windward*, via New Zealand and Cape Horn. She described the length and monotony of the voyage, the difficulties of navigation, and the intense cold in a latitude of nearly sixty degrees south. Her simple, elegant speaking style was praised as 'excellent'. Her talk ended with projections of photographs of town and country scenes in Tasmania and New Zealand. The reporter from *l'Indépendance belge* was so impressed with her talk he claimed to be a convert to the emancipation of women and female suffrage, and suggested Tasma should stand in the coming Senate elections.[66]

Perhaps as a result of her 1889 speeches, or perhaps through Auguste's journalistic contacts (Jessie's diary is unclear), Jessie and Auguste were offered a trip to the East. After a stormy passage on a trading ship, the *Vandertaelen*, through the Bay of Biscay and the Mediterranean, they arrived in Athens by train from Patras on 10 April 1889. In Athens they climbed to the Acropolis by moonlight, received a visit from the Greek Prime Minister, Charilaos Tricoupis, and called on his sister.

After a few days they sailed on to Constantinople (Istanbul) where, through Auguste Couvreur's standing as a foreign correspondent, they were entertained by high ranking Turkish officials and diplomats, including the American minister to Turkey, Oscar Solomon Straus, a friend of President Cleveland and brother of Isidor and Nathan Straus, owners of Macy's department store in New York. 'I like Mr & Mrs Straus', Jessie wrote, 'the former interests me'.[67] Fellow guests at the minister's residence included the 'fabulously wealthy' Cornelius Vanderbilt and his wife, the French Ambassador, Comte de Montebello, and the Dutch Ambassador, Comte de Tets.

Before she left Turkey, Jessie gave a copy of the just released Tauchnitz edition of *Uncle Piper of Piper's Hill*[68] to Oscar Straus and his wife Sarah (née Lavanburg). Although not mentioned in her diary, Jessie must have developed a rapport with Oscar Straus, as they came to an arrangement for her to translate his *The origins of the republican form of government in the United States of America*, first published in 1885 and republished in 1887, into French. It was produced in Brussels in 1890, translated by 'Madame Auguste Couvreur'.[69]

Jessie's diary contains only one or two entries on Constantinople, since she wrote articles which she hoped to get published. She sold the articles 'Women in a Harem' to publisher Richard Bentley the following year, but their publication has not been traced.[70] They would make interesting reading on the position of women in Turkish society, as Jessie had some unusual experiences there, including an evening spent with 'the Ladies of the Harem of the Turkish Minister for Justice', a visit to a Turkish bath 'among all the fat [T]urkish ladies—in delightful deshabille' with Sarah Straus as a companion, and a visit to the 'dancing and howling dervishes', which she described as 'appalling' and a 'form of epilepsy or hysteria'. When she left Turkey she wrote, 'Nothing remains but a feeling of écoeurement [disgust] at the dirt, backwardness and material and moral corruption which cling to the capital'.[71]

Jessie and Auguste spent a further month in Athens later in 1889 when Auguste was appointed a special correspondent for the *New York Herald*, mainly to report on the situation in Crete. From their arrival on 21 October, Jessie was critical of the arrangements under which Auguste had to compete for news with a Mr Stanhope, also representing the *New York Herald*. It is clear she had a far better appreciation of the impediments to successful reporting in this situation than her husband. She correctly believed all the paper wanted was 'sensational information telegraphed as a "primeur" ', whereas Auguste was used to writing feature material at a more leisurely pace.[72] Eventually the situation was resolved, when Stanhope left Athens.

Jessie was in her element staying at the very grand Hotel de la Grande Bretagne. Here she met 'Actresses, Excellencies and Serenes' at very turn. She met the immensely popular English writer, Rider Haggard—'very amusing with his monocle—but not, I should say, a model of all the virtues', and made friends with Mr Fitzgerald of the *Manchester Guardian*, who pleased on two counts: he was both entertaining and radical in his views. As well, she met 'heaps' of other interesting men, reflecting, 'I like hearing them and I like mixing among them—but what would have been keen pleasure and delicious excitement some years ago is such a modified feeling now. Can it be that *all* my sensations are blunted?'[73]

Soon after the arrival of the Couvreurs, Athens was inundated by royalty, diplomats, special envoys and politicians, for the wedding of the Duke of Sparta, heir to the Greek throne, and Princess Sophy, daughter of the German Empress, the first Royal wedding to be held in Greece. Jessie and Auguste, 'in full court dress, with all his decorations', attended the wedding at the Cathedral, sitting in the 'loge des diplomates'. Afterwards, they attended the Court Ball. Jessie wrote that she had never 'assisted before at such a brilliant spectacle', but analysing the brilliance she decided 'it all lies in so many yards of costly stuff and so many clusters of precious stones'. She wrote a three part series on the wedding, which was published in the Melbourne *Argus*.[74]

Again she was the guest of Mademoiselle Tricoupis and, with Auguste, an experienced and enthusiastic archaeologist, walked again up to the Acropolis. She was oppressed as she went 'at the contemplation of the enormous blocks of marble, and the reflection that they had been hewn and set up by human hands'. She visited all the museums, the ruins at Eleusis and at the Temple of Jupiter. She commented on the latter: 'One marvels at the disproportion between these mighty monuments, and the miserable habitations that surround them'.

Jessie was also entertained by Madame Sophia Schliemann who, with her famous archaelogist husband, Henry, had discovered and excavated the ancient city of Troy. The Schliemanns' eleven-year-old son, Agamemnon, came to escort Jessie across the street to the Schliemanns' beautiful mansion, Iliou Melathron. Among its expanses of austere marble, she met Sophia Schliemann, thirty years younger than her husband, 'cordial, plain, and somewhat faded-looking', and their daughter, Andromache, 'a Hebe in appearance'.[75]

When she returned to Brussels, Jessie heard that her next book, A *Sydney Sovereign*, was about to be published. As she had been at the beginning of 1889, she was pessimistic in mood. 'May it be as successful as the first!' she wrote. 'I am the more anxious about these poor little works of mine that I have a desperate misgiving as to the likelihood of producing any others. I am not sure even the power remains'.[76] It is remarkable with the multitude of other activities and demands on her time recorded in her diary that she had time to write at all.

10

Tasma is surpassed by few British novelists

Brussels, 1890–93

When they were published, Tasma's novels received great critical acclaim. It seems important to record extracts from some of these reviews, not only because of this remarkable but forgotten reception of an Australian novelist, but also because of the circumstances of their survival. I was lent the reviews by a descendant of Jessie's sister. They were collected by Jessie herself and pasted into a book of cuttings, 'Appréciations de la presse anglaise du *Uncle Piper, A Sydney Sovereign, In her Earliest Youth, The Penance of Portia James, A Knight of the White Feather, Not Counting the Cost*'. They have been kept with many loose cuttings, some still stamped with the name of the press cutting agency, Romeike and Curtice.

The pages of Jessie's press cuttings book, now tattered at the edges and faded with age, are full of reviews amazing both in quality and quantity. The majority are in English, others are in French, and one or two are in German. Without this record, it is doubtful whether it would be possible to trace them. Certainly it would take many months of research to locate them in the newspapers of the time. Reviews are important to all writers, perhaps particularly so to Jessie, who had only fragile confidence in her writing ability. It is an added advantage that we also have in her diary her comments on some of the reviews, as well as on the progress of her writing.

The critical response to Jessie's first novel, *Uncle Piper of Piper's Hill*, seems amazing even now. It brought her fame 'in a single week'[1] and made her 'perhaps the most popular living Australian novelist'.[2] *Uncle Piper of Piper's Hill* first appeared as a serial, 'The Pipers of Piper's Hill', in the *Australasian* from 7 January to 12 May 1888, where it was so popular that the journal's circulation jumped.[3] It was released as a book, under the title of *Uncle Piper of Piper's Hill: An Australian Novel*, late in 1888,[4] by Trübner of London.

Its immediate success with critics and the public surprised both Jessie and her family,[5] and the publishers soon had to produce another edition. The sophistication of the writing, the vividly drawn characters and the charm of its story appealed. It was set among the mansions of South Yarra near Blairgowrie, and in the rectory in the country town of Barnesbury (based on Malmsbury). The gentle irony in the central story of the English Cavendish family with their aristocratic pretensions, dependent in the colony of Victoria on the self-made wealth of ex-butcher Tom Piper, and the intellectual and slightly daring heroine, reluctant to tie herself to marriage, brought enthusiastic praise from critics. Many were surprised to find not a convict, bushranger, Aborigine, or kangaroo in sight, and no sound of a 'coo-ee'; they disputed its claim to be 'An Australian Novel'. These critics were seemingly unaware that it portrayed aspects of Australian life hardly touched in Australian fiction up to that time. *Uncle Piper* dealt with urban life among the *nouveau riche* of an Australian city and the subtle effects of exposure to Australian life on the values and manners of English migrants.

Uncle Piper of Piper's Hill was hailed as 'the novel' of the season.[6] Tasma was described as 'the Australian George Eliot' by Rolf Boldrewood,[7] the Australian writer recently celebrated as the author of *Robbery Under Arms*, and in an English newspaper as 'the Australian Jane Austen'.[8] She was compared with writers as diverse as Charles Dickens and Olive Schreiner.

The *Pall Mall Gazette* [9] said there was every indication that Tasma would 'take her place among the first and best of Australian writers of fiction'. The *Spectator* [10] ranked *Uncle Piper* with Marcus Clarke's *For the Term of His Natural Life* and Rolf Boldrewood's *Robbery Under Arms*, calling it only the third novel of 'remarkable merit to come . . . from the Antipodes'. It was 'the very last kind of book we expect from the intimation that it is an Australian novel, and one such as we rarely have the chance of welcoming from any quarter'. It was 'a curiously close study of character, spiced with humour of a dry and seemingly unconscious kind', the *Spectator* said.

The London *Times* [11] said *Uncle Piper* was 'written in pleasing style, and distinguished by an originality the more uncommon because applied to a simple plot'. The *Guardian* [12] said that the tale 'was thoroughly charming', the characters 'delightfully drawn', and that it was comparable with George Eliot's *Scenes of Clerical Life*. The *World* [13] said it was 'a capital sample of the novel of character'; the *Academy* [14] that it was 'a work of considerable promise'; the *Glasgow Herald* [15] that it was 'simple and unforced, amusing and pathetic' and the characterisation 'skilful and complete'; and the *Athenaeum* [16] that it was a 'well-written story, equal in one substantial volume, to an ordinary two or three'.

There were many other favourable comments but, most important for its success, people began talking about *Uncle Piper of Piper's Hill*. Less than three months after its release the London *Figaro* [17] wrote, 'Already people are talking about "Uncle Piper of Piper's Hill" at the dinner-table, and great curiosity is being displayed as to who its author or authoress can be—both unerring signs that the book is "catching on" '. Several notes speculating about the author, often assumed to be male, appeared in literary gossip columns. Refuting references to Tasma being a man, Arthur Patchett Martin, who had known Jessie in Melbourne when he edited the *Melbourne Review*, claimed that the English clergyman in *Uncle Piper of Piper's Hill*, the Reverend Francis Lydiat, was a 'life study' based on a clergyman who had migrated to Melbourne in an advanced stage of consumption contracted during his work in the East End, and died there; he also claimed to know a butcher on whom Tom Piper was based.[18]

In Australia the *Australasian*, which knew Tasma's identity, before quoting a review from the *Saturday Review*[19] began with the ill-informed and tendentious comment: 'In every case the author is assumed to be masculine, which "Tasma" will no doubt accept as a compliment, as the ambition of female novelists is to write like men'.

In Brussels, the *Journal de Bruxelles*[20] referred to the enormous success of *Uncle Piper of Piper's Hill* and the unanimous acclaim of English critics. It praised the portrayal of character, comparing Uncle Piper's young daughter Louey with Eva in *Uncle Tom's Cabin*. It also praised Tasma's descriptions of exotic scenes, such as the avenue lined with Moreton Bay figs and Murray pines leading to Piper's palatial residence in Melbourne. In a very long review in the *Indépendance belge*,[21] Gérard Harry, under the heading 'Un Roman Australien', compared Tasma's adoption of her pseudonym to Melba using the name of her native city as a patriotic statement of origin. He predicted a brilliant future for the Australian novel if Tasma's work was an example. He praised her restrained use of local colour and compared her characterisation with Dickens. Reviews appeared in several other Brussels papers[22] and in *La nouvelle revue*[23] in Paris, in which Léo Quesnel wrote that *Uncle Piper of Piper's Hill* placed Tasma in the front rank of Australian storytellers.

Jessie's fame spread in Brussels. At a social event she was told a friend had 'pleurer a chaudes larmes' [cried hot tears] over one of the later chapters of *Uncle Piper of Piper's Hill*. Hearing that books were being talked about, a lady sitting next to Jessie commented: 'J'ai les femmes auteurs en horreur . . . Et vous, Madame?' ['I regard women authors with horror . . . And you Madame?'] Jessie replied: 'Je te regrette Madame, parceque c'est justement de mon premier petit livre que Madame Berardi est en train de parler.' ['I beg to differ because it is precisely of my first small book that Madame Berardi is speaking.'] Jessie wrote in her diary, 'It would have made a famous "things one would rather have left unsaid" but it shows how backward the modern conventional Bruxelloise must be. There is not an up country township in Australia where such a remark would be made.'[24]

Jessie commented in her diary on some of the reviews. The *Glasgow*

Herald review was 'very favourable', the *Athenaeum* 'faint praise but not enough to damn'. The long review by Gérard Harry in the *Indépendance belge* she thought was 'amusingly [F]rench—and somewhat patronising and with a weakness for the character of Sara because of her beauty'. She continued: 'Judgment of the *World* very favourable, of the *Academy* favourable and encouraging'.[25]

By the middle of February she had heard from Trübner that the first edition of *Uncle Piper* had sold out and they intended 'to stereotype it and issue a second edition immediately'.[26] Further editions followed, including an edition by Tauchnitz of Leipsig, a firm that specialised in producing popular editions in the style of latter-day paperbacks. The absence of international copyright laws allowed foreign publishers to publish pirated editions, but Bernard Tauchnitz paid authors, and obtained permission from Jessie to publish *Uncle Piper of Piper's Hill*.[27] Four editions were published in New York, but it is doubtful if Jessie received any money from these. She was to complain that her returns from *Uncle Piper* were small. The initial run seems to have been 750 copies, and the second edition of 500 copies yielded her only £20.[28]

Jessie's fame as an author led to several features being written about her. Being a 'British' novelist in Brussels, she was usually compared with English novelists who had lived there, such as the now forgotten Irish-born Charles Lever, author of the then very popular *Charles O'Malley: The Irish Dragoon* and many other works. She was also compared with Charlotte Brontë. One interviewer concluded, 'it is not impossible that one of "Tasma's" literary efforts in the Chaussée de Vleurgat may yet attain the immortality of "Villette" '.[29] The picture presented in these articles was an idealised one of Jessie and Auguste as a devoted couple, united in their work, sitting at opposite ends of the same table as they worked, she at her novels, he at his writing on economics. The reality was a little different, as Jessie's diary revealed.

Immediately the critical and public success of *Uncle Piper of Piper's Hill* became apparent, Trübner began planning the release of a follow-up book, a collection of Jessie's already-published short stories. Released late in 1889, *A Sydney Sovereign and other Tales* took advantage of the fame of Tasma, but also publicised *Uncle Piper of Piper's Hill*. At the front were four pages of extracts of reviews of *Uncle Piper*, headed by the announcement that the second edition was NOW READY at six shillings a copy.

The title story, 'A Sydney Sovereign', had first appeared as a novella in the *Australasian* between 15 January and 19 February 1887. The other stories, dated to the years when Jessie first began writing—'Barren Love' from 'Hash': A Mixed Dish for Christmas was her first published story, 'How a Claim was Nearly Jumped in Gum-Tree Gully', 'Monsieur Caloche' and 'A Philanthropist's Experiment' had all appeared in the *Australasian* in 1878.

'A Sydney Sovereign' was not a favourite with reviewers, who all preferred Jessie's earlier stories. Its main interest is in the use of the Isle of Wight and the Barrington name, both of which were embedded in Huybers family folklore. Jessie had grown up hearing tales of Charlotte's connections with the Simeon family, including Lady (Louisa) Simeon, heiress to Sir Fitzwilliam Barrington of Barrington Hall, Essex and Swainston on the Isle of Wight.

Early in October 1889, Jessie received the proofs of *A Sydney Sovereign*. Although dated 1890, it was published in time for Christmas 1889.[30] When the reviews began appearing, she singled out a mildly critical one and her confidence in her writing ability was shattered. She became depressed about whether she would be able to keep writing in the face of continued anxiety about her family. 'Some good notices of my collection of tales, though the *Athenaeum* calls them morbid and inconclusive—as well as petty and pathetic', she wrote.

> I think sometimes I am worn out before my time. There is such a curious lack of *deep* interest in things. Is it a phase, or is it a settled state? To secure the bien-être of Mother and the rest would be the only thing, I believe, engraved on my heart. As far as other things are concerned, I don't feel very strongly.[31]

The review in the *Athenaeum* was an exception in not being enthusiastic. Even it concluded that the stories made 'a fair bid for favour' and were 'easy, straightforward, simple as a rule' although the humour was 'rather strained', and there was 'a distinct dash of cynicism'.[32]

Several reviewers singled out 'How a Claim was Nearly Jumped in Gum-Tree Gully' and 'Monsieur Caloche' for praise, and many compared Tasma with Bret Harte, famous for his colourful stories about the American West and the Californian goldfields. The *Scottish Leader* said 'How a Claim was Nearly Jumped', 'Monsieur Caloche' and 'Barren Love' were worthy of Bret Harte at his best, having 'all his breadth of contrast, his cunning blending of comedy and tragedy, his faculty of the portrayal of heroic moods in what might seem uncongenial surroundings, while they are wholly free of his tendency to monotony of treatment'.[33] *Literary World* said 'How a Claim was Nearly Lost' with its 'dry humour, its underlying pathos . . . its unostentatious realism' suggested 'that a Bret Harte of the Southern Seas may do for the New Continent what the great novelist of the West has done for the New World'.[34] The *Lincolnshire Herald* also thought Tasma would do for Australia what Bret Harte had done for California.[35] The *Pictorial World* considered 'How a Claim was Nearly Jumped in Gum-Tree Gully' the best story and, like other reviewers, saw the influence of Bret Harte.[36] The *Glasgow Herald* described the stories as 'graphic' and 'fresh and original'.[37]

The *Indépendance belge*, which had praised the characters in *Uncle Piper* as being drawn with the truth and finesse of Dickens, said the stories in A

Sydney Sovereign combined a happy blend of a storyteller's imagination and realist observation. Tasma was 'capable of renewing the English novel by her freshness and originality'.[38] The *Belgian News*, however, found the stories disappointing.[39]

Uncle Piper of Piper's Hill and *A Sydney Sovereign* were published by Trübner of Ludgate Hill, a scholarly publisher founded by German-born Nicholas Trübner. He was an Oriental scholar, interested in religion and philosophy.[40] After his death in 1884, his widow kept the firm operating with the help of partners, including a young employee, William Heinemann, who in February 1890 left Trübner to begin his own successful publishing firm. He knew Jessie as a highly successful Trübner author and in May 1890 offered her the large sum of £300 as an advance on another novel. Although she replied that she could make no arrangement until the work was 'begun & completed', she was to have two novels published by William Heinemann.[41]

Before Heinemann's offer, during a visit to Trübner in March 1889, a few months after the release of *Uncle Piper of Piper's Hill*, Mr Duffing (whom she described as the 'real Trübner'), told her Trübner wanted a three volume novel.[42] Jessie appears to have already written most of this book, which was published as *In Her Earliest Youth*, since she received a payment from Trübner during 1889 and it was published as a serial in the *Australasian* from 4 January to 7 June 1890. It was released in book form within a few months of *A Sydney Sovereign* by Kegan Paul, Trench, Trübner and Company, the successor to Trübner. When Jessie received her copies of *In Her Earliest Youth* in April 1890, she remarked on the exorbitant cost of 'thirty-one shillings and sixpence' for the three volumes, adding, in one of many complaints about the poor returns from her books, 'Naturally "Je n'y suis pour rein" though I am to have—or am supposed to have—halves in halves!'[43] It was a usual tactic of publishers at the time to issue three volume novels. Their sale was almost exclusively to the library trade, lending libraries being able to lend and charge for each volume separately. Single volume editions of *In Her Earliest Youth* were issued soon afterwards. From the publishers' records, it seems that initially many more copies of *In Her Earliest Youth* were printed than of *Uncle Piper of Piper's Hill*.[44]

In Her Earliest Youth is an important book in Jessie's life. It is the first of several books in which she was to portray in fictional form some of the tensions of marriages similar to her own to Charles Fraser. The last such treatment was to appear only after her death. *In Her Earliest Youth* begins with the courtship of the incompatible Pauline Vyner and George Drafton in Sydney, then follows their married life on the huge, drought-stricken Rubria station on the Murray. There are interludes in Melbourne for the races. The heroine, Pauline Vyner, is intellectual, interested in ideas, philosophy, literature and painting, and she marries against her better judgment. She has of a sense of obligation to George Drafton, a horse-mad gambler and drinker uninterested in ideas, because he has saved the life of the child uncle she loves. Though seriously tempted by an older English aristocrat, Sir Francis Segrave, Pauline draws back from leaving her husband, again because of concern for her young uncle. Eventually she finds qualified happiness with George Drafton, after they have children together.

Reviewers recognised the ending for what it was. 'The story has that satisfactory conclusion which most readers of fiction refuse to be deprived of without a warm feeling of resentment', the *Manchester Examiner* wrote.[45]

It is interesting that although *Uncle Piper of Piper's Hill* is now regarded as Tasma's outstanding novel, unmistakeably superior to her others, when first published, *In Her Earliest Youth* was praised at least as much, if not more highly. The scenes of pioneering Australian bush life on a huge squatting run made it exotic for European readers. The London *Times* noted that Australian life, 'whether in busy Melbourne, the sunny suburbs of Sydney, or at the squatter's station on the Murray' made the novel 'refreshing' to those who longed for a change from 'English tales of English society'. The *Times* concluded its review by stating that Tasma was 'surpassed by few British novelists—we should be inclined to say by none who deal with the same range of subject'.[46]

The *Manchester Examiner* said *In Her Earliest Youth* was 'an exceptionally able novel' that would 'enhance the literary fame of the newest continent'.[47] The *Scotsman* said that 'the elaboration of character and incident' was excellent, and that there was 'a certain affluence of intellect in the book' which placed it 'above the level of most good stories'.[48] The *Glasgow Herald* said it was 'very far indeed above the average';[49] the *Woman* that it was 'very fresh and vigorous' and 'the cleverest novel' of the year.[50] The *World* thought it was better than *Uncle Piper of Piper's Hill*. It displayed 'all the qualities of its predecessor' but was 'broader, livelier, and faces human nature and its types more boldly in the open'.[51] The *Academy*, which described the book as 'the cleverest as well as the most ambitious' Tasma had written, noted that it was 'really a profound indictment of ill-mated marriages'. Unaware of Tasma's personal experience of such a marriage, the reviewer added, 'though the author probably does not mean it so, literally'.[52]

The portrayal of character was singled out in most reviews. The *Daily News* applied an English judgment to the characters, describing George Drafton as 'a weak, boisterous, slangy, horsey colonial of a frequent but most undesirable type', ignoring his capability in handling a huge station. The pleasure-seeking but otherwise idle Englishman Sir Francis Segrave was 'a refined, cultured, man of the world', said the *News*. It also noted the character of Pauline Vyner's grandmother, Madame Delaunay, describing her as 'most original'.[53] The *Times* noted the resemblance between the repulsive Josiah Carp, George Drafton's uncle of *In Her Earliest Youth*, and the equally irritable but basically good-hearted Tom Piper in *Uncle Piper of Piper's Hill*, both self-made vulgarians.[54]

The *Indépendance belge* continued to compare Tasma's writing with that of Dickens. The character portrayals of the 'charming and coquettish' grandmother, Madame Delaunay, and the 'loving and loyal' though slang-ridden George Drafton 'would not disgrace the gallery of Dickens', the reviewer wrote.[55]

Reviewers noted what they saw as obvious flaws in the story, particularly the appearance of Pauline's father as a runaway seaman, apparently included to pad the story out to three-volume length, and the happy ending. While the latter was regarded in most reviews as saving the heroine from an immoral future and providing the uncontroversial conclusion required by readers, the *Pall Mall Budget* was more realistic. The story 'flickers out rather ineffectually . . . If "Tasma" had but the courage to work it out, there is stuff for a true tragedy in her initial situation', the reviewer said.[56] The *Manchester Guardian* thought the ending a triumph for loyalty, 'though it is a sorry life to which it condemns poor Pauline'. Nevertheless it was 'a very powerful story, and a most graphic account of life in fashionable Melbourne'.[57]

English reviewers had found that *Uncle Piper of Piper's Hill* contained English characters portrayed in a setting they found not particularly Australian. *In Her Earliest Youth*, with its main setting an outback station, conformed to their view of what an Australian novel should be.

Despite the release of two books closely following one another, and the continuing success of *Uncle Piper of Piper's Hill*, Jessie remarked many times on the pittance she received from her writing. At the beginning of 1890 she wrote that she had 'a hundred odd pounds of my own now, made by *Uncle Piper* and *In Her Earliest Youth*. But I dare not lay any [of] this sum out—though I would be very happy in the possession of a real skin jacket'. A letter from Professor White, former United States minister in Berlin, praising *Uncle Piper*, pleased her—'from a man of his stamp praise counts for a great deal'—but also provoked another complaint. 'But how little *material* benefit I have reaped from my work despite the fact that the Americans have issued four different editions of it'.[58]

Early in 1890 she began writing 'a sensational story' which appears to be the novel later published as *A Knight of the White Feather*. She recorded that she was 'very dispirited' about her work:

> It seems so hard to find inspiration in my present milieu. I think a good deal about making my little allowance go as far as possible, and in bending my energies in the direction of 'des économies de bouts de chandelles' lose sight of the necessity for reading and studying. When I have got through my household work, and written a bit in the morning—very laboriously and with less satisfying results than of yore—it is time for one o'clock dinner—and the whole afternoon is taken up with silly calls. The evenings have been unprofitable.[59]

At the end of the year Jessie was still worried about lack of progress on this novel:

> I have begun a long tale—mais je patauge [but I flounder]—and no one who has not experienced it can understand the dreary depression induced by finding inspiration and power of work slipping away. The days glide by, and to outward appearance are well filled up with household tasks—a little writing, a little reading, a little visiting, a little piano thrumming, a little talking to Mother, and a little dawdling. But no one but I myself know how little is really achieved in them. Perhaps it is a pity I have written a book or books that had the success of mine. They make people suppose I am capable of accomplishing so much more. Whereas I feel more hopeless than ever about it myself.[60]

Towards the middle of 1890 there came a respite from the oppression of a project that was not progressing. Following a meeting with Alexander Meyrick Broadley, a barrister and former sub-editor of the *World: A Journal for Men and Women*, begun in London in 1874 by novelist Edmund Yates, the direction of Jessie's writing changed. Broadley was in self-imposed exile in Brussels, after being accused of complicity in the Cleveland Street homosexual scandal in which the Prince of Wales was involved. He lived in the avenue Louise in a house he had decorated with Oriental embroideries, old china and, as Jessie described them, 'other approved bric-a-brac'.[61] Broadley urged Jessie to write short stories for the *World*, and 'godfathered' her first story, 'A Wool-King's Widow',[62] which Edmund Yates accepted 'with a flattering note of acknowledgement'. She was pleased with the pay of four guineas, which she thought excessive for 'a short and trivial story'.[63]

The *World* provided her with an opportunity to make money from short stories. These were easy to write compared with concentrating on writing a novel: 'I am trying—oh so hard!—to get into some kind of swing of regular work—and can't manage it. There are so many interests that call me off', she wrote in June, and the following month she still could not get her 'mind into the story-writing groove'.[64] Jessie's second story 'His Modern Godiva' was published in the *World* on 23 July 1890, and Broadley told her he had orders from Yates to keep her 'nose to the grindstone'.[65] Edmund Yates was lavish in his praise of her stories. When he accepted 'The Lady of the Christmas Card',[66] published in December 1890, he told Jessie it was '[M]aupassant-like in its strength and reticence, its passion, power and simplicity'. But such praise was still no help in writing a novel. She wrote in her diary, 'the inspiration for the longer work refuses to come. I am living through too sad a romance of my own'.[67]

The *World* again came to her rescue when she was asked to write a full-length novel, to be published as a serial. Abandoning for a time her attempts at work on *A Knight of the White Feather*, she wrote *The Penance of Portia James* in just six weeks. The first episode was published in the

World on 29 July 1891, and the story continued weekly until 18 November 1891. Jessie was thrilled: 'I have just earned two hundred pounds in six weeks—by writing a serial story for the *World*'.[68]

The Penance of Portia James, set initially in London, is the story of a young Australian woman who keeps a promise to marry wealthy Australian squatter and mine owner John Morrisson. The promise had been made years before, and she honours it because, apparently, he had waited patiently for her, although she finds him repugnant. When, immediately after the wedding, she discovers he has a mistress, Mary Willett, and a child, she runs away to her artist friend in Paris. Anna Ross is a feminist who believes marriage is the 'most foolish and suicidal step' a woman can take, and the entire system of marriage 'an outrage to common sense'. 'Why should we bind ourselves to belie for the remainder of our natural lives our real natures, our real selves?' she asked. In writing the scenes set in the artists' colony in Paris, Jessie was able to draw on the life she and her sisters and brothers had lived near the Luxembourg Gardens and later in the area of rue du Montparnasse and rue de Vaugirard. She described the freedom of this milieu in *The Penance of Portia James*: 'There could be no Mrs Grundy where people did not even acknowledge the existence of that formidable abstraction'.[69] Portia, faced with the problem of supporting herself, becomes an artists' model. She eventually returns reluctantly to her husband, the motivating factor, as in *In Her Earliest Youth*, being the love of children. In this case, John Morrisson's child needs motherly care after the death of her own mother.

The Penance of Portia James, dedicated to Edmund Yates 'in appreciation of past kindnesses', was published in book form by William Heinemann to coincide with the ending of the serial version in the *World*. It was not as universally praised as her previous books, several reviewers advising Jessie to return to an Australian background. The *Academy* thought that 'neither in style nor in plot' was *The Penance of Portia James* the equal of *Uncle Piper of Piper's Hill* or *In Her Earliest Youth*; 'with all its faults', however, it had 'individuality and charm'.[70] The *Daily News* thought 'the good points much outnumber the bad'—one of the bad points being the author's habit of interpolating long asides.[71]

The *Times* linked Rosa Praed and Tasma:

> It is singular that almost the only two Australasian novelists who have found readers in the old country are women. Mrs Campbell-Praed is one; the lady who writes under the *nom de plume* of Tasma is the other. 'Uncle Piper of Piper's Hill' proved that 'Tasma' is worthy to rank, if not among great novelists, at all events among novelists of taste and feeling.

The rest of the review gave details of the story of *The Penance of Portia James*, but did not make any judgment on its merit. The reviewer commented that the ending was 'a tribute to convention rather than the solution that our sympathies demand'.[72]

The *Athenaeum* accepted the convenient ending (the death of Mary Willett) although it was 'a little old-fashioned to kill awkwardly disagreeable ladies in omnibus accidents in order to make things straight'.[73] The *Lady's Pictorial* reviewer 'was wicked enough to hope that some day John Morrisson will be killed in Australia, and then Portia will be free to make a better man happy', but Tasma had given the 'proper' ending.[74] *Literary Opinion* thought *The Penance of Portia James* more conventional and hackneyed than *Uncle Piper of Piper's Hill*, but noted it was well written, and a 'very readable book'.[75]

Despite the qualifications of the critics, *The Penance of Portia James* remained popular throughout the 1890s and was reprinted up to 1899.

The enormous publicity and critical acclaim generated by her three novels and collection of short stories made Jessie's stories prized additions to several Australian collections published in London. She contributed 'Monsieur Caloche' to Philip Mennell's *In Australian Wilds and other Colonial Tales and Sketches*, published in 1889.[76] 'John Grantley's Conversion', a slight story about an upper class Englishman who arrives in Australia to dissuade his younger brother from marrying a colonial and instead falls in love with the girl's sister, its main interest being the sympathetic treatment of the girls' radical Irish ancestors, went to *Under the Gum Tree: Australian 'Bush' Stories*, edited by Harriette Anne Patchett Martin (1890).[77] 'An Old-Time Episode in Tasmania' was published in *Coo-ee. Tales of Australian Life by Australian Ladies*, also edited by Harriette Anne Patchett Martin (1891).[78] A convict story, it is set at Cowa on the outskirts of Hobart, the same setting that Jessie was to use as the home of the Clare family in *Not Counting the Cost*.

Tasma was represented by 'Bertha and the Snake' in *Over the Sea. Stories of Two Worlds*, an illustrated collection of short stories for children edited by Arthur Patchett Martin.[79] She also contributed a chapter to a serial novel, *The Fate of Fenella*, which began in the 1891 Christmas number of the *Gentlewoman* with a chapter by Helen Mathers.[80] It was described as the 'Most Extraordinary Novel of Modern Times', every chapter being written by a 'Well-Known Writer of Fiction, without consulting his or her collaborators, the result being a remarkable and interesting novel and literary curiosity'. Some of the better-known contributors included Justin McCarthy and Arthur Conan Doyle. Jessie contributed the second last chapter, 'Sick unto Death'.

In 1892, *A Knight of the White Feather*, the novel Jessie had found so hard to write, was published by William Heinemann. Set in Melbourne and a property in the Victorian bush, it is the story of a marriage more drastic in its outcome than in Jessie's other novels. Linda Robley, who has the choice of two cousins, appears to choose wisely in accepting John Fullerton, a quiet man who shares her intellectual interests, rather than his cousin Jack, a reckless man of action with very conservative views on women. Following an incident on her wedding day, Linda begins to doubt whether John has courage, and thinks nostalgically of Jack, who is later killed fighting in a South African war. Eventually, John redeems himself by courageously saving his son from drowning, but losing his own life. After the loss of both men she loved, Linda is confined to a mental asylum outside Paris. She wonders about physical and moral courage, the ending leaving in doubt whether she will recover and marry Jack's friend, Captain Greville, who combines some of the characteristics of both John and Jack Fullerton.

The French-educated Linda Robley is the most intellectually advanced of Tasma's heroines. She is a disciple of Auguste Comte's theory of Positivism, on which she gives lectures, and she has women friends, particularly Mrs Lesbia Wiseman, who hold advanced views on the role of women. Mrs Wiseman supports women's suffrage, women doctors, women writers and women lecturers, 'women who can do anything but a little fancy work or piano-playing'.[81]

Some reviewers were enthusiastic about *A Knight of the White Feather*, but most were equivocal. The *Literary World* praised the 'freshness' of its Australian setting, stating it was 'an exceptionally powerful novel' which deserved 'to rank among the few first rate novels of the season'.[82] The *Sheffield Daily Telegraph* said the literary style was 'faultless', but the story itself was 'not as good as its predecessors'.[83] The *World* said *A Knight of the White Feather* was 'the strangest, and in some respects the strongest' Tasma had written. The conclusion was 'bold and entirely unconventional'.[84] *Vanity Fair* and the *Spectator* both commented on Linda Robley's lack of strong feelings. The *Vanity Fair* reviewer said that Linda acted 'with a certain aloofness from sentiment and with a half amused indifference which are more characteristic of an indolent and unemotional man contracting a temporary *liaison de convenance* than of a woman concerned with the most momentous circumstance of her life. There is no absorption of self . . .'[85] After making a similar point, the *Spectator* reviewer concluded: 'We shall hope to meet with work from "Tasma's" pen again.'[86]

The *Natal Mercury*, which reviewed the Colonial edition, the first to be released in Heinemann's Colonial Library of Popular Fiction, said Tasma had written 'an uncommonly good novel'.[87] The *Sydney Morning Herald* saw a resemblance in Tasma's 'extremely clever story' to Charles Dickens's *Pickwick Papers*, and found the end 'a strong situation' which made amends for some rather tame passages earlier.[88] The *Belgian News* reviewer preferred *A Knight of the White Feather* 'with its bright Australian atmosphere, redolent of rushing rivers, broad plains, blue skies, rambling homesteads, and healthy robustness of colonial life, to the more refined Belgravian and Parisian surroundings of *The Penance of Portia James*'.[89]

The London *Times* reviewer was sceptical of a Positivist heroine. 'It has been reserved for "Tasma", one of the cleverest of Australasian novelists, to introduce into fiction, if not the first Positivist heroine, at all events the first Australian variety of the species.' The reviewer noted the moral ending, 'Conjugal virtue, as usual in Tasma's novels, is saved from a fall, but at the price of a terrible tragedy, which opens Linda's eyes to the worth of her husband'. The review concluded, ' "Uncle Piper", which we regard as Tasma's masterpiece, rather throws "A Knight of the White Feather" into the shade'.[90]

Tasma received most of her reviews in English newspapers and periodicals. When she spoke to the Women Writers' Club in London in May 1893, she remarked that many Australian authors received only belated recognition in Australia. They were neglected until 'the seal of success had been set upon their works' by English readers.[91]

In each of Jessie's novels to this stage children had played important parts either as characters with major roles—Louey in *Uncle Piper of Piper's Hill*, and Uncle Chubby of *In Her Earliest Youth*—or in deciding the fate of the heroine. Examples of the latter are the baby left motherless after Mary Willett's death in *The Penance of Portia James*, and Linda and John Fullerton's son who, in *A Knight of the White Feather*, provides the opportunity for his father to prove himself a man of courage.

Jessie's skill in depicting children was often remarked upon, and in her own life she showed the greatest interest in, and affection towards, children. Two of only a handful of Jessie's letters which appear to exist were written to her niece Fauvette Loureiro. They are reproduced here because of their rarity and because they illustrate the rapport with children which enabled her to write so convincingly about them. When sending a doll to Fauvette, aged five, then living in Melbourne, Jessie wrote:

> I think she is well-behaved, but you must not let her have her own way too much, because as you will be her mama, you will know what is good for her, better than she can herself.
>
> I have made her enough clothes to last for a long time. You will find two little nightdresses among them, as I suppose you will like to put her to bed at night. I think if I were you, I would make her wear the dressing-gown in the morning, with the pink flannel petticoat and the little silk one for under-wear. Then there is a grey house-dress, with a white pinafore for the afternoon, and when you want her to be very fine, you can put on her the claret-coloured silk. The little pink foulard is for very warm weather.
>
> Two very kind ladies, called Delphine Couvreur and Victorine Couvreur, helped me make the dolly's frocks—and they will be very pleased if you are pleased with them.
>
> I must tell you one thing about your doll. You can turn her head any way you please, and you can make her sit or stand up. But her legs will be a little stiff after the journey, so you must push them forward hard to make

her sit up straight. When her face needs cleaning, one must rub a very little button on it with a soft cloth.

Give Vasco a kiss for his aunt Jessie and with one for yourself, my dear little Fauvette, I am your loving Aunt Jessie.[92]

In another letter to Fauvette she wrote:

Your sister birds have promised to carry this letter with Aunt Jessie's best love, and the hope that your Mother, Father and Vasco will find 1894 a far brighter and happier year than 1893.

I was very glad to receive your nice little letter, telling me about the adventures of your kitten. We have a beautiful grey and black cat here, and whenever I stroke her, she raises her bushy tail like a plume high in the air, and waves it backwards and forwards. I would often let her come upstairs, but she has the bad habit of scratching away at the carpet as though she wanted to make a hole in it. Sometimes she disappears for a night and a day, but whenever she is in the neighbourhood, and hears my voice calling 'Bishka-Bishka'—she turns around, sticks up her tail and comes running back along the top of the garden wall as fast as she can.

The day after tomorrow will be Christmas Day. Uncle Auguste and I have been into town buying little presents for his nephews and nieces next door. The street where all the prettiest shops are to be found is very steep and narrow. Mother knows it well, for long before you were thought of, she and I used to go down it together to look at the pretty things so beautifully arranged in the shop windows. It ought to be bitterly cold just now, but instead, we have bright windy weather. I walked all the way home up the Avenue Louise under the bright gas lamps thinking how nice it would be if I could gather round the table at Christmas all our dear ones in Australia. As you are all so far away I have not even troubled to make a Christmas pudding but went out and ordered one at the English shop here all ready made and tied up in a basin so that one has nothing to do but drop it in a pot.

Will you give Vasco a kiss for me. I have often carried him in my arms when he was a little fellow not two years old and I can remember how quickly he used to scramble up the stairs at Cromwell Road [London] on hands and knees and give dear Mother another kiss and tell her how I should come to meet her with you and Vasco on either side. Uncle Auguste sends his love to you too. I hope you will write again before long, my dear little Fauvette to your affectionate Aunt Jessie.[93]

Jessie published her remarkable sequence of books—*Uncle Piper of Piper's Hill*, *A Sydney Sovereign*, *In Her Earliest Youth*, *The Penance of Portia James* and *A Knight of the White Feather*—in less than four years. While she wrote she also gave lectures, maintained a demanding social life, experienced the restlessness that made temporary liaisons attractive and agonised about her family, members of which were about to re-enter her life with further distractions.

After living with Jessie for about two years, Charlotte Huybers left

Brussels in 1892, to stay with her son Edward in London, and then to sail to Australia. While Jessie always found her company stimulating, Charlotte's restless, critical nature also made her a disturbing influence, particularly in making known her antagonism to Jessie's marriage.

Charlotte arrived in Melbourne, where her children, and their families, Koozee and Arthur Loureiro, Edith and Jean Reverdy, her eldest son Willie and his wife and their children were living, to find the Depression of the 1890s had affected all three. Arthur Loureiro's patrons had all but disappeared, some, like Charles R. Staples who had bought several of his paintings, to bankruptcy and gaol. Loureiro was reduced to earning a living teaching painting at the Presbyterian Ladies' College and at his daughter's school, Genazzano Convent.[94] Edith and Jean Reverdy had arrived at the beginning of the Depression. While Edith had succeeded in gaining casual employment as art critic for the Melbourne *Age*, Jean's wood carvings had not gained a following in Melbourne.[95] Willie's employment with merchant Jules Renard had ceased, and he was struggling to keep his large family as a mercantile agent.

Alfred Huybers, seriously ill with cancer of the neck, arrived in Melbourne from Hobart on 4 May 1893, intending to live with Koozee at Cabana, but he died eight days later. Willie took his body back to Hobart for burial in a vault at Queensborough cemetery.[96] In his will, Alfred Huybers left his £800 insurance policy to Rebecca Chance, who appears to have shared his life from the time of Charlotte's departure nearly twenty years before. The income from the rest of his estate he left to Charlotte during her lifetime, the proceeds after her death to be divided in one-fifth shares between William, Jessie, Koozee, Edward and Edith apart from legacies of £200 to Rebecca Chance and £100 each to his unmarried sons, Frank and John.[97]

Although small, the income from her husband's estate provided Charlotte with the means to return to Europe after not much more than a year in Australia. She, Edith and Jean Reverdy and their son sailed on the *Ville de la Clotat* on 31 January 1894, for Marseilles.[98] Charlotte's passion for educating those around her was as strong as ever. She took with her Elsie, Willie's eldest daughter, so that she could experience European culture.

Edith and Jean Reverdy lived for some time in Paris then left to join John Huybers, who was in Boston. Reverdy stayed there only a short time. Edith may have already met Pierre Valerio, an Italian-born artist, with whom she later lived in Boston and New York. Charlotte and Elsie went to live with Jessie in Brussels. They joined a household in which some of the tensions of the early 1890s, caused by financial constraints, had disappeared.

In January 1892, Auguste Couvreur had been appointed London *Times* correspondent in Brussels, a city in which the *Times* had not previously had a full-time correspondent.[99] This was not only a prestigious appointment but provided Auguste and Jessie with a more regular income and a more established position in society. The *Times* wanted to add Couvreur with his unrivalled experience of European politics, economics and diplomacy to their staff and at first suggested stationing him in Berlin. When he refused, they agreed he should be their Brussels correspondent.

During the period when her mother was in Australia and her husband working as *Times* foreign correspondent, Jessie had a less stressful atmosphere in which to write. It was during this time that she began *Not Counting the Cost*, the novel which depicts, through the fictional Clare family, some aspects of the life of the Huybers family in Hobart, and through the fictional Charles Frost something of her courtship with and marriage to Charles Fraser.

The equilibrium of this period was not, however, to last.

11

Remain at The Hague until further orders

Brussels, London, The Hague, 1894–96

Auguste Couvreur's appointment as representative of the London *Times* in Brussels promised so much, yet was to be of tragically short duration. The *Times* regarded its foreign correspondents as an élite group, but even in this company Auguste Couvreur was regarded as exceptional. He served the *Times* with outstanding success during 1892 and 1893, but towards the end of 1893 became seriously ill. Although he struggled to continue his work and his involvement in the causes so important to him, increasingly he was confined to a chaise longue in the drawing room. One of his last public acts was to call on Liberals to unite in defence of their fundamental political and economic convictions. His illness was diagnosed as incurable cancer of the stomach from which, in the final stages of the disease, he suffered great agony.

When he died on 23 April 1894, aged sixty-six, his outstanding contribution to Belgian politics and international relations was praised in lengthy obituaries in Brussels and overseas papers.[1] Jessie inserted a large family notice in the *Indépendance belge*[2] in her own name, that of Auguste's sisters and his brother, and her mother, Charlotte Huybers, concerning the funeral arrangements. The notice listed Auguste's impressive number of decorations. A man of great intellect, he was admired throughout Europe for his work for free trade and towards European federation, and in Belgium for his work for a great number of organisations.

On the day of the funeral, large crowds crossed the entrance hall of 254 chausée de Vleurgat to the long narrow room comprising the drawing and reception rooms and library. Here the coffin was scarcely visible under masses of flowers. All the politicians Couvreur had worked with visited the house—Buls, Vanderkindere, Montéfiore-Lévy and Goblet d'Alviella, as well as innumerable artists, painters, engravers, sculptors, architects, historians, archaeologists, geographers, librarians and archivists, directors of government departments and institutions, many of his colleagues in journalism, all the pupils from the school for young women which he had founded, and Freemasons from various lodges. Representatives from different groups gave addresses, praising his contributions to radical and reformist politics in Belgium, and his championship of international movements promoting free trade and co-operation, and the study of economics and the social sciences. His colleagues in journalism praised his magnificent dispatches from international congresses, his cheerfulness as he began early each morning to prepare the foreign news pages, and his great encouragement of young journalists. Following the addresses he was accorded military honours by an army detachment as an Officer of the Order of Leopold. He was buried in the family tomb at the cemetery of Saint-Josse-ten-Noode.

The burden placed on Jessie of nursing her husband through his final illness, followed by the strain of the public funeral, must have been enormous. During the illness it is almost certain that she would have written and filed his dispatches to the *Times*, at first under his guidance, and later, as he became increasingly ill, on her own initiative. She had been familiar with his work since their marriage, had entertained the people who were his contacts, and shared his views on politics and social issues.

When Auguste died, she was faced with the immediate cessation of his salary as *Times* correspondent, which, despite her own money-making efforts through writing, had been their regular source of income. She believed, however, that she was capable of taking over as *Times* correspondent in Brussels. This was an almost unheard-of role for a woman in the 1890s, and she had to persuade the *Times* to accept her.

Jessie's involvement with the London *Times* is usually noted in a sentence in accounts of her life. I believed that there was at least a possibility that in an organisation of the standing of this celebrated paper, records of her employment might have survived. Through an initial letter to the *Times* (now News International), I learned that not only were there employment records, but that books containing the letters sent from London to *Times* foreign correspondents still existed. Late in 1991, I went to the London *Times* archives in Wapping, and in the letter books read about 150 letters written to Jessie in Brussels by the manager, Sir Charles Frederick Moberly Bell, and the manager of the Foreign Department, Sir Donald Mackenzie Wallace. Bell had overall control of her employment, mainly her placement, employment conditions and payments. Wallace had direct control of her work and was responsible for the fate of her contributions. The correspondents' letters, including Jessie's, to which these *Times* managers replied unfortunately have not survived, but it possible to learn a great deal through the outgoing letters of Jessie's work for the *Times* and realise the extreme importance the paper placed on the competence, integrity and standing of its correspondents.

Supplementing this—an equally exciting discovery—I was able to trace through hundred-year-old bound volumes of the *Times* Jessie's day-by-day contributions to the Foreign News page. In these volumes each of her contributions, from the smallest, of a few lines, to major articles of a column or more, were ringed in blue and 'Couvreur' written across them. In this way I was able to follow her amazingly prolific and important contributions to the *Times* over more than three years.

Her appointment in itself was remarkable. Not only was she a woman, but a woman whose experience in writing for newspapers had been confined to feature articles and short stories written at a leisurely pace. Overnight, she was transformed into a foreign correspondent from whom instant reports were required on subjects needing a very wide background in European affairs, political philosophies and trends, economics and personalities. Achieving and sustaining such an appointment must have been far from easy.

Jessie began her efforts to be employed by the *Times* by writing to Charles Frederick Moberly Bell,[3] a forty-seven-year-old man with a distinguished background as *Times* correspondent in Egypt. He had an especially keen interest in foreign affairs, and a deep conviction that he was responsible for upholding the best traditions of the *Times*, and maintaining its influential role in public life. Jessie probably knew him well through her husband's association with the paper, and would have met him either on visits to London, or on Bell's visits to Brussels.

On 27 April, only four days after Auguste's death, Bell replied to Jessie's request to be appointed London *Times* correspondent in Brussels.[4] His letter was full of sympathy but guarded. 'I am sure it is quite unnecessary for me to say', he wrote, '(1) that personally I have every desire to meet your wishes (2) that I must consider the question quite apart from any considerations of personal sympathy. The tone of your letter shows me that it was unnecessary for me to say this—I only do so because a dry business letter at such a moment is difficult though necessary'. He detailed the history of *Times* representation in Brussels which, until the appointment of Auguste Couvreur, had not been of sufficient importance to warrant a correspondent. 'Then we met your husband', Bell wrote. 'We were all so very strongly impressed with his ability and extraordinary knowledge of foreign affairs in Europe that we felt we must do our utmost to secure his services'. But now 'in the absence of an exceptional man like your husband', the agencies would keep the *Times* sufficiently informed.

Despite this apparent rejection of Jessie's request, Bell finally came to the equivocal offer which the *Times* was prepared to make. 'But, if you care, when you feel yourself able, to begin sending us telegrams which you think will be interesting we will of course pay you the cost of the telegrams and at the end of the next month, let us say, we will consider the matter again. You may rely on us to do what we think fair and to pay whatever we think them worth. By beginning in time in this way we *may* be able to come to some sort of an agreement'.[5] Aware of Jessie's ability and standing as a fiction writer, he added that she should think of sending short stories for the Weekly Edition. Jessie, however, desperately needed a regular income, not an uncertain return from short stories.

Despite the trauma associated with the illness, death and burial of her husband, she almost immediately took advantage of this trial offer. Her first story appeared in the *Times* on 14 May 1894 (dateline Brussels, 11 May). At the end was the ego-boosting signature in italics—*Our Correspondent*— although the story itself was only a three-sentence communiqué on debates proceeding in the Belgian parliament.

Jessie followed this with an avalanche of reports which appeared almost daily over the following six weeks. Usually short in the form in which they appeared in the paper, many dealt with proceedings in the parliament which, fortunately for Jessie's efforts to become established, were of considerable interest, since a general election was to be held later in the year, with voting extended for the first time to all male adults. During the months preceding the election there were innumerable parliamentary debates on voting methods, many party meetings, and statements on possible alignments of groups with either of the major Liberal or clerical camps, as well as proposals for the introduction of protective tariffs. All these provided a rich source of stories for Jessie. She also wrote on the Belgian Congo, a topic that was to grow in importance over the next few years, and on some of the violent episodes which occasionally erupted in Belgian life, associated with strikes by poorly paid workers in industrial towns or disputes between political parties.

Her own views were not hard to discern. There was usually an ironic tone to her reports on the clerical (Catholic) parties, and her reports on the proposed introduction of higher tariffs were hostile. On one occasion she wrote, 'the partisans of commercial liberty are being united to prevent a moribund Parliament from bequeathing to the nation a *loi de famine* in the guise of the proposed new duties'. This was not the standard dispassionate *Times* reportage, and it is not surprising that she should be taken to task.

Once Jessie began sending dispatches, she came under the direction of the manager of the Foreign Department, Donald Mackenzie Wallace, another distinguished *Times* man. In 1876 he had written a definitive book on Czarist Russia, before becoming *Times* correspondent in St Petersburg and then Constantinople. He was noted for his calm judgment and encyclopaedic knowledge of foreign affairs. He sent Jessie a stream of notes, always polite, generally encouraging, but sometimes quite critical, in which he undertook her education as a *Times* correspondent, a role which he often stressed was 'a *metier*' to be learned.[6] He gave her advice on matters ranging from such minor procedures as the width of the margins she should leave, the printing of foreign names in capital letters, to the great need for conciseness.

On one occasion he wrote, 'To plunge at once *in medicus res* is a good old maxim'.[7] Valentine Chirol, a senior *Times* correspondent and later stand-in manager for Wallace, made the same point, at greater length. 'You have so much consideration for the exigencies of our work that I need hardly say the shorter compass with which you can deal adequately with the subject the better the chance of our being able to use your article', he wrote. 'It is an ungracious thing to say but it is not ungraciously meant'.[8]

Wallace was quick to point out that some of Jessie's early reports did not demonstrate the detached attitude expected of a *Times* correspondent. Most correspondents held strong opinions, but in these early reports Jessie had not developed sufficient subtlety to disguise her opinions and prevent them from intruding too obviously. When she sent a long general article on the political situation in Belgium, Wallace wrote that it was 'very interesting and instructive' but not suited for publication in the *Times*. 'I have no doubt that all you say is true and accurate, but there is a tinge of rhetoric in the tone and the despatch reads rather as if it was a leader in a party organ. Our correspondent', he emphasised, 'should be a calm, dispassionate observer who appears at least to belong to no party'. Following this criticism, he softened the blow with the urbanity and politeness usual in his letters. 'Forgive my giving you this little hint', he wrote. 'It may be useful to you in future'.[9]

Jessie was quick to learn. She took back the article, rewrote it, and submitted it again. Wallace wrote that her revised article was 'an immense improvement on its predecessor. Indeed it is very good and I hope to get it published as soon as the prorogation of Parliament leaves us more space for foreign intelligence'. He added, 'I am very glad to see that any hints have been so perfectly understood and turned to such advantage'.[10]

'The Political Situation in Belgium', Jessie's first major contribution, over one column in length and signed at the top 'From Our Brussels Correspondent', appeared on 31 August 1894. It is a very clear account of the confusion into which Belgian politics had been thrown with the advent of universal manhood suffrage, requiring previously narrowly based parties to appeal to newly enfranchised groups. This had precipitated the formation of new parties and splits among former allies holding different views on the major questions of education, tariffs, military service and colonial policy.

By the time this article appeared, Jessie had been offered a definite, although not generous, financial arrangement by Bell. She was to be paid £200 a year plus expenses. The payments were made about the middle of each month and covered expenses for the previous month plus salary for the current month.[11]

Her frequent, almost daily reports, sometimes of only a few sentences, continued to appear during the summer months in the lead-up to the October election. Pre-election news predominated, but reports on the Congo, and fighting on the Upper Nile, were frequent. She also covered the meetings of organisations such as the Labour Party, the Progressivist Congress, the Congress of Free Thought, the International Peace Congress and the International Science Congress. This continuous stream of stories culminated in her report on the result of the Belgian elections, which appeared on 16 October. 'The result of the general election in Belgium has been the complete overthrow of the Liberal Party save in the capital, where the ultimate triumph of Liberals or Clericals will probably be decided by a second ballot a week hence', she began.

Soon after the election Jessie visited London,[12] where on 29 October she received a telegram from Moberly Bell inviting her to a dinner at which Sir Donald Wallace was to be present.[13] She may well have felt she had been accepted into the *Times* establishment.

Back in Belgium, she sent off another flood of stories as the second round ballots for the election proceeded and the new parliament assembled for its opening on 14 November. Reports of parliamentary debates followed, as the government began to introduce the conservative policies on which it had been elected.

When she complained that some of her stories were not used, Wallace reassured her, 'Don't be unnecessarily worried . . . It is the common lot of correspondents . . . Of late Belgium has had more than its share of space'. He suggested that she could do 'a short concise graphic account of the chief political changes which have taken place since the present crisis began'.[14] When Wallace received this article, he thanked her for her 'admirable account of the situation in Belgium'. He had found it 'so interesting and instructive' that he was trying 'to get the Editor to find space for publishing it *in extenso*'. 'In any case it will be extremely useful for reference', he added.[15]

This was just one indication among many from Wallace Jessie was to receive of the tremendous pressure on space in the *Times*'s Colonial and Foreign News section. It rarely covered more than a page, and was often confined to only three columns of a six-column page. News from all over the world, all the countries of Europe, America and Asia, colonial territories in Africa, Asia and Australasia, vied for this very limited space. Wallace was to reassure Jessie several times that all *Times* correspondents had 'to suffer' on occasions by not having their telegrams published. In a favourite phrase, he spoke of these lost stories as the 'massacre of the innocents', on one occasion telling Jessie that 'there will be a fearful massacre of the innocents'.[16] Although often counselled to send less material, Jessie must have been conscious that anything she missed would be sent by the Reuter's correspondent in Brussels. This competitive situation made her rather tenuous position far from relaxing.

Although Wallace had been non-committal on the publication of Jessie's major article on 'The Political Situation in Belgium', it appeared in full on 27 December 1894. She wrote of the crushing of the Liberals by the clerical parties on the one hand and by the socialists on the other, and the division of both sides of politics into factions representing a wide spectrum of opinion:

> Thus, if we analyze the Clerical party we find it composed, first, of the old, inflexible Conservatives, who rally round the Church as their citadel, and for whom all change is anathema. The organ of this party is the *Bien Public*, of Ghent. Secondly come those who, while sanctioning certain reforms, oppose the principle of the intervention of the State in labour questions. This party acknowledges M. Woeste as its head. Thirdly (and this is a new departure), we find in the Clerical camp the ardent Christian democrats, whose ambition is to give a Christian bias to the Socialistic movement. These men are led by Abbé Pottier in Liége and the Abbé Daens in Alost. I may add that in Belgium where what is called 'le bas clergé' is mostly of peasant origin, the passionate espousal of the cause of the underfed, overworked Belgian peasant or artisan by his brother and friend the curé is very comprehensible.
>
> The same threefold division exists in the Liberal camp, where we find the rigid doctrinaires of the *laissez-faire* school, the Liberal opportunists who admit State intervention on behalf of the hours of women and children but not of men, and the Radicals, or Democrats, who, however, are being slowly assimilated by the Socialists, and whose ultimate absorption by them is as certain as that of the serpent in the Zoological Gardens who was swallowed by his friend.
>
> The divisions in the Socialist camp are not clearly defined as yet, but the intransigents will inevitably become separated from the opportunists, and the idealists from the men of action.
>
> Such are the heterogeneous elements of which the new Chamber is composed.

Like the Liberals, radicals and socialists on the opposition side, the clerical party was divided on the main issues facing parliament, including the reform of electoral law in the communes; changes to compulsory military service, with exemptions on payment of specified fees putting the burden of military service on the poor; and the perennial problems of free trade versus increased tariffs, and subsidies to church schools.

In a retrospective paragraph Jessie noted that the great issues that had 'furnished subject-matter for battles without end between Clericals and Liberals in the past . . . the great questions of liberty—religious, industrial, and commercial'—would have to be considered by the new parliament. She noted that the 'last stronghold of ecclesiastical tyranny' had been stormed

As an Officer of the Order of Leopold, Auguste Couvreur was given a military funeral following his death on 23 April 1894. He also held decorations from other countries: Commander of Charles III of Spain, Commander–Saviour of Greece, Chevalier of the Lion of the Netherlands and Chevalier of Saints Maurice and Lazar (Italy). Many tributes were paid to his outstanding contribution to Belgian politics, and to economic and social causes. (*L'Illustration Européenne*)

Jessie was engaged as Brussels correspondent for the London *Times* by Charles Frederic Moberly Bell, the distinguished manager and later managing director. Bell had a deep conviction that he was responsible for upholding the best traditions of the *Times*, although his reputation was affected by his secret support for an uprising in the Transvaal backed by Cecil Rhodes. (London *Times*)

As correspondent for the London *Times* in Brussels, Jessie came under the influence of Sir Donald Mackenzie Wallace, manager of the foreign department. An erudite scholar and experienced correspondent, he sent Jessie a stream of advice aimed at moulding her into a model *Times* correspondent. (London *Times*)

Flora Shaw became the London *Times* colonial editor in 1893, a most unusual appointment for a woman. Previously a correspondent for the *Manchester Guardian* in Egypt, she was sent as part of her training for the *Times* position to South Africa, Australia, New Zealand and Canada. Some articles she wrote while in Australia were published in book form as *Letters from Queensland* (1893). She also wrote *The Story of Australia* for The Story of the Empire series (1897). In 1902, she married Lord Lugard. (London *Times*)

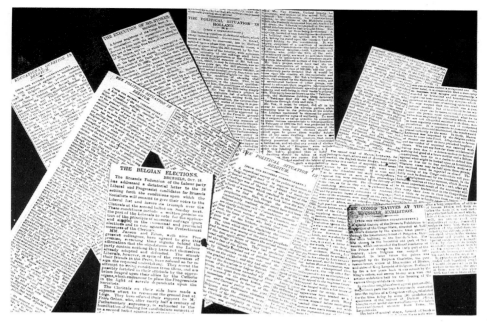

Jessie covered Belgium and Holland for the London *Times*, sending an almost daily stream of dispatches. Sometimes she had the opportunity to write longer articles, including several summaries of the current political situation. She was sent to The Hague to cover Dutch reaction to the controversial Jameson Raid in the Transvaal, and filed many stories on the international ramifications of incidents in the Congo.

The courtyard at the Ecole Couvreur. Auguste Couvreur was one of its founders, when it was called the Ecole professionale des jeunes filles. It was renamed in his honour after his death. (*Ecole Couvreur*, 24 December 1913)

Jessie moved to 161 chaussée de Vleurgat, Brussels, after her husband's death. Her mother lived with her, and several other family members joined her. It was to be her home until her death.

This illustration of Tasma appeared with an obituary in the *Star*. The obituary noted that Tasma's earliest associations were with Tasmania when it was a penal colony, yet she 'lived in the whirligig of time to be the correspondent of the *Times*' in Brussels. (*Star*, 29 October 1897)

two years before with the secularisation of burial grounds, allowing Protestants, Jews and free-thinkers to be buried alongside Catholics. On a subject close to her heart, however, she reported no progress. 'Ecclesiastical prejudice has frustrated hitherto all attempts to introduce cremation into Belgium, but it is to be hoped that the right of regulating the manner in which the body is disposed of after death may be claimed among other liberties', she wrote. The article was nearly two columns in length, by far the longest and most important she had written for the *Times*.

By the time this was published Jessie was ill with influenza. When she told Bell, he replied that she must not resume work too soon. 'Your work has been excellent', he wrote, 'and you are fairly entitled to a month's holiday'.[17]

Her flow of material nevertheless continued, almost without a break. Some of it was based on extracts from Belgium newspapers, a technique she could justify when used to indicate public opinion, but not as a source of information. Wallace told her on 17 January 1895: 'Do not trouble to send us so many extracts from the Belgian Press . . . It would be much better if you could describe the various elements of public opinion very briefly in your own words'. He also advised her to send fewer stories as there was great pressure on space: 'In general, by the way, you must "take in sail", for the Law Courts are again open, the political campaign is beginning', he wrote.[18]

A few months later Wallace asked her 'to refrain from mentioning Parliamentary incidents which have little or no interest for the British public and to confine yourself to the *grandes lignes* which anyone can understand. The details of Belgian politics and Belgian legislation are rather beyond the ordinary John Bull, and you have been giving lately perhaps a little too much of them'.[19] These notes from Wallace give the impression that few of Jessie's dispatches were used but they continued to appear very regularly. They mainly concerned the efforts of the new government to change the electoral law by raising voting eligibility to males over thirty, and to change the electoral system in the communes, a move which culminated in a general strike followed by rioting, during which police fired on workers.

Whatever restrictions there might be on the amount of Belgian news the *Times* would print, there was perennial British interest in the Congo, the colony which had been a personal domain of the Belgian King since 1885. In January 1895, a proposal came before the Belgian parliament for the annexation of the Congo, since King Leopold found the administration of the vast territory beyond even his royal purse. Belgium was obliged by an agreement reached in 1890 to provide finance to the Congo, but had no say in its use. Over the months this proposal was debated in parliament, and opposition grew in the country, Jessie sent off many dispatches. On 16 March, she reported that there were rumours in the lobbies of parliament that the annexation proposal would not go ahead. This, in fact, happened, Jessie's dispatches reporting the deferral of parliamentary consideration (20 May), further doubts about annexation being passed (23 May), a ministerial crisis and the resignation of the Count de Merode as foreign minister (27 May) and newspaper opinion against annexation (28 May).

Other material she sent on the annexation issue was used in leaders.[20] A few months later when she sent off another major article on the Congo, Wallace wrote, 'If space cannot be given for it, it might be used for a leader'.[21] The lengthy *Times* leader based on Jessie's material appeared on 4 June 1895, following the indefinite postponement of the debate on annexation. It gave in detail the history of the financial involvement of Belgium in the Congo, and reactions for and against annexation.

When Wallace wrote to tell her 'your Congo letter used for a leader', he said he would be delighted to see Jessie when she visited London that week.[22] During this visit to England she also had dinner on 25 June with Bell and the *Times* colonial editor[23] who, surprisingly for this conservative newspaper, was also a woman. Flora Shaw, a remarkable woman in her early forties, had developed a very influential role in *Times* policy on colonial matters, particularly Africa, since being recruited by Moberly Bell. She had met him in 1888 while representing the *Pall Mall Gazette* and the *Manchester Guardian* in Egypt, where Bell had been London *Times* correspondent for over twenty years. Shaw became recognised as an authority on Mediterranean issues, and began studying the politics of Africa at a time when the scramble for colonies among European powers was in full swing.

After he was appointed assistant manager of the *Times* in 1890, Bell worked towards manoeuvring Shaw into a permanent position on the paper, a previously unheard-of position for a woman. In 1892 he arranged for her to go to South Africa, Australia, New Zealand and Canada as *Times* special correspondent, to write a series of articles as part of her training for a more permanent position. Several articles she sent from Australia, published in the *Times* in December 1892 and February 1893, were later published in book form as *Letters from Queensland by* The Times *Special Correspondent*. When she returned to London in 1893, Shaw became colonial editor, with responsibility for appointing colonial correspondents and organising their work.[24]

Jessie may have met Flora Shaw in Brussels in 1889, when Shaw represented the *Manchester Guardian* at an international conference convened by King Leopold to formulate a code of international law on the slave trade. At the London dinner, she must have made a great impression on both Bell and Shaw, as future events were to show. Almost immediately Bell began to make more use of her talents, and was to ensure he had her strategically placed to report Dutch reaction when, with the secret knowledge and support of the *Times*, an attempted *coup d'état* was engineered in the Transvaal. Before this meeting, Jessie, at the direction of Bell, had spent time in Holland, where the *Times* did not have a correspondent. Her added responsibility was recognised when he increased her monthly payment to £20, in view of her 'enlarged diocese'.[25] Jessie's first major article on Holland—a lengthy two-column article on 'The Political Situation in Holland'—was published on 19 August 1895. It was concerned mainly with the 'burning question of electoral reform' and provided detailed background on the political situation which had led to the electoral reform bill coming before parliament. Her article ended with a shrewd assessment of the comparative trends in Dutch and Belgian politics:

> With regard to the parallel I have drawn between [Belgium] and Holland in respect of their political evolution, it is perhaps a little to be wondered at that neither nation should have profited more from the fact of posses-sion of an object-lesson in politics in its next-door neighbour. We seem to see the same efforts sterilized in each during the course of long years through the same influences, while upon such questions as those of secular *versus* denominational schools, personal service enforced in the army, and the extension of the franchise, the same arguments are employed recipro-cally in the Dutch and Belgian Chambers. The same outcry was raised in each by the Clerical party against the neutral schools established by the Liberals, and the same lesson was read to the latter by the majorities, who, in restoring the Clericals to power, proved that the country was not yet ripe for the disentangling of morality from dogma. Many other points in common might be found in the development of the political parties in the Dutch and Belgian Chambers . . .
>
> If imitation be the sincerest form of flattery, then Holland and Belgium should regard each other with sentiments of sincere mutual admiration.

During the middle part of 1895, Jessie's main news from Belgium con-cerned a new education bill. This culminated in a long article entitled 'The Educational Question in Belgium'[26] in which she detailed the plans of the governing clerical parties to revert from neutral communal schools intro-duced by the Liberals in 1879, to schools based on religious teaching. She described the bill as denying the liberty of conscience guaranteed by the Belgian constitution. 'It is a repetition of the same claim to control men's minds, against which succeeding generations of Belgians have risen in turn. Even should the law receive the sanction of the majority, as is more than likely, its opponents will continue to agitate for its repeal, and the struggle of which the nation was so tired, will recommence with renewed force', she wrote.

In August 1895 an event occurred in the Congo that was to dominate relations between Britain and Belgium for many months, creating a diplo-matic impasse. It was the execution by hanging by Belgian military of a British trader, Charles Stokes, alleged to have been supplying arms to insurrectionists. Jessie was assured of almost daily stories for the length of the controversy. Stokes, an Ulsterman and former lay missionary and later arms dealer, was at the time of his arrest in the service of Germany. Charging Stokes with assisting the enemies of the Congo by selling arms to Arab slavers, Captain Lothaire, leader of a military party against an Arab chief, tried and executed him. The British and German governments protested strongly, but Lothaire was acquitted both on trial and appeal. Both trials were regarded in Britain and Germany as biased.[27]

Both France and Germany became involved at a diplomatic level in the Stokes affair, leading at one stage to contradictory statements appearing from Jessie in Brussels and the *Times* correspondent in Berlin, the very experienced and highly favoured Valentine Chirol. Jessie's claim that Germany had made representations to Brussels over the affair was denied from Berlin,[28] although it was later acknowledged that her story had been correct. Wallace, however, warned her, 'as a general rule we do not like our correspondents to get into controversies'.[29]

International concern over the Stokes execution ensured that most of Jessie's despatches on this subject were published, many of them at some length. Such concern was responsible for King Leopold visiting both London and Paris, and the payment of an indemnity by Belgium to Stokes's family and Germany, without admitting responsibility. Jessie's information also formed the basis for a lengthy *Times* editorial on the Stokes affair, published on 3 September 1895. In general her despatches questioned the legality of Lothaire's actions in trying Stokes by court martial and, by summarily executing him, denying him any right of appeal.

The following year, Lothaire returned to Belgium, where his second trial and second acquittal in Brussels provided Jessie with many more stories. Information from her despatches was incorporated into a leader published on 7 August 1896. Later, she had a further string of human interest items published, after Lothaire, who had become a public figure in Brussels, became engaged, then reneged on the engagement, and was sued for breach of promise.

Towards the end of 1895, Bell's strategy in having Jessie file stories from Holland became clear. He directed her to an important secret assignment. It concerned the sensational Jameson Raid in South Africa. Cecil Rhodes was its principal conspirator, in an attempted overthrow of the Boer government in the Transvaal, to which Bell and Shaw lent support. On 23 December 1895,[30] five days before the raid occurred, Bell wrote to Jessie telling her to remain at The Hague 'until further orders'. Her task was obviously to report Dutch reaction to events in South Africa, but she knew nothing of this impending action.

> Your letter of 20th to Sir Donald saying that you were going to Amsterdam '*Tomorrow*' and speaking of your return to Brussels in 2 or 3 days has puzzled me for it leaves me without any address where I can be certain to find you for these two or three days and as I told you that I wanted to have you at our disposal for the month it is a little wicked! of you to

remove yourself from the end of the cable! I have however wired you that I want you to remain at The Hague until further orders—In fact as you force me to be explicit, The Hague is the place at which I wish you to be useful to us and if you will please return there you shall soon be informed why. Meanwhile I have to beg you to be very cautious not to create the impression that you are there except as an accident and for the sake of studying Dutch politics as to which we are up to the present badly informed.

Jessie had previously received sealed instructions from Shaw on the background to the proposed moves by Jameson and Rhodes in the Trans-vaal.[31] Bell, however, was so extremely cautious about spreading news of the raid that he dissembled in the rest of his letter to her. After raising Jessie's curiosity as to the reason for her being needed at The Hague, he proceeded to ask her to study the current situation regarding British Guiana, a territory the English had earlier taken from the Dutch. 'It is important to have the Dutch on good terms with us just now and to smooth over any difficulty that may arise', he wrote. 'Ignorance is the source of most quarrels and we look to you to inform us about Holland and to inform Holland about us.'

While he was giving Jessie these directions, Bell was also organising *Times* correspondents in other capitals, so that the *Times* would have dispatches from strategic centres as soon as events erupted in South Africa. This occurred towards the end of December, when Leander Starr Jameson, with the connivance and support of Cecil Rhodes, organised a force of some 500 men to invade the Transvaal, a move planned to coincide with a rising of Uitlanders in Johannesburg. This rising failed to take place, but Jameson went ahead, crossing the Bechuanaland border on 28 December. On 2 January 1896 his small force was surrounded by Boers and compelled to surrender. The success of the Boers in dealing with the raiders prompted the German Kaiser to send President Kruger of the Transvaal a telegram of congratulation, which aroused much resentment in Britain.

A subsequent parliamentary select committee inquiry, during which Flora Shaw was questioned at length concerning the prior knowledge and com-plicity of the *Times*, resulted in severe censure of Rhodes. It was largely due to Shaw's clever handling of questions that the *Times* and the Colonial Office escaped having their roles exposed and censured.

In her first dispatch from The Hague following the raid, Jessie reported a very hostile reaction, including a description of Dr Jameson's men as 'a band of medieval marauders'.[32] In a lengthier article, published on 9 January, she described the flags hung out at Amsterdam to celebrate the Boer victory, and the unanimous acclaim from the newspapers on 'the repulse of Dr. Jameson and his "freebooters" '. Her article included a scoop in the form of an interview with a resident of Pretoria with interesting local knowl-edge.[33]

In a dispatch published on 11 January, she wrote that the Dutch government had adopted a more moderate attitude. 'It has been found possible to reconcile the declaration of sympathy with the Boers with a recognition of the desire of the British Government to do the best that was possible in the most trying circumstances', she wrote. Returning to Brussels that day, she sent a further dispatch on the reaction in the Flemish part of Belgium to the Jameson Raid. The Flemish, she reported, expressed the hope that the Republic would shake off 'the British yoke' and form 'an offensive and defensive alliance with the Orange Free State'.

Meanwhile, during 1896 and 1897, with the political situation remaining relatively settled, Belgium's clerical government having passed most of its controversial legislation, the country provided only limited scope for news of international interest, except at election time. In mid-1896 there were elections for half the Chamber of Representatives, about which Jessie wrote at length, forecasting the return of the clerical parties. She added, coming close to defying Wallace's warning against identifying with any political group, 'But because the Clerical *regime* proves the most enduring it must not therefore be inferred that it is the most conducive to the advancement of the nation. A review of the labours of the last Session shows that a consistently retrograde policy has marked its administration throughout'. The election took place on 6 July, and from then until the middle of July there were several stories on the results which, as Jessie had predicted, resulted in a win for the clerical party.

When Belgian news was scarce, there was usually news of the Congo or, increasingly, of the Dutch East Indies, where Jessie reported unrest and minor revolts. A major exhibition in Brussels in 1897 provided news items and material for a long article, 'The Congo Natives at the Brussels Exhibition'; it appeared on 14 August 1897. In normal times Jessie's dispatches on the Brussels Exhibition would have received much more space, but they coincided with war between Turkey and Greece, covered at enormous length in the *Times* and leaving little space for other foreign news.

When Valentine Chirol relieved Wallace in 1897, he asked Jessie to write about King Leopold's financial involvement in the Congo rubber trade, and allegations that 'Congo officials feel therefore assured that any excess of zeal on their part to stimulate the collection of rubber will be, to put it mildly, viewed with considerable leniency'.[34] Jessie's article was unfortunately timed. When it appeared it was a relatively small piece, most of the *Times* being given over to the Diamond Jubilee of Queen Victoria.[35]

Jessie also continued to report from Holland at intervals, and on 1 December 1896 had a major article, 'The Political Situation in Holland', published. Wallace told her it made 'excellent reading'.[36] As usual when she had the opportunity to write at length, Jessie wrote well and interestingly. The article conveyed the tumult of political argument taking place in Holland preceding the first election to be held with adult male suffrage. She predicted that, as in Belgium, 'the inevitable consequence of extending the franchise will be to deliver over the country to the dominion of clericalism and protection'. In some perceptive comments, she also reported the importance all sides attached to religious arguments to bolster their cases, 'every occasion serves for a theological tilt'. 'We may take it for granted that in Holland, as elsewhere, the elements at strife are broadly represented by the principles of conservatism, radicalism, and socialism. But these distinctions of a purely political character are further complicated by the spirit of religious partisanship infused into them'.

Wallace had several times warned Jessie that she relied too much on quotes from the Belgian press instead of giving the '*essence* in your own words'.[37] On one occasion he told her it was unnecessary 'to go to the *Indépendance* or the *Etoile* or any other papers for confirmation of our correspondents' statements'.[38] Later he wrote in the most explicit terms he had so far used. She quoted too much from papers 'of little or no European reputation', he wrote. Then he spelled out in detail points he had made before. 'As for facts, no paper . . . should be quoted, for it is the correspondent's duty to verify the statements before reporting them. If he finds they are true there is no necessity for mentioning any paper, and if they are false there is no necessity for referring to them at all'. He added, indicating that she had complained of the dullness of Belgian news at the time, 'I can well agree that in dull times you are often hard up for "copy" but in these cases it is better to send less'.[39]

Taking material from Brussels newspapers landed Jessie in serious trouble when on 10 November 1896, the *Times* published a fairly lengthy item on the 'Opening of the Belgian Chambers'. She had copied it from another paper, and sent it the previous day. It purported to give a preview of the speech from the Throne due to be delivered at the opening of parliament. However, the item put such a seal of approval on all the controversial issues which had plagued the government during its term referring to 'the excellence of the system of military reform' (which had just been shelved by the government), the likely early annexation of the Congo state (also shelved), and other similar matters, that it is surprising Jessie sent it—and indeed that the *Times* published it.[40]

At first Jessie did not seem to see the item for what it was—a sarcastic skit on the government's proposed program. Immediately she did realise, she sent a telegram to the *Times*, but too late to save the article from being printed. The following day the *Times* had to publish a retraction, which it did in the least conspicuous way possible: 'The speech from the Throne published last night in the newspaper *La Gazette* was a skit. The terms of the speech are not yet known'.[41]

The same day, 11 November, Wallace wrote to Jessie, 'The Editor was rather annoyed to learn from you last night that we had published a "skit" as a piece of serious news. That shows how dangerous it is to transmit to us news taken from another paper without verification and without quoting your authority'. [42] When Jessie replied, he wrote using a term he had used before, 'I have no doubt you will be careful in future. The duties of a *Times Correspondent* are a *metier* which must be learned by experience'.[43]

It is hard to believe Jessie would have made this error of judgment in normal circumstances. The work of a foreign correspondent was demanding at the best of times. Her brother Edward was to describe the foreign correspondent's profession as like the doctor's: 'you are liable to sudden night calls, and moreover you must ever be on the watch'.[44] Three years of reporting for the *Times* had made great demands on Jessie's time, energy, mental alertness, and mobility. She was then a woman in her late forties and, although she had supported herself by journalism and lecturing for considerable periods of her life, she had never before experienced the around-the-clock demands of a foreign correspondent's life.

Her work for the *Times* had proceeded against a background of a constant stream of advice and comment from Sir Donald Mackenzie Wallace. While at times encouraging and always polite, it sometimes amounted to harassment tinged with condescension towards a woman.

Jessie's very creditable, sometimes inspired, reporting was also achieved against a background of highly disruptive personal and family matters. It was later acknowledged by the *Times* that she was 'most conscientious and painstaking', and fulfilled her duties 'ably'.[45] But eventually the unceasing demands of her work and family took a sad toll on her health.

Towards the end of 1896, at the time the 'skit' episode took place, Jessie became seriously ill.

12

I have been so cast down by my long illness

Brussels, 1897

There is little doubt that the illness which overtook Jessie, previously a healthy woman, was related to her highly stressful life. The extraordinary demands on her time, energy and commitment in fulfilling the very high standards of reporting for the London *Times*, the constant advice and polite criticism from her mentors there, and the intrigue behind being sent to The Hague to cover the repercussions of the Jameson Raid, provided stress enough. During the three years following her husband's death, her work had also proceeded against a background of domestic upheaval, particularly family concerns and regarding accommodation. Remarkably, she also continued to write novels.

When Auguste Couvreur's will became known, the house that had been her home was, to Jessie's dismay, left by her husband to his sisters, not her.

I have not been able to discover the reason for this. It seems to indicate an estrangement before Couvreur's death. However, after it, Jessie referred to him, for instance, as 'my dear husband' when disposing of a miniature of him in her will. Wills of deceased persons are not public documents in Belgium as they are in Australia or England, and my efforts to obtain a copy of Auguste Couvreur's will through a descendant of a relative (enormously helpful with other information, such as copies of obituaries, which provided a great deal of information about Couvreur's life), and in other ways, were unsuccessful. I did, however, obtain the record of one of his benefactions. The information concerning Auguste's house being left to his sisters comes from Jessie's niece, who stated Jessie 'was very disappointed the house was left to his sisters'.[1] This is also apparent from the fact that she moved after his death.

There is also something of a mystery about the house Jessie and Auguste

145

Couvreur were living in when Auguste died. It was numbered 254 chaussée de Vleurgat, yet seems almost certainly the same house in which they lived in their earlier married life, then numbered 230 chaussée de Vleurgat. I was able to inspect 230 chaussée de Vleurgat while visiting Brussels in 1991. It appears to be the house Auguste and Jessie lived in as described in various articles and other sources. Number 254 no longer exists, having been replaced by apartments, but from the style of older houses in the street, it would have been similar to 230. Possibly renumbering accounts for the discrepancy.

Despite no evidence of an estrangment, apart from the disposal of his house, Auguste Couvreur also left the considerable sum of two thousand francs to the Ecole professionale des jeunes filles, the school he had founded, to be used for the development of courses in painting and drawing. The school was later renamed in his honour the Ecole Couvreur.[2] Jessie seems to have been left little.

In the latter part of 1895 she moved from 254 chaussée de Vleurgat to a rented house on the opposite side of the same street, Number 161, closer to the avenue Louise. She took her possessions, mainly furniture, paintings and books with her. During this period Jessie's mother lived with her. Although a woman to whom Jessie remained closely attached and solicitous all her life, she was also, with her swings of mood from elation to depression, and her dominating personality, a person incapable of maintaining an aura of calmness.

Other members of Jessie's family also descended on her. First came her brother, Edward, again having trouble keeping regular employment. Following the success of the Victorian Exhibit at the Paris Exhibition in 1889, for which he was made Officier de l'instruction publique by the French government,[3] he had spent a period at the Victorian agent-general's office in London, then was appointed, in March 1891, secretary to the Imperial Tobacco Corporation of Persia. Within a year, however, the corporation was in liquidation. By this time, Edward had already suffered a severe attack of nervous debility, an illness that was to recur during his life. After a long, anxious period of unemployment, he was appointed London representative for a group of Belgian paper mills, of which Auguste Couvreur had been a director, his brother-in-law, Adolphe de Vergnies, being chairman. Within nine months, however, Edward was again unemployed, when the London office was closed in June 1895.

Later that year he visited Brussels, spending seven weeks with Jessie, with the idea of emulating her as a foreign correspondent. After submitting some articles, he was appointed Brussels correspondent for the London *Daily Chronicle*. He moved temporarily into 264 chaussée de Vleurgat only a few houses from Jessie, then when Jessie moved to 161 chaussée de Vleurgat, Edward, his wife Julia and their children joined Jessie and her mother in

Jessie's house. In retrospect, one advantage that flowed from this arrangement was the fleeting glimpse of Jessie's life provided through the childhood memories of Edward's daughter, Ethel Marie (known as Dickie), born in Hobart in 1885, and then about eleven. Dickie in her old age remembered her Aunt Jessie in Brussels lifting her up on her horse when she returned from her early morning rides. (Had the rides with Charles Buls resumed?) She remembered Jessie sitting in front of a mirror brushing her dark hair, so long that it reached the floor, and she remembered hearing of Cecil Rhodes's proposal of marriage. The latter memory, if correct, and not a misinterpretation by a young girl of an overheard remark, suggests the alleged proposal may have occurred about the time of Jessie's involvement in the *Times* intrigue with Rhodes concerning the uprising in the Transvaal rather than before her marriage to Auguste Couvreur. Dickie also remembered her grandmother Charlotte, with her long corkscrew curls, appearing eccentrically dressed at Jessie's dinner parties. She wore her oldest clothes, old shoes and gloves with holes in the fingertips.[4]

Jessie's kindness in accepting her brother, with whom she had a close relationship, as well as his family into her home, is typical of the overriding importance she gave to family responsibilities—even at the expense of her own interests. Although Eddie seemed unconcerned about the problem of having two close family members living in the same house as the correspondents of two rival London dailies, to Jessie this was a crisis. It was a possible threat to her continued employment, which was crucial in earning enough money to keep herself. She wrote to Bell, probably anticipating that the matter would be raised with her when her brother's position became known. Bell replied that he appreciated her 'very right feeling'. He presumed that 'in a small place like Brussels' it would be almost impossible for Jessie and her brother to avoid coming across the same people, discussing the same topics, and holding the same views, so there was 'a great chance that there will be a remarkable similarity between the correspondence of The Times and of The Chronicle'. However, he continued:

> Still I do not think I have any right to prevent it. All I would ask is that you would both do your best to differ as much as possible and as our news on most subjects are widely different to those of the Daily Chronicle perhaps you can best consult the wishes of both your employers by so doing.

He continued, with the innate superiority of a *Times* man:

> I have no doubt also that the correspondent of The Times will receive some preference over the correspondent of the Daily Chronicle and this preference is an asset which belongs to us and which you will guard. If in the course of the next three months I should see that it was not possible to continue the double arrangement, I would let you know in time, perhaps by then they may have transferred your brother to some more important centre.[5]

Additional family members also temporarily joined Jessie's household. In 1896, Edith and John, both of whose lives were in crisis, visited Brussels from Boston. John was still attempting unsuccessfully to make a living as an artist in the United States. Edith wanted a legal end to her marriage to Jean Reverdy. She had had a second child in 1895,[6] but may by 1896 already have been living with sculptor Pierre Valerio, an Italian-born naturalised American. Edith visited Reverdy in Paris but was unable to persuade him to agree to a divorce.

Jessie and her mother were finally left to themselves when, after Edith and John had returned to Boston, Edward and his family moved to a house opposite Jessie's, at 166 chaussée de Vleurgat. The additional strain of having so many members of a temperamental and sensitive family staying with her, combined with the exacting demands of her job and uncertainty about its continuance, had already had an effect on Jessie's health, the seriousness of which was to become apparent before the end of 1896. It was very likely responsible for her lapse of judgment regarding the publication of the 'skit' of King Leopold's speech.

Despite the constant demands of reporting for the *Times*, the crush of family problems, and the disruptive tension in such a crowded house, Jessie also continued her own writing. When Charlotte rejoined her in Brussels in 1894, she was writing a short novel for children, 'Gran'ma'[s] Tale', set in the Tasmania of her childhood, and *Not Counting the Cost*, the novel which seems most closely based on her own family.

On 13 March 1895, Jessie signed an agreement with Richard Bentley and Son, who had published Mrs Henry Wood's enormously popular *East Lynne* and some of Charles Dickens's works, for publication of either a one or two volume work. She received an advance of £63, reserving the rights to editions in foreign languages.[7] In fact, when the novel was published a few months later, it was issued in three volumes, one of the last novels to be published in this form, a vogue which had in fact run its course and was no longer in demand from libraries.[8] When D. Appleton and Co. bought the American copyright they published a single-volume edition.

Not Counting the Cost follows the story of the Clare family during their life in Hobart, their voyage by sailing ship to Europe and their residence in Paris on the Left Bank near the Luxembourg Gardens. In Europe they live in poverty while they search for a relative who has a valuable inheritance they believe is rightfully theirs. In an effort to earn money for her family, Eila Frost, the married daughter who has left her estranged husband in a mental asylum in Hobart, enters a dubious beauty competition. There she meets the deformed, decadent, rich Hubert de Merle, a long lost relative who wants to make her his mistress.

Even this bald outline indicates parallels between the early history of the Clare family and the Huybers family in Hobart and on their voyage to Europe, and the circumstances of their life in Paris. There are also other parallels in, for instance, the Clare family's search for their wealthy relative, which has something of the almost mythical quality of Charlotte Huybers's Simeon connections. This quality is reinforced by the final comments in *Not Counting the Cost* on the enigma of Hubert de Merle: 'I have a feeling sometimes that he wasn't a real person at all'.[9] The novel also has overtones of the attraction exerted on Jessie's sister Edith by the decadent world of Joris-Karl Huysmans. In the book the situation is resolved with the arrival of Reginald Acton, who had loved Eila in Hobart, and a colonial prevails over European decadence.

Some reviewers wrote enthusiastically about *Not Counting the Cost* but others were critical, particularly those who saw in the heroine, Eila, the independent minded New Woman, someone defying convention to lead a life of her own. The New Woman was a threat to male domination in real life and in fiction.

Among the more favourable reviews, the *Daily Chronicle* said *Not Counting the Cost* was Tasma's 'best story' but believed it would be improved by cutting when issued in one volume.[10] The *Daily Telegraph* said it was a 'brilliantly imaginative and subtly introspective romance' with 'highly-finished character-sketches'.[11] The *Standard* thought it long-winded, but 'a clever, entertaining, and original story', worthy to be classed with the author's *Uncle Piper of Piper's Hill*, and adding that 'we count that as being very high praise'.[12]

The *World* said *Not Counting the Cost* was Tasma 'at her best'. After describing the plot as 'quite out of the ordinary', and the characters as 'full of life and personality', the reviewer referred to the 'everlasting marriage question' stating that the author had avoided with 'skill, grace and reasonableness all the repulsive and wearisome "problems" of which novel readers and reviewers are so heartily sick'.[13]

The *Scotsman* said the novel would be 'pleasant and palatable enough but for the taint of "New Womanishness" ', the reviewer being particularly critical of Eila's considering the possibility of becoming de Merle's mistress.[14] The *Academy* reviewer agreed, stating that although Tasma had the knack of writing 'interesting novels', and the story was 'amusing and full of variety', Eila 'treads near the edge of the precipice' when she considers becoming de Merle's mistress.[15] The *Spectator* praised the Tasmanian chapters and the Clare family's life in Paris, but also criticised the moral attitude of Eila, who could leave her husband in Tasmania in a mental asylum and contemplate becoming mistress to the deformed but rich Hubert de Merle, to help her family, without having any feeling 'approximating to love' towards him.[16]

Among critical reviews, the *Athenaeum* said *Not Counting the Cost* was not so well constructed as some of Tasma's stories, and the end was 'hardly managed in a satisfactory fashion', but that it was 'worth reading and worth remembering, above all for its simple delineation of character'.[17] The *St*

James Gazette reviewer thought it was heavy reading, and an argument against the three-volume novel which encouraged spinning out material that would gain conciseness and clearness by compression.[18] The *Queen* said it would not be reckoned among 'this talented lady's highest achievements', lacking 'some of the *verve* and brightness which usually stamp her work'. Eila Frost's 'advanced views on the marriage tie, and her Socialistic attitude towards other people's property' needed more skilful treatment, the reviewer wrote. The Paris scenes made 'excellent reading' when they did not 'soar too far into the regions of fairy tale, with opulent monsters of cousins and silver kings for heroes'.[19] The *Morning Post* also raised the question of Hubert de Merle's unreality. He was 'clearly a creation of fairy lore', the reviewer wrote.[20]

In *Not Counting the Cost*, Jessie had created a heroine more active in taking charge of her own life than those of her other novels. The work itself was more complex and ambitious in scope than some of her other books but, perhaps partly because of the critical moralistic view taken by some reviewers, it was not as successful. Her other novel set in Paris, *The Penance of Portia James*, was reprinted several times throughout the 1890s, but *Not Counting the Cost*, apart from one American edition, was not.

It may have been because of this comparative lack of success that for her next book Jessie reverted to a wholly Australian setting. Such reversion, combined with the presentation of a darker view of a mismatched marriage similar to that between George Drafton and Pauline Vyner (*In Her Earliest Youth*) may also suggest that *A Fiery Ordeal* is at least partly the reworking of some earlier material. Set outside Baynton, a fictional town similar to Malmsbury in Victoria, an unhappily married couple, Ruth and Jim Fenton, live in a dilapidated homestead overlooking a lagoon. Fenton is a drunkard, a gambler at cards and on racehorses, a reckless spendthrift living on credit and borrowed money, and a jealous husband. He attacks his wife, knocking her head against a wall. Ruth Fenton had been interested in intellectual ideas, but at Tarooma finds no mental stimulus. When their financial position becomes desperate, Fenton disappears. Ruth contemplates legal action to free herself from her marriage, but the situation is resolved when Fenton reappears as a wild, deranged apparition. In his madness he sets alight to the bush. Ruth narrowly escapes from the raging bushfire in which Fenton perishes.

The succession of novels about ill-matched marriages, particularly *In Her Earliest Youth*, *Not Counting the Cost* and *A Fiery Ordeal*, written so long after Jessie's first marriage had ended and her own life had taken on so different an aspect, invites the question of why this topic should dominate her fiction. Why did the major male characters in varying degrees have Charles Fraser's faults? Did Jessie have a residual feeling of deep-seated hurt from her own ill-matched marriage which she had to express, in the case of A *Fiery Ordeal* close to twenty years after she had left Charles Fraser? In her last two novels both husbands become insane and die, leaving the heroines free to remarry. The husband also dies, although heroically, in the preceding novel, A *Knight of the White Feather*. Is it reading too much into her fiction to wonder whether in having these characters die Jessie was freeing herself of rankling memories of her unhappy years with her first husband?

There are also questions that could be raised concerning A *Knight of the White Feather*, the book Jessie found so hard to write. Was this because she was expressing something she found difficult to face—that a man of action could have some attraction over a man with overriding intellectual interests? Does the novel reflect some of Jessie's own ambivalence in her relations with men?

To readers aware of Jessie's own life, it must also have been apparent that she defied convention far more than her heroines. No doubt writing to the perceived needs of the market—and reviewers—for moral endings, she did not feel free to allow her heroines to divorce and remarry as she had herself.

It is impossible to know how Jessie's writing would have developed had she lived to write further novels. Had she in her five novels written away her memories of life in the Victorian bush? Would she have next turned to subjects drawing on her rich experiences of European society? Would she have written of the intrigues involved in being a foreign correspondent for the *Times*, or, on a more personal level, the contradictions implicit in Cecil Rhodes's alleged offer of marriage, her sister Edith's life among the Decadents in Paris, the intense mother-son relationship between Charlotte and John, or the complexities of her own relationships with men? Perhaps she may have explored the limits to which a woman could develop in the social climate of the challenging *fin de siècle*. Would her future as a novel writer have been in the portrayal of colonial heroines confronting disturbing aspects of European civilisation? Would she have portrayed women not as victims trying to escape from unhappy marriages but as participants in the sophisticated world of European politics and society, with its distinctive mores and strangely restrictive social conventions? These are questions only since Jessie did not survive to answer them. Perhaps as she sometimes indicated, her talent was exhausted.

In the latter months of 1896, Jessie became ill with a complaint diagnosed as anaemia. Her brother wrote that her illness caused 'a collapse of her system sad to witness'. From the few references to her illness—an entry in Edward Huybers's diary, a letter from Edward and a letter Jessie wrote herself[21]—it appears she developed ischaemic heart disease. It caused severe attacks of the frightening pain of angina pectoris.

In July 1897, just after she had signed the contract for publication of A

Fiery Ordeal, she had a 'nervous crisis', probably precipitated by a heart attack. From this time there appears, in retrospect, to have been little hope, with the treatment then available, that Jessie would recover, although her brother wrote that there were alternating periods of hope.

Medical interpretation of Jessie's illness indicates that she suffered from long-standing angina pectoris due to coronary heart disease, causing severe paroxysmal constricting pain when the flow of arterial blood to the heart muscle was interrupted. The 'nervous crisis' which occurred in July 1897, the physical symptoms of which were congestion of the lungs, has been interpreted as 'undoubtedly cardiac failure caused by her long-standing coronary heart disease'.[22]

During one of the periods when she was free of the worst effects of this ominously threatening disease, Jessie wrote to her brother Willie, then manager of Markwald's mercantile business in Brisbane.[23] She believed that she had regained her health, but in fact her death was tragically close:

> I ought to have answered your letter before but I have been so cast down by the weakness following my long illness that I had not the heart to do so. Now I seem to have turned the corner but it will take time to recover my strength, which both physically and mentally has been temporarily shattered.

As usual she was more concerned about the family's problems than her own. She expressed fury at William's treatment by his employer, a copy of one of whose letters he had sent her:

> What would one not give for you to be able to treat the communication of the former with the contempt it deserves! The money grubber and the cad are imprinted in every line, and it seems pitiful that you should have to defend yourself in the words one would employ in writing to an equal and a gentleman. But it is a question of bread and butter—and that goes before everything. It seems too that as Markwald's business has been benefited by your connection with it, self-interest alone should prompt him to alter his tone.

Then she turned to news of their brother Frank, tragically languishing with a broken back in Thargomindah Hospital, more than 1000 kilometres west of Brisbane, following a fall from a horse. Already, he had one leg shorter than the other as a result of two previous horse riding accidents:

> I would a thousand times rather see him dead than condemned to the living death of a totally paralysed man, with nothing to live for but the end of maintaining the tormenting consciousness of existence. I know how I would feel were I in the same case. It may be however that there is a hope of his recovering to a certain extent the use of his limbs which would make all the difference. Meanwhile I suppose the best that can be done is to make an arrangement by which one can ensure his being looked after well. Mother has had a heavy outlay already and I need not

say I will do my utmost to help. But it should be known that he belongs to a family of which every member is working more or less for his daily bread, and those who are implicated in the accident (for which none of us are in the smallest degree responsible) such as the man whose horse he was riding, should be called upon to contribute their share.

Eddie is resolved to find other work in addition to that he does for the *Chronicle*, being aware of the fact that notwithstanding his excellent relations with his employers one can never reckon with absolute certainty upon the continued success of a paper. If he had not been here to help me with the *Times* when I was at the worst, I don't know what I should have done, for without the *Times* I would have no *fixed* income to live upon, and the responsibility of a yearly mortgage of £60 to pay with which I am saddled for life. What strikes me as so deplorable in our family is the continual and relentless evil fate that seems to pursue it, and the way in which its members seem to be *forced* to be their own undoing. Both Eddie and Edith might have made safe and honourable alliances; they might have married well and congenially, and been welcomed into families with plenty of money and plenty of affection for them. And in each instance they *spurned* the proffered good and went out of their way to ally themselves with what was infinitely beneath them, and to drag poor and squalid connections into the family. To see one's belongings deliberately shipwreck their lives in this way casts such a shadow over one's own life, that sometimes one could almost wish to be quit of it. Now Frank has ruined his life—quite needlessly—I will try & write less gloomily next time.

She ended the letter 'au revoir—Jessie' but this was the last letter she was to write to Willie, and her last known personal communication.

During the next month, she suffered excruciating pain from further attacks of angina pectoris. Finally, she had a myocardial infarction or coronary thrombosis—a heart attack—and died in severe pain on 23 October 1897, just a few days short of her forty-ninth birthday.[24]

With her long-living parents and her own unusually active lifestyle for the era, she appears to have been unfortunate to have developed coronary heart disease at a comparatively early age. The extraordinary stresses of her life undoubtedly contributed. A few days after her death Eddie wrote to Willie:[25]

It must have been a sad shock for you to hear that Jessie has passed away from us. We are completely stunned by the blow. For Mother who feels the term of her life drawing to a close it is especially sad, but she bears it with great fortitude. Jessie's health has long given us anxiety. For at least a year she has been anaemic and had altered greatly in appearance—about 3 months ago an attack of congestion of the lungs put her life in danger and since then she did not rally. Without our knowledge she had heart trouble which the doctors kept from us and finally a clot formed in the lung [this was almost certainly a clot in a coronary artery] which brought on 'angina pectoris' from which only a temporary rally can be expected in any case— for the last week the cruel sufferings were mitigated by morphine injections but her strong brain struggled for life to the last.—Let us hope she was spared much of apparent suffering. Julia was our mainstay and held her hand for 36 hours almost without a break at the last.

In line with her long-standing views, Jessie specified in her will that after her death her carotid artery was to be cut by a physician to prove that death was 'without doubt'. She asked to be cremated, but if that was too difficult that her body be placed in a light coffin filled with charcoal, wood and quicklime to ensure quick destruction, with minimum emanations. In an earlier will she had raised the possibility of cremation in Paris if it were still illegal in Belgium, and had said that her ashes should be scattered to the wind. Although not included in Jessie's instructions in her will, Edward arranged for the Church of England burial service to be read in her home by the Anglican clergyman in Brussels, a service attended at his request by the British minister to Belgium, Sir F. Plunkett. Then Edward arranged for her body to travel by train from Brussels to Paris to Père Lachaise crematorium. Eddie continued:

> Her death is the subject of articles in all leading papers both here and in England etc. and yet how pitiful all seems now she is beyond our reach!
> Her poor savings were inconsiderable. The heirs are you, Koozee, Edith and I and she says in her will 'in case there is over £100 each'[26] which shows how trifling were her worldly goods compared with the love borne her by everyone . . . All her income expires at her death, and had it not been for the 'Times' her position would have been a very poor one—in fact any trouble with the house rent would have left her penniless.

There were many tributes to Jessie, none more touching than Eddie's comment in his diary, 'She was so much to her own [family] and of a nature so completely exceptional that the family light seems gone for ever'.[27]

The London *Times* referred to her success as a novelist, particularly her 'remarkable insight into character', her portrayals of children, and to 'the best novel she ever wrote', *Uncle Piper of Piper's Hill*, which when published in England had become 'instantly a great success'. As a journalist she had been 'most conscientious and painstaking' and 'alive to all political, intellectual and social movements'. The obituarist added, 'Though she had, like her husband, strong liberal convictions of the Belgian type, she showed judgment and moderation in her comments on the conduct of other parties—virtues which are not common in a country where political passions run exceptionally high'.[28]

In other obituaries, Jessie was described as 'one of the foremost of the rising and influential school of Australian novelists'; 'a most interesting figure from the ranks of contemporary novelists'; 'the Olive Schreiner of Australasia'; 'the senior member of the now numerous band of Australian lady novelists' and 'as unlike the typical literary woman, as she could possibly be, excepting in the intense interest she took in all leading topics of the day, and in everything that appertained to the welfare of her own sex'. As a journalist she was described as 'one of two women who occupied the unique position of foreign correspondent to the Times'. Obituarists also remarked on her 'considerable conversational powers', her 'genuine gift for platform oratory' and her handsomeness and beauty.[29]

An advance copy of her last novel, *A Fiery Ordeal*, arrived at Jessie's home as she lay dying, and the book was released shortly after her death. The proofs appear to have been read by her brother Eddie. As her executor he signed a contract with Appleton's for the American edition of the book. On the day of her death, he wrote to Richard Bentley, the publisher, expressing the hope that 'this latest work may meet with public approval and that you will do the same towards furthering the sale as with her other novels'.[30]

Jessie's death occurring almost simultaneously with the release of *A Fiery Ordeal*, the reviews almost became obituaries. One reviewer wrote that unless Jessie had left completed manuscripts behind, *A Fiery Ordeal* would be 'the last novel from her pen'. Another wrote that her fame rested 'mainly on her presentation of life in Australia', and *A Fiery Ordeal* bore this out. It was 'interesting and effective, but not in any way sensational'. The tale was told 'with considerable dramatic power', the characters 'drawn with sufficient, if not exceptional, strength'. Another reviewer wrote, 'If in the next century Australian society becomes literary, and recognizes the debt it owes to the writers of romances who have described Australia, while Mrs Campbell Praed will be the representative of Queensland, it is in Victoria rather than in Tasmania that Madame Couvreur will be remembered'. One reviewer commented on the convenient ending: 'Australian novelists always have bush fires in reserve to burn up every trace of an inconvenient husband'.[31]

Jessie made three wills. The first, dated 24 September 1894, six months after her husband's death, gave detailed instructions in French about her method of burial and the disposal of her estate, including her jewellery and clothes, mainly among her married sisters and brothers. She made a will in English in June 1897, and another in French on 16 August 1897 during her last illness, making similar provisions to the 1894 will with minor variations, the last being the only legal expression of her wishes.[32]

Whatever the legal situation, however, Charlotte remained in Jessie's house and once she had at least partly recovered from the death of her 'best beloved child', she oversaw the disposal of Jessie's personal possessions. This led to a rift with Edward, who had been named executor, which was never healed, and also appears to have led to a haphazard distribution of Jessie's jewellery and clothes, not in the precise way she had specified.[33] In her 1894 will, Jessie had asked that letters, journals and so on, either written to her or in her hand, and in her possession at the time of her death, be destroyed. It is fortunate that Charlotte did not entirely carry out this wish.

Though enormous amounts of Jessie's correspondence, manuscripts and other material must have been destroyed, some valuable material survived in Charlotte's hands. When she later returned to Australia she brought with her Jessie's 1889–91 Brussels diary and her *Windward* diary, both of which have remained in her sister Koozee's family and are valuable sources for her life. She also brought the unpublished manuscript of 'Gran'ma'[s] Tale', which was kept in her brother William's family, to be published nearly forty years after her death. Charlotte also brought back the painting of Charles Ogleby which had accompanied her to Australia in 1852, and had travelled with her until she gave it to Jessie when she settled in Brussels.[34] Jessie's most valuable possessions were her books, paintings and items of furniture, but these appear to have been sold precipitately rather than through accredited connoisseurs as she had specified, and probably brought less than their true value.

Apart from copies of some of her books in the Bibliothèque Royale Albert I in Brussels, and reports of her lectures and reviews of her books in the pages of hundred-year-old copies of *l'Indépendance belge* and other newspapers and periodicals, no traces of Jessie remain in Brussels. The house at 254 chaussée de Vleurgat has been demolished. Number 230, the address on her diary, and 161, where she died, remain, but residents know nothing of the Australian author, lecturer and *Times* correspondent who lived there.

Epilogue

Jessie's family was so important to her during her lifetime that it seems appropriate to record what happened to them. Five months after Jessie's death Charlotte Huybers, a sad figure, was still living in Jessie's house in Brussels. On 10 February 1898, Eddie noted in his diary: 'Jessie's furniture & objets d'art were sold & Mother remains alone in the deserted house opposite but will, we trust, live with some other member of the family'.[1]

Shortly after Jessie's death, Charlotte heard that another of her children, Frank, had died in Thargomindah Hospital from the results of a fracture of the dorsal (middle) spine caused by his fall in a bush steeplechase four months before. His death on 27 September 1897 had preceded Jessie's, but word of it did not reach Europe until after her death. Only a wardsman witnessed Frank Huybers's death. He was buried in Thargomindah Cemetery on the Bulloo River in the bush he loved, his great artistic talent unknown to those around him. On his death certificate he was described as a boundary rider.[2] Some time after his death, his brother and sister living in Australia, Koozee and William, joined to pay for a simple monument on his grave.[3]

Charlotte Huybers sailed for Melbourne on 26 September 1898, on the *Friedrich der Grosse*. She stayed for a while near Koozee at Kew, visited Willie in Brisbane, then returned alone to the Hobart she had left with five of her children twenty-five years before. She took lodgings in Macquarie Street. Her unsettled nature did not allow her to remain there long, however. She moved again to Melbourne, taking lodgings near Koozee who, after a period of stability almost unequalled in the family, was about to experience the turbulence that had enveloped to some extent all of Charlotte's children. In the early 1900s, her husband, Arthur Loureiro, who had been ill, returned to Portugal leaving Koozee with their three children,

Vasco, Fauvette and five-year-old Inez, without support. With a resilience and resource that equalled Jessie's, Koozee, who had been art critic for the Melbourne *Age* since Edith left Melbourne early in 1894,[4] turned to writing articles for the recently begun *Age* women's page under the name of 'Marmite' (French for cooking pot).[5] These articles were paid for at a penny a line and in cuttings she kept Koozee marked the amount she would receive for each.[6] These very tiny payments eventually must have been too small to keep her younger children and she was forced to take successive positions as a governess in country households. In letters to her daughter, Fauvette, she expressed the humiliation she felt there.[7] When she became ill, she returned to Melbourne and died at Kew from cancer of the throat on 28 March 1907, in the latter stages of her illness becoming insane.[8] Her sister Edith wrote of her 'deep tenderness and devotion', her 'caustic humour', and her 'contempt for *social* morality'.[9]

Koozee's daughters, Fauvette and Inez, joined their father in Portugal, but soon became unhappy and returned to Melbourne, where Fauvette supported Inez by taking positions, as her mother had done, as a governess. Fauvette was in Melbourne when her grandmother, Charlotte Huybers, died on 21 July 1908 at the age of ninety-one.[10] Charlotte was confined to a wheelchair for the last years of her life.

Fauvette Loureiro was, apart from her young sister, the only Huybers descendant living in Victoria. She took charge of funeral arrangements, which were almost identical with Jessie's. In her will, Charlotte gave instructions that her carotid artery be cut to make sure life was extinct, that she be wrapped in a gown she had ready, and placed in the light wicker basket which had accompanied her since she had arrived in Hobart nearly sixty years previously. She was then to be cremated. Charlotte was the sixth person and the second female to be cremated in Melbourne, the first being in 1905.[11] To the end of her life Fauvette remembered travelling on the train with her grandmother's body to Springvale Necropolis, accompanied by curious crowds who flocked to follow this strange rite. After cremation, which took place in the open, Charlotte's ashes were buried in the Church of England section of the Springvale cemetery.

Charlotte's antagonism to her son Edward appeared to extend beyond the grave. He is not listed as one of her children on her death certificate. In his diary and the two versions of his autobiography, Edward credited his mother with the development of the artistic and literary talents of her children, but added: 'it is largely owing to want of mental balance in dealing with the ordinary affairs of life, so characteristic in our mother, that I ascribe the non-fulfilment of great promise in several of my brothers and sisters'.[12]

On a journey to Europe Fauvette Loureiro married a Hungarian photographer, Philippe Erdos. Her husband died in 1911, shortly after the birth of their only child, Renée. Her sister Inez, a trainee nurse, died from

influenza in London soon after. Vasco Loureiro joined the AIF in World
War I as Sapper Louis Vasco in the 11th Field Co. Engineers. Wounded at
the front in 1918, he was recovering from his wounds in hospital in England
when he died suddenly of meningitis on 3 August 1918. One watercolour
and ten of his black and white drawings of fellow soldiers are in the
Australian War Memorial, Canberra.

William Huybers, to the end the solid, stable family member, died on
10 February 1913, at the age of sixty-six, in Toowoomba. In 1919, his eldest
son, Alfred Stutzer Huybers, began a mail order business, Queensland
Pastoral Supplies, publicising his business in his periodical, *Queensland
Pastoral Review*, which circulated in country districts. In this paper he
published Jessie's suspenseful short novel for children, 'Gran'ma'[s] Tale',
over seven episodes, from February to August 1936. Told in the form of a
grandmother's story to her grandchildren, it is set in Van Diemen's Land
in a home similar to Highfield, where a ticket-of-leave man brought in for
sentencing for a misdemeanour escapes to a cave on Mount Knocklofty. A
child's forced kindness to the convict in getting food, wood and matches
(there is a delightful juxtaposition of an advertisement for Bryant and May's
matches in the *Queensland Pastoral Review* with this incident in the story)
is repaid later when the escaped convict turned bushranger spares her life
and that of her friends. Written in 1894, but either not submitted to a
publisher or not accepted, it seems appropriate that this most Australian
of stories should be belatedly published in a paper circulating in the
outback.

Of the rest of the family, John Huybers, during the first decade of the
twentieth century, led a bohemian existence. He lived in a small apartment
at the back of a house near the sea in a poor quarter of South Boston,
looking like 'a tramp' but retaining his 'wonderfully deep sympathy for
humanity'. Edith thought of asking him to live with her in New York, but
restrained herself when she thought of him 'lying on his bed in the evening
smoking a corn cob pipe and making an intimate of some Jewish youth
who works at a cigar factory'. It made her realise that 'our ways & aims in
life would never agree'.[13]

One day on a street in Boston, John Huybers discovered a talented
sixteen-year-old Greek boy, George Demetrios, working in a menial position. Huybers took him in as a protégé.[14] He wrote Demetrios's story,
which was published in 1913 as *When I was a Boy in Greece* by George
Demetrios, illustrated by John Huybers.[15] Through his friendship with
Demetrios, John Huyber's interest in Greece flourished. During World War
I, after working in New York in the United States Press Censorship Office
with his brother Edward, he went to Greece. There, as correspondent for
the *New York Evening Post*, the *Christian Science Monitor* and the *Weekly
Review*, he became involved in the Greek independence movement, and a
close friend of the Greek Prime Minister, Eleutherios Venizelos, who led

Greece into World War I on the side of the Allies. John Huybers died suddenly in Greece from a heart attack on 27 May 1920, at the age of sixty. The Greek government erected a monument over his grave at Piraeus, and Venizelos wrote a panegyric published in Athens papers.[16]

Edith, living in New York where she was for some time on the staff of the Museum of Fine Art, a writer for *Art in America*[17] and a translator, became secretary of the Huybers Memorial Fund Committee. This was set up by an influential New York group to raise funds for an endowment at the American School in Athens, to the memory of John Huybers.[18]

She was by then Edith Valerio, apparently having persuaded Jean Reverdy to divorce her. Eight years after she had begun living with Valerio, and after having three sons, Sylvio, Angelico and Gregorio, she was still, however, complaining in letters that Reverdy refused to divorce her.[19] Her son, Maurice Reverdy, remained with her in America.

In later life Edith left the United States to live in London and then in Brussels, where she died on 3 February 1939 at the age of seventy-seven. Her brother Edward wrote, 'Poor dear Edith! Her life was "manquée" [spoiled] to a great extent by her unbalanced temperament'.[20] At her death she was working on a translation into French of Marcus Clarke's *For the Term of his Natural Life*.

Edward Huybers was the last of that generation of the Huybers family to die. For some years, from 1900, he held Jessie's former position as Brussels correspondent for the London *Times*. Later he ran an English language periodical and then with his wife a school, both unsuccessful ventures, in Brussels. During the early part of World War I he was a war correspondent in Rome and then in Paris, but his position was made redundant by newsagencies with their pooled news. His marriage with Julia failed during this time, and after her death in 1917 he married Ella, who had been his companion for some time. Throughout his life he was plagued with mental illness, and confined for ten years in various English mental asylums, suffering from 'depersonalisation'. In his final years, however, he reached a state of 'calmness'. Edward's life, which at times held so much promise, was chequered, indeed tragic. To his death in 1941 at Monkland Vicarage near Leominster, Herts, he maintained a diary or family chronicle which he had begun with his childhood reminiscences while living at Blairgowrie in Melbourne in 1877. It is an invaluable record of the Huybers family's movements, and events affecting them. His daughter, Dickie (Ethel Morris), who as a child remembered staying with her Aunt Jessie in Brussels in 1896, lived to record her impressions seventy years later [21] when the first stirring of interest emerged, since her death in 1897, in the talented writer and extraordinary woman known as Tasma. Jessie Couvreur was 'a personality of consummate charm', Edward wrote, 'whose work should have left a more lasting record'.[22]

Notes

REB	Book of cuttings kept by Tasma, containing reviews of *UPPH*, *SS*, *IHEY*, *PPJ*, *KWF* (Renée Erdos)
REC	Collection of loose cuttings, containing reviews of *NCC*, *AFO*, obituaries, plus reviews of other novels by Tasma (Renée Erdos)
SS	*A Sydney Sovereign* by Tasma (Trübner, London, 1890 edn)
UPPH	*Uncle Piper of Piper's Hill. A Novel* by Tasma (Heinemann, London, 1892 edn)
VPRS	Victorian Public Records Series
Windward	Jessie Fraser's *Windward* diary 1873 (Renée Erdos)

INTRODUCTION

1 Greco, p. 6; ' "Tasma" (Mme Auguste Couvreur)' *Queen, The Lady's Newspaper*, 13 January 1894.
2 London *Times*, 2 May 1890.
3 Margaret d'Alviella to Jessie, 24 November 1889 (R. Erdos).
4 Rolf Boldrewood, 'Heralds of Australian Literature', in *Australian Association for the Advancement of Science*, 4th meeting, Hobart, 1892.
5 See *Queen*.
6 Gérard Harry, 'Un Roman Australien', *l'Indépendance belge*, 13 January 1889.
7 Margaret Harris, introduction to *Uncle Piper of Piper's Hill*, Pandora, London, 1987.
8 Suzanne Falkiner, *The Writers' Landscape*, Simon and Schuster, East Roseville, NSW, 1992.
9 Brisbane *Courier*, 7 April 1933.
10 Letter from J. Gencourt, Secrétaire Général, Association des Membres de l'Ordre des Palmes Académiques, to author, 8 January 1992.
11 *Galignani's Messenger*, 16 November 1890.
12 These remarks were made in the context of a review of a book by Alexandre Dumas. 'Les femmes qui tuent et les femmes qui votent', *Victorian Review*, vol. 4, no. 1, August 1881.
13 *PPJ*, p. 193.
14 *Bulletin*, 19 November 1991.

1 HOW MAGNIFICENTLY WELL MY DEAR ONE TAUGHT KOOZEE AND EDDIE

1 Named after Trucanini, thought to be the last surviving full-blood Tasmanian Aboriginal woman. In giving a character this name Tasma was probably seeking to honour the Aboriginal race, by then virtually destroyed by European settlers. To present-day readers the gesture seems insensitive.
2 *NCC*, pp. 5–6.
3 ibid., pp. 16, 19.
4 ibid., p. 2.
5 ibid., p. 6.
6 ibid., p. 4.

Notes

7 Birth certificate 68/1848, Hornsey and Highgate sub-district, Edmonton district, Co. Middlesex. The address is given as 164 Southwood Lodge, Southwood Lane, apparently an old numbering system, since Southwood Lodge was later no. 52 Southwood Lane. Jessie spelt her second name Katherine.

8 John Richardson, *Highgate. Its History since the Fifteenth Century*, Historical Publications, New Barnet, Herts, 1983, p. 135.

9 I am indebted to Mrs Sue Whitington, Southwood Lodge, Highgate for this observation, and also for the information that Southwood Lodge earlier this century was the Lloyd Thomas Rest Home for Women and Girls. A plaque stating that the Home had been established through a bequest by Helen Strachan and Lloyd Thomas for use as a house of rest and recreation for women and girls from the East End of London still hangs in the kitchen.

10 *Queen*, 13 January 1894; REC, undated, unsourced (in French).

11 Baptism record, St Pancras, Co. Middlesex. Charlotte had two younger brothers, Richard Louis, baptised St Pancras Old Church, 24 July 1820, and Charles Orme, baptised at St Luke's Church, Old Street, Finsbury, 6 March 1823. The younger brother does not appear to have survived childhood. He is last mentioned in a letter dated 22 March 1824 (Charles Ogleby to Charlotte).

12 PROB 11/1540. Edward Simeon died 14 December 1812, probate 26 January 1813.

13 Edith Valerio to Fauvette Erdos, 26 December [?1935] (R. Erdos).

14 Robson's *Commercial Directory, Street Guide and Carriers' List* (London).

15 Charles Ogleby to Charlotte, 22 March 1824.

16 ibid., 17 July 1832. Charles believed his son would get 'a better Education in many respects in Paris'.

17 Burke's *Peerage and Baronetage*, 1970, p. 2447.

18 Charles Ogleby to Charlotte, 17 July 1832.

19 Patricia Clarke and Dale Spender (eds) *Life Lines. Australian Women's Letters and Diaries, 1789–1840*, Allen & Unwin, Sydney, 1992, p. xxii.

20 Daphne Bennett, *Emily Davies and the Liberation of Women 1830–1921*, André Deutsch, London, 1990, p. 156.

21 Sir Richard Simeon to Charlotte Ogleby from Swainston, Isle of Wight, 13 January 1833.

22 PROB 11/1820, Charles Ogleby. Jane Johnson, a former servant in the Simeon household and a beneficiary in their wills, was a close friend of the Ogleby family.

23 She was not living with her mother at the time of Adelaide Ogleby's death on 15 July 1845 at 4 Belgrave (now Belgrove) Street, St Pancras, aged 56. (Death certificate No. 132/1845 Grays Inn Lane sub-district, St Pancras, Co. Middlesex). Charlotte also does not appear to have been living with her mother at the 1841 Census.

24 Marriage No. 34/1846, Hendon district, Parish Church, Stanmore, Co. Middlesex. The witnesses were Bransby William Powys, attorney of Guilford Street, Russell Square, friend and lawyer to both the Simeon and Ogleby families, and Emma Drew.

25 Edward Simeon to Charlotte Ogleby from Carshalton House, Co. Surrey, 5 July 1846.

26 Birth record (E. Jones).

27 See *Queen*, 13 January 1894.
28 Described as 'tutor' on marriage certificate; as clerk in a mercantile house on Jessie's birth certificate; as 'agent for foreign wines' at the 1851 Census.
29 Charles Alfred Huybers (William was added later), born 80 Nichols Square, Shoreditch, 16 April 1847, Haggerstone West sub-district, Shoreditch district, Co. Middlesex, baptised St Leonards, Shoreditch, 14 July 1847.
30 1851 Census, Parish of Hornsey.
31 Alfred Huybers to Charlotte, c/o David Morian, 2 rue des Champs, Porte de Laeken, Brussels [1848].
32 PROB 11/2142; death duties IR 26/1916.
33 Greco, p. 5A.
34 *Hobart Town Courier*, 8, 11 December 1852. The *Australasia* left Plymouth on 21 August 1852.
35 See *Queen*.
36 For example, JC diary, 18 February 1889.
37 'British Novelists in Belgium. "Tasma" at Home', *Galignani's Messenger* (Paris), 16 November 1890; 'Some Australian Women. "Tasma" ', *Illustrated Sydney News*, 25 April 1891.
38 Greco, pp. 4–5. Long after transportation ceased in 1853, prisoners still serving their sentences were a common sight in Hobart.
39 John Levett, 'The Tasmanian Public Library in 1850', in *Books, Libraries and Readers in Colonial Australia*, Graduate School of Librarianship, eds Elizabeth Morrison and Michael Talbot, Clayton, Vic., 1985, p.1. During the next eight years footpaths were flagged with paving stones, a night soil service began, and street lamps were gas-lit.
40 *Hobart Town Courier*, 30 August 1853, death notice.
41 Vivienne Rae-Ellis, *Louisa Anne Meredith. A Tigress in Exile*, Blubber Head Press, Hobart, 1979, p. 160.
42 *Illustrated Tasmanian Mail*, 28 March 1933. Cleburne House was built by Richard Cleburne, who operated a wine and spirit and general merchant's business there until his death on 31 December 1855. The business was carried on by his two sons until the premises were leased to Alfred Huybers towards the end of 1859.
43 *Mercury*, 6 August 1887, p. 4, notice of auction.
44 *Illustrated Tasmanian Mail*, 28 March 1933; 'The Captain', *In Old Days and These*, Monotone Art Printers, Hobart, 1930.
45 Roberts & Co, *Catalogue of the Library of A. Huybers, Esq. consisting of valuable French and English Works by the most popular authors to be sold by Roberts & Co., on Friday, August 19, 1887*, Hobart, 1887.
46 Greco, p. 5.
47 Charlotte Huybers to Willie, 10 Addenswick Road, Ravenscourt Park, London, 17 August [1898].
48 ibid.
49 ibid.
50 NCC, pp. 16–17.
51 For example, ECH diary, p.6, Jessie's description of commonplace surroundings in Brussels.
52 See *Queen*.

53 Greco, pp. 5A-B, 15.
54 NCC, p. 34.
55 EAH diary, p. 5.
56 In a letter to Charlotte Ogleby, 17 July 1832, Charles Ogleby mentioned entertaining John Julius Stutzer, Snr, to dinner. For an account of the extra-ordinary life of J.J. Stutzer, classical scholar, linguist, journalist, see *Mercury*, 30 May 1867, 9 November 1874, *Argus*, 24, 26 May 1867.
57 EAH diary, p. 3.
58 Frank C. Green, *The Tasmanian Club 1861–1961*, n.p., Hobart, 1961.
59 EAH diary, p. 7.
60 ibid., p. 5.
61 Greco, p. 6.
62 ibid., p. 7.
63 *Mercury*, 7 February 1866; *Illustrated Tasmanian Mail*, 28 March 1935.
64 EAH diary, p. 8.
65 The two properties, Highfield (5 a. 3 r.) and Barton Vale (4 a. 3 r.) comprised the grant of 10 a. 2 r. to William Harris, brass founder of Hobart, in December 1844. Harris sold the rear portion to shipowner George Watson and the Highfield portion to James Crooke of Bacchus Marsh, Victoria. In June 1858, Crooke sold Highfield to Captain George King RN, but appears to have retained an interest (information from Frank Harris, Kingston Beach, Tasmania).
66 Highfield was described in the *Mercury* on 6 October, 1 December 1860, 18 February, 21 May 1862, when advertised to let by Mrs Harriet King. The Hudspeth family rented the property from her.
67 Although described as Captain King's property, the land was owned by James Elijah Crooke, Harriet Matilda King, widow of Captain King, William King and Marcus Richard Loane, MD of Port Sorell. After Marcus Richard Loane's death, his heir, Marcus Walpole Loane, failing to obtain payment of money owed, took possession of the property on 17 March 1866 and sold it to Alfred Huybers four months later (Memorial 5/4241, Tasmanian Titles Office).
68 For example, on 3 June 1853, while on a trip to Launceston, Alfred had written to Charlotte '& what would I already not have given to be again quietly at your side to scold & play with our dear angels?'
69 Edward Huybers obliterated the few lines in his diary in which he commented on Rebecca Chance.
70 NCC, p. 13.
71 ibid., p. 89.
72 ibid., p. 27.

2 SHE COMMITTED THE CROWNING ERROR OF HER LIFE

1 Charlotte Huybers to Willie, 17 August 1898.
2 Presbyterian baptisms in the District of Port Phillip 1838–44, 187.
3 Bertine Hay, *History of the Fraser and Agnew Families*, privately published, 1972.
4 G.M. Hibbins, *A History of the City of Springvale. Constellation of Communities*, City of Springvale/Lothian, Port Melbourne, Vic., 1984, pp. 31–2.

5   Hay.
6   Ian Brand, *The Convict Probation System: Van Diemen's Land 1839–1854*, Blubber Head Press, Hobart, 1990; A.G.L. Shaw, 'The Origins of the Probation System in Van Diemen's Land', in *Historical Studies Australia and New Zealand*, vol. 6, no. 21, November 1953.
7   Tasmanian Archives card index—Fraser.
8   R. C. Hutchinson, 'Mrs Hutchinson and the Female Factories of Early Australia' in *Tasmanian Historical Research Association Papers and Proceedings*, vol. IX, no. 2, December 1963. According to this article, the Frasers' management had been 'far from satisfactory'.
9   NCC, p. 37.
10 ibid., p. 40.
11 Hibbins, p. 27. Based on an entry in Thomas Journal, 12 August 1840.
12 See Hay.
13 Carolyn R. Stone and Pamela Tyson, *Old Hobart Town and Environs 1802–1855*, Pioneer Design Studio, Lilydale, Vic., 1978, pp. 190–2.
14 *Mercury*, 21 March 1883; 'William Degraves', *ADB* 4; *Australasian Sketcher*, 18 July 1873.
15 *IHEY*, pp. 6–7.
16 [John Phillips] *Reminiscences of Australian Early Life by a Pioneer*, A.P. Marsden, London, 1893, pp. 100–3.
17 Victorian Parliamentary Debates 1860–74; *ADB* 4; Garryowen, *The Chronicles of Early Melbourne 1835 to 1851*, vol. 2, Fergusson and Mitchell, Melbourne, 1888, p. 919.
18 *PPJ*, p. 28.
19 *IHEY*, p. 69.
20 Greco, p. 9.
21 *Mercury*, 10 June 1867; *The Cathedral Church of St David*; *A Short Guide to the Cathedral Church of St David*, plus notes 1803–42 and 1842–63; marriage certificate.
22 REC, undated, unsourced cutting.
23 FBB, p. 5.
24 *Mercury*, 27 June 1867.
25 NCC, p. 38.
26 ibid., p. 39.
27 *IHEY*, pp. 84–7.
28 NCC, p. 39.
29 ibid., p. 34.
30 ibid., p. 35.
31 ibid., p. 41.
32 ibid., p. 40.

3   HE SHOWED NO POWER OF ADAPTABILITY TO HER TASTES

1   Montpellier, under its present name of Skelsmergh Hall, and nearby Degraves Mill are classified by the Historic Buildings Council of Victoria and the

National Trust; the Australian Heritage Commission has registered the Mill and listed Skelsmergh Hall as a Reported Place.

2 Personal inspection; unsourced newspaper cutting, 28 October 1954.

3 *History of Kyneton 1836–1900*, Kyneton, Vic., 1934–35 (based on contemporary newspaper reports) states that the Riverview mill opened in 1857 and the Montpellier mill in 1860.

4 ibid., note following entry for 9 April 1860.

5 *Kyneton Guardian*, 16 January 1869.

6 ibid., 17 March 1869.

7 For information on William Piper, see J. O. Randell, *Pastoral Settlement in Northern Victoria, Vol. II, The Campaspe District*, Chandos Publishing, Burwood, Vic., 1982, p. 46; 'Kyneton in the Fifties' by Old Timer, Kyneton Historical Society's collected newspaper cuttings, p. 180.

8 *History of Kyneton*, 24 November 1857.

9 ibid., January 1864. Mrs Arthur Davitt, formerly Marie Antoinette Helene Heseltine, was superintendent of pupils at the Model and Normal Schools until 1860, and then a teacher.

10 *Kyneton Guardian*, 30 January 1869.

11 ibid., 14 December 1867. Furphy was awarded a prize in a competition run by the Kyneton Young Men's Association for the best poem on 'The Death of President Lincoln'.

12 For Ada Cambridge's movements, see Margaret Bradstock and Louise Wakeling, *Rattling the Orthodoxies. A Life of Ada Cambridge*, Penguin, Ringwood, Vic., 1991, p. 32; Audrey Tate, *Ada Cambridge. Her Life and Work 1844–1926*, Melbourne University Press, Carlton, Vic., 1991, p. 52. A reference in Jessie Couvreur's Brussels diary suggests the possibility of an acquaintance or friendship (JC diary, 7 October 1889).

13 *Kyneton Guardian*, 9 November 1867.

14 ibid., 16 October 1867. Fraser read 'The Two Adjutants'.

15 ibid., 28 December 1867.

16 *Illustrated Australian News*, 1 September 1891.

17 Melbourne *Leader*, n.d. The barrow was purchased by a Kyneton resident, Mr MacBean of Mollison Street.

18 EAH diary, p. 10.

19 ibid., pp. 13–14.

20 Jessie to Charles Fraser (letter in possession Mr Bill Falkiner, Brisbane). Some of the people mentioned in the letter: Dr Jas. B. Motherwell, physician, Collins Street; J.H. Aylwin, granite mason, importer; Robt W. Nutt, Solicitor; Kilpatricks, jewellers, 30 Collins Street West.

21 'William Degraves (1821–1883)', ADB 4, p. 40.

22 Union Bank of Australian records: J. McMullen (UBA Inspector and General Manager) to W.R. Mewburn, No. 528, 1 February 1870 U/103/10; McMullen to John Bramwell (London Manager) No. 531, 23 April 1870 U/103/10; McMullen to Bramwell No. 564, 5 December 1870 U/103/11; McMullen to Bramwell No. 531, 23 April 1870 U/118/6; Union Bank Board Minutes (London), 14 June 1870 U/7/10; J. C. Raymond (UBA Sydney Manager) to McMullen No. 822, 13 September 1870 U/62/12; McMullen to Bramwell, No. 591, 12 July 1871 U/118/6.

23   Union Bank of Australia records: McMullen to Bramwell No. 605, 1 January 1872 U/118/7; McMullen to Bramwell No. 623, 18 June 1872 U/103/13; McMullen to Bramwell. No 645, 30 January 1873 U/118/7; McMullen to Bramwell 27 February 1873 U/118/7; Union Bank Board minutes, London, 17 June 1873 U/7/10, 24 March 1874 U/7/11; McMullen to Bramwell No. 691, 26 March 1874 U/118/7; McMullen to Bramwell No. 692, 3 April 1874 U/103/15. Although the appeal went against Degraves, costs were not awarded against him. The Union Bank agreed to pay McMullen's costs (minutes, London, 25 August 1874 U/7/11); Melbourne *Age*, 6–13 June 1873; Melbourne *Argus*, 6–14 June 1873, 24, 26 March 1874. The *Argus* published a scathing editorial criticising both parties to the appeal on 26 March 1874.

24   Victoria, *Parliamentary Debates*, 23 October 1872, p. 1870. In a debate on the Diseases in Stock Bill Degraves said 500 of his cattle being overlanded from Queensland had died at Wagga Wagga, NSW from pleuro-pneumonia caught in that state. Another member (O'Shanassy) claimed the stock had brought the disease with them from Queensland.

25   'Queensland. La dernière née des colonies Australiennes, son bétail, son coton, son sucre' in *Bulletin de la société de géographie commerciale de Paris*, Paris, 1883.

26   Victoria Land Titles Office. Yarraman portions 20, 21, 26, 27, 51 and 52, Parish of Dandenong, Book 195, p. 963; D.J. Mickle, 'Origins of the name "Yarraman" and some Yarraman history', in *Gippsland Gate*, vol. 5, no. 4, June 1976; diary entries by William Lyall, Andrew Hudson quoted pp. 58–9. The property stretched from what is now the suburb of Noble Park towards Keysborough, bounded by Heatherton Road on the north, Corrigan Road on the west, Gladstone Road on the east, and followed a stepped boundary as far south as Kirkham Road (letter to author from Gillian Hibbins, 15 April 1991). There is now a Yarraman railway station and a Yarraman Road in this area.

27   EAH diary, p. 11. 'In 1870, towards the winter, Mother went again with the children to Melbourne, and this time stopped with Jessie at Oakville near Dandenong.' Mrs Huybers, Misses Huybers (2), Master Huybers and nurse, *Southern Cross*, Hobart to Melbourne, 4 May 1870; Mrs Huybers and two children, *Southern Cross*, Melbourne to Hobart, 3 October 1870; Miss Huybers (Koozee) from Melbourne to Hobart 29 October 1870 (*Mercury* shipping notices).

28   Frank to Willie Huybers, 28 February 1873 (E. Jones).

29   Victoria Land Titles Office. Mortgages by Charles Forbes Fraser: £2000 Book 195, p. 964; £600 Book 206, p. 293; £500 Book 195, p. 993.

30   *IHEY*, p. 341.

31   JC diary, 24 July 1890.

32   *AFO*, p. 33.

33   *IHEY*, p. 109.

34   *Queen*, 13 January 1894.

35   Lucy Sussex, 'Tasma's First Publication', in *Australian Literary Studies*, vol. 15, no. 3, May 1992.

36   EAH diary, p. 12.

37   For example, Mr Fraser, *Southern Cross* from Melbourne to Hobart, 4 February 1870; Mr Fraser *Tamar*, Hobart to Melbourne, 14 February 1870; Mr Huybers,

Tamar, Hobart to Melbourne, 11 March 1870; Mr Fraser, Mr Huybers, *Derwent,* Melbourne to Hobart, 24 March 1870.

38 Victoria Land Titles Office, Book 207, p. 887. Fraser sold the land subject to mortgage. It was then converted to Torrens title. Sands and McDougall, *Melbourne Directory*: Charles Fraser appeared only once in 1871 listed in the Oakleigh district.

39 NLA MS 1540, Catherine Deakin's diary. The school was run by the Misses Thompson in Kyneton until 1862, when it was moved to South Yarra (*History of Kyneton,* 3 December 1862).

40 Sands and McDougall, *Melbourne Directory.* Degraves was listed at 182–4 Collins Street East (Ebden House, now numbered 41–3 Collins Street, part of the Collins Place development) until 1869, and from 1870–5 at Dandenong Road, later Alma Road, St Kilda (in 1872 *Directory,* at Oakleigh, Dandenong Road).

41 *History of Kyneton,* 18 May 1872.

42 EAH diary, p. 13.

43 Windward, p. 1.

44 *Mercury,* 24 December 1872, Mrs Fraser, Melbourne to Hobart, *Southern Cross,* 23 December 1872.

45 On 23 August 1873, the *Kyneton Guardian* reported that 'Charles Forbes Fraser of Montpellier added to his stud stock by purchasing Ringleader'.

46 *History of Kyneton,* 27 November 1873.

47 *IHEY,* p. 128.

48 ibid., pp. 243–4.

4 WHAT A CHANGE THIS YEAR HAS BROUGHT

1 NCC, pp. 154–60.

2 Letters dated 28 February 1873 (E. Jones).

3 EAH diary, pp. 14–15.

4 L. Norman, *Pioneer Shipping of Tasmania,* Shearwater Press, Hobart, 1989, pp. 101–2.

5 *Mercury,* 4 March 1873.

6 Frank C. Green, *The Tasmanian Club 1861–1961,* n.p., Hobart, 1961, p. 17; 'W.L. Crowther', *ADB* 3, pp. 501–3.

7 Green, p. 18. Charles Champagne Des Voeux, who had property in Queensland, left Tasmania for England soon after his son. He became the sixth baronet and Fred (Sir Frederick Henry Arthur Des Voeux) succeeded him as the seventh baronet in 1914. Then a general staff officer, he had been a major in the 6th Dragoon Guards, and decorated in the Afghan War (1879–80).

8 'Charles Edward Walch'; 'Garnet Walch', *ADB* 6, pp. 337–8; letters from Geoffrey Stilwell to author, 12 August (family tree), 4 September 1991.

9 Windward, 18 April 1873.

10 ibid., 10 May 1873.

11 ibid., 6 April 1873.

12 ibid.

13 ibid., 19 April 1873.

14 ibid., 6 April 1873.
15 ibid.
16 ibid., 19 April 1873.
17 JC diary, 3 April 1889.
18 Windward, 6 April 1873; 'Le Tasmanie: Voyage par le cap Horn' in *Compte-Rendu des actes de la société royale belge de géographie*, vol. 16, no. 2, 1892, March-April, pp. 65–6; *l'Indépendance belge*, 24 March 1892.
19 Windward, 21 May 1873.
20 ibid., 8 April 1873.
21 ibid., 18 April 1873.
22 ibid.
23 ibid., 19 April 1873.
24 ibid., 27 April 1873.
25 ibid., 21 May 1873.
26 ibid., 31 May 1873.
27 ibid., 6 June 1873.
28 ibid.
29 ibid.
30 ibid., 17 June 1873.
31 'Barren Love', in ed. Garnet Walch, *'Hash'. A Mixed Dish for Christmas* with Ingredients by Various Australian Authors, P.E. Reynolds, Melbourne, 1877.
32 Windward, 4 July 1873.
33 *NCC*, p. 162.
34 Windward, 4 July 1873.
35 ibid., 30 June 1873.
36 London *Times*, 30 June 1873.
37 Windward, 30 June 1873.
38 Emily Faithfull accused Admiral Codrington of raping her in a case in which he sued his wife Helen, a friend of Emily Faithfull's, for divorce on the grounds of adultery. She later withdrew the claim, and she remained active in feminist causes until her death in 1891.
39 Windward, 7 July 1873.
40 ibid., 8 July 1873.
41 ibid.
42 ECH diary, 19 February 1875.

5 ARE WE THE SAME PEOPLE I WONDER?

1 ECH diary, 19 February [1875], recounting events of the family's nineteen months in Brussels from July 1873.
2 ibid.
3 ibid.
4 ibid.
5 ibid.
6 Translation of inscription on monument.
7 ECH diary, 19 February 1875.
8 ibid., 5 March 1875.

9   *IHEY*, pp. 232–3.
10 ECH diary, 19 February 1875.
11 JC diary, 20 April 1890.
12 Although Jessie lived in Brussels for nearly two years, from 1873 to 1875, and for the last third of her life, this was the only fiction she set in this city. By contrast Charlotte Brontë, who lived in Brussels for less than two years, set her 1853 novel *Villette* there.
13 ECH diary, 19 February, 5 March 1875.
14 ibid., 19 February 1875, stating that they were to live in the Champs Elysées.
15 ibid., 20 March, 10 April 1875.
16 ibid., March, 17 July 1875.
17 ibid., 15 May 1875.
18 ibid., March 1875.
19 ibid., 24 April 1875.
20 ibid., 10 April 1875.
21 ibid., 15 May 1875.
22 'A Hint for the Paris Commissioners', *Australasian*, 24 November 1877.
23 ECH diary, 15 August 1875.
24 JC diary, 26 May 1890.

6   HER WHOLE BEING WAS IN A STATE OF REVOLT

1   EAH diary, February 1877, pp. 9–10.
2   ibid., p. 16.
3   ECH diary, 25 February 1876.
4   EAH diary, summary, February 1877, p. 17.
5   Greco, p. 5B.
6   ECH diary, 25 February 1876.
7   *Kyneton Guardian*, 10 March 1874. Fraser also leased an adjoining small property known as Pethybridge's dairy farm. Pemberley was originally part of the Colliban run, pioneered by squatter Alexander Mollison, who sold it to James Orr in 1848. In 1857, Orr transferred the station to his son Henry, who renamed it Pemberley. (J. O. Randell, *Pastoral Settlement in Northern Victoria.*, Vol. 1, *The Colibon District*, Queensberry Hill Press, Melbourne, 1979, pp. 182–5, 230–6).
8   *Kyneton Guardian*, 4 September 1875.
9   ibid., 15 November 1876.
10 Roslyn Stevens compiler, *History of Malmsbury*, n.p. 1987.
11 Malmsbury bluestone was used in the construction of many well-known Victorian buildings, including St Patrick's Cathedral, Melbourne.
12 ECH diary, letter to father [March 1877].
13 St John's, built in local bluestone, was opened on 28 January 1866, completed on 7 November 1873, and consecrated on 20 March 1877 by Bishop Moorhouse (*Kyneton Guardian*, 25 March 1877).
14 *Argus*, 14 December 1883. *Fraser v. Fraser* divorce evidence. 'In 1877 her husband told her that there had been connexion between him and a servant girl, which had resulted in the birth of a child' (also *Age*, 14 December 1883).

15 *PPJ*, pp. 7, 82.

16 *AFO*, pp. 1, 4–5, 8–9, 18.

17 ibid., pp. 20–1.

18 ECH diary, 25 February 1876; *Argus*, 6 January 1876. Charlotte, John and Edith sailed on 5 January 1876 on the *Southern Cross* for Hobart.

19 E.M. Robb, *Early Toorak and District*, Robertson and Mullens, Melbourne, 1934; John Butler Cooper, *The History of Prahran 1836–1924*, Modern Printing Co, Melbourne, 1924; Betty Malone, 'Prahran's Heritage No. 4. From Como House to Como City, A Study in Diversity', Prahran Historical and Arts Society, 1989.

20 Letter Jane Clark to Enid Jones, 24 January 1985 (copy from Jane Clark).

21 *Table Talk*, 14 March 1890; H. M. Humphreys, compiler, *Men of the Time in Australia*, Vic. series, 2nd edn, McCarron, Bird, Melbourne, 1882, pp. 220–1. Walch was secretary of the Melbourne Athenaeum until 1879, resigning to stage 'Victoria in 1880'.

22 EAH diary, October 1877, p. 19: 'We saw a good deal of "The Vagabond" while he was in Melbourne, and now his name is familiar all over Australia'.

23 Julian Thomas (John Stanley James), *The Vagabond Papers*, ed. Michael Cannon, Hyland House, Melbourne, 1969; 'John Stanley James (1843–1896)', *ADB* 4, pp. 469–70.

24 Gowen Edward Evans, the only son of the Reverend Gowen Evans, of Potterspury, Northants, was born in 1826, and educated at Lincoln College, Oxford.

25 C.P. Smith, 'Men Who Made "The Argus" and "The Australasian" 1846–1925', LL MS 10727 MSB 312; Philip Mennell, *Dictionary of Australasian Biography*, Hutchinson, London, 1892, p. 151. Evans was admitted to the Victorian Bar in 1867.

26 Obituary, *Australasian*, 9 October 1897.

27 JC diary, 12 September 1889.

28 ibid., 26 May 1890.

29 *IHEY*, pp. 230, 241.

30 These paintings (some with slightly different titles) were part of the National Gallery collection: 'Pilgrim Fathers' (Cope) acquired in 1864; 'Rachel at the Well' (Goodall, R.A.) 1867; 'View of Rotterdam' (Webb) 1868; 'Italian Brigands' (M. Layraud) 1873; 'The Descent of Moses' (John Herbert) 1877 ('Votes and Proceedings of the Legislative Assembly of Victoria 1871–1881, quoted in Ann-Mari Jordens, 'Cultural Life in Melbourne 1870–1880', MA thesis, University of Melbourne, 1967).

31 Patricia Clarke, *Pen Portraits. Women Writers and Journalists in Nineteenth Century Australia*, Allen & Unwin, Sydney, 1988, pp. 207–10.

32 *Australasian*, 19 January 1878.

33 ibid., 3 August 1878.

34 *Australasian*, 1 June 1878, 'A Novel by M. Zola', The Contributor. *Queen*, 13 January 1894, stated that the review caused a controversy, but this has not been located.

35 James Edward Nield, 'On the advantages of burning the dead', in *Transactions and Proceedings of the Royal Society of Victoria*, vol. 11, 1874, pp. 18–27; Harold Love, *James Edward Nield. Victorian Virtuoso*, Melbourne University Press,

Melbourne, 1989, pp. 310; Graeme M. Griffin and Des Tobin, *The Australian Response to Death*, Melbourne University Press, Melbourne, 1982, p. 65.

36   Edgar Allan Poe, 'The Premature Burial', in *Selected Tales*, ed. John Curtis, Penguin, UK, 1956, pp. 322–36; see also, Thomas Embling, 'Premature Interments', in *Victorian Review*, May 1882, published four years after Tasma's article.

37   *Australasian*, 30 March 1878.

38   Edward Huybers left his position in William Huybers's stockbroking office when business fell away, and took a job at the Commercial Bank.

39   *Kyneton Guardian*, 3 April 1878.

40   EAH diary, 14 July 1878.

41   'Monsieur Caloche' has been republished many times: in Mennells's *In Australian Wilds* (Hutchinson, London) in 1889; in Tasma's own *A Sydney Sovereign* (Trübner, London) in 1890; and in this century in *Australian Round-Up* (ed. Colin Roderick, Angus & Robertson, Sydney, 1953); in *From the Verandah* (ed. Fiona Giles, McPhee Gribble, Melbourne, 1987); in *Eclipsed* (ed. Connie Burns and Marygai McNamara, Collins, Sydney, 1988); in part in *Her Selection* (ed. Lynne Spender, Penguin, Ringwood, Vic., 1988; and in *The Penguin Best Australian Short Stories* (ed. Mary Lord, Penguin, Ringwood, Vic., 1991).

42   Clarke, *Pen Portraits*, p. 102.

43   *Melbourne Review*, vol. 4, January 1879, p. 109.

44   Mennell, *In Australian Wilds*, p. 9.

45   *Fraser v. Fraser*, divorce evidence, *Age, Argus*, 14 December 1883.

46   EAH diary, 18 May 1879.

7 SHE HAS COME OUT AS A CONFÉRENCIÈRE WITH MUCH SUCCESS

1   *KWF*, p. 12.

2   Well over half the articles Jessie sent to the *Australasian* from Europe included reports of lectures she had attended.

3   Clara Aspinall, *Three Years in Melbourne*, L. Booth, London, 1862, p. 21.

4   JC diary, 15 February 1889.

5   'A Passing Glimpse of Cape Town. Part I., The Traveller', *Australasian*, 6 September 1879, p. 295; 'II', 13 September 1879, p. 326; 'III', 20 September 1879, pp. 357–8.

6   Sir Graham Berry, Premier of Victoria, had left on a mission to London to obtain British acquiescence in the reform of the Legislative Council in December 1878; the bushranging Kelly gang were at the height of their notoriety when Jessie left Victoria. Ned Kelly was not captured until June 1880.

7   'Home Impressions. A Sermon, a Play, and a Wedding' (The wedding of the title—of Captain Frederick Gustavus Burnaby, famous British traveller and soldier—is mentioned only briefly as a peg for remarks on other subjects), The Sketcher, *Australasian*, 11 October 1879, pp. 454–5; 'Home Impressions. (Concluded)', The Sketcher, 18 October 1879, p. 487.

8   Called rue de l'Observatoire in *Not Counting the Cost*, and now avenue de l'Observatoire.

9 Frank had left to work on Waverley, a Tasmanian station owned by Charles Fraser's nephew, Charles Agnew, while Jessie was still at Pemberley. Frank later returned to Pemberley, where he became a steeplechase rider of note. He left Victoria on 13 February 1880 on the *Sobraon* to join the family in Paris to train as an artist (EAH diary, 11 January, 27 June 1880).

10 Shirley Fox, *An Art Student's Reminiscences of Paris in the Eighties*, Mills and Boon, London, 1909, pp. 72–4.

11 Jane Clark, 'Arthur José de Souza Loureiro 1853–1932', *Art and Australia*, vol. 23, no. 1, Spring 1985; Jane Clark and Bridget Whitelaw, *Golden Summers. Heidelberg and Beyond*, International Cultural Corporation of Australia, Melbourne, 1985, pp. 20–1; *Illustrated Sydney News*, 1 August 1891; 'Artur José Loureiro (1853–1932)', *ADB* 5, pp. 104–5.

12 'Notes from Paris. The Comédie Française in England from a French point of view', *Australasian*, 10 January 1880, pp. 38–9.

13 'Art Gossip and the Paris Salon. No. 1 Realism', Fine Arts, *Australasian*, 11 September 1880, pp. 326–7 (no other parts have been located).

14 'Literary Notes from Paris', The Traveller, *Australasian*, 16 April 1881, p. 488.

15 'Notes from Paris', The Traveller, *Australasian*, 21 February 1880, p. 231.

16 'A Communistic Gathering', The Sketcher, *Australasian*, 5 March 1881, p. 294.

17 'Notes from Paris', The Traveller, *Australasian*, 21 February 1880, p. 231.

18 'Professor Nordenskiold's North-East Passage', The Traveller, *Australasian*, 12 June 1880, p. 744, 19 June 1880, p. 774.

19 EAH diary, 26 March 1881.

20 'Professor Nordenskiold's North-East Passage', preliminary comments, p. 744.

21 'The Familistère of Guise', The Traveller, *Australasian*, 21 August 1880, pp. 230–1.

22 'A Zinc Factory in Belgium', The Traveller, *Australasian*, 21 May 1881, p. 647.

23 In ' "Tasma". Mme Jessie Couvreur', published in *Queen*, 13 January 1894, it is said that this article, which led to Jessie being asked to lecture, was published in *La nouvelle revue*. The first article of Jessie's to appear in this publication was her short story 'L'amour aux Antipodes', published in August 1880, a month after her first lecture. The publication of the article on fruit growing in Tasmania has not been traced.

24 Mme Tasma, 'L'Australie et les avantages qu'elle offre a l'émigration Française', *Bulletin de géographie commerciale de Paris*, 20 July 1880.

25 FL MSS F372. Edward A. Huybers cuttings 1880–1900, No. 1, *Société de géographie commerciale de Paris*, Seance du 21 Decembre 1880 (quotations from cuttings have been translated from French to English).

26 ibid., No. 21, 'Nouvelles du Monde'.

27 See *Queen*. She also spoke in Italy and probably in Holland although no reports of these speeches have been found. The *Queen* article includes Holland on the list of countries in which Jessie spoke.

28 'Bordeaux, in its Relation with Australia', The Traveller, *Australasian*, 11 June 1881, p. 743; 18 June 1881, p. 775.

29 See *Queen*.

30 FL MSS F372 No. 9, 'Anvers, 17 Mars. Cercle artistique. Madame Tasma'.

31 ibid., No. 10, 'Cercle Artistique et Littéraire. Conference de Madame Tasma'.

32 ibid., No. 9.

Notes

33 ibid., No. 3, 'Arts, Sciences & Littérature. Cercle Artistique et Littéraire'.
34 EAH diary, 28 March 1881; FBB, p. 140.
35 FL MSS F372 No. 19 (no heading).
36 ibid., No. 6, 'Chronique de la Ville'; also No. 5, 'Belgique'; No. 7, 'La France, 25 Mars 1881'.
37 ibid., No. 15, *Echo du Parlement*.
38 *Australasian*, 16 July 1881.
39 JC diary, 29 April 1890; FBB, p. 140.
40 FL MSS F372, No. 2, 'Société de geographie d'Anvers'.
41 ibid., No. 8, 'Soirées populaires'; 'Madame Tasma aux Soirées populaires'.
42 ibid., No. 3, 'Arts, Sciences & Littérature'; No. 4, 'Lettres, sciences et arts'; No. 10, 'Cercle Artistique et Littéraire. Conférence de Madame Tasma'; No. 11 untitled [Anciens Normalistes]; FBB, p. 123.
43 ibid., No. 12, 'En Australie. Causerie Populaire', Paris, 31 March [1881]; also No. 14 'Association philotechnique Conference'.
44 ibid., No. 16, 'Au Cercle'; No. 17, 'Arts, Sciences et Lettres'; No. 18, untitled.
45 *l'Indépendance belge*, 11, 13, 16, 17, 18, 21, 23, 24 September 1880, one month after the story had appeared in *La nouvelle revue* (August 1880), pp. 848–83.
46 Winifred Stephens, *Madame Adam (Juliette Lamber), La Grande Française from Louis Philippe until 1917*, Chapman and Hall, London, 1917; Juliette Adam (Lamber), *My Literary Life*, D. Appleton and Co., New York, 1904, NLA Mfm 1424, Reel 625, No. 4991, History of Women series; *La nouvelle revue*.
47 'Literary Notes from Paris', The Traveller, *Australasian*, 16 April 1881, p. 488.
48 'The "Actualités" of Paris', The Traveller, *Australasian*, 30 July 1881.
49 'Autumn in Paris', The Traveller, *Australasian*, 14 January 1882.
50 *Illustrated Sydney News*, 1 August 1891.
51 *Launceston Examiner*, 17 September 1884; *Argus*, 15 September 1884. Koozee stayed in Hobart until after the birth of her second child, Fauvette, early in 1885.
52 Information on Loureiro from Renée Erdos; see Jane Clark; *Illustrated Sydney News*, 1 September 1891; ADB 5, pp. 104–5; Clark and Whitelaw, *Golden Summers*; *Table Talk*, 19 October 1888.
53 EAH diary, 11 January 1880; 26 March 1881; 5 February 1882.
54 'Professor Tyndall on Molecules', Scientific, *Australasian*, 15 April 1882, p. 455.
55 Tasmanian Supreme Court: Will, John Degraves; EAH diary, 14 January 1883.
56 EAH diary, 14 January 1883.
57 Melbourne *Argus*, 14 December 1883.
58 Victoria. *Acts of Parliament* No. 268/1864–65, An Act to consolidate the Laws relating to Marriage and to Deserted Wives and Children and to Divorce. This Act continued the provisions of the 1859 Act, amended in 1861, An Act to amend the Law relating to Divorce and Matrimonial Causes, Victoria, Acts of Parliament No. 125/1861.
59 Patricia Branca, *Women in Europe since 1750*, Croom Helm, London, 1978, p. 169.
60 Victoria. *Parliamentary Papers* 1860–61/3. Dispatch from Secretary of State for the Colonies to both Houses of Parliament notifying that Her Majesty had been advised not to assent to the Act to amend the Law relating to Divorce

and Matrimonial Causes in Victoria. The offending part was withdrawn and the Act passed without provision for divorce after four years' desertion.

61 Margaret James, 'Marriage and Marital Breakdown in Victoria, 1860–1960', PhD thesis, La Trobe University, March 1984 (Family Information Centre, Institute of Family Studies).

62 It is possible Jessie was given free trips or trips at reduced fares to and from Melbourne on the Messageries Maritimes line. This received a large subsidy from the French government, partly as a result of Jessie's lectures, in which she urged direct shipping links with Australia. She also wrote two articles on her voyage which publicised the line.

63 *Galignani's Messenger*, 16 November 1890; REC, undated, unsourced obituary (in French).

8 SHE GOES HOME UNFETTERED BY ANY TIE

1 Count Goblet d'Alviella, 'Nécrologie Auguste Couvreur', *Société d'archéologie de Bruxelles annuaire*, vol. 6, Bruxelles, 1895.

2 *Biographie nationale*, L'académie royale des sciences, des lettres et des beaux-arts de Belgique, Bruxelles; no. 43, suppl. 15, 1983–84, pp. 228–9. Couvreur was vice president from 22 March 1881–18 June 1884.

3 Hélène Couvreur (née Corr), died 22 July 1880 at 26 rue des Deux Eglises, Brussels, death certificate from Joris Couvreur.

4 Information on Auguste Couvreur from *Biographie nationale*; Goblet d'Alviella; *Biographie coloniale belge*, no. 4, Bruxelles, 1955, p. 163; Edouard Sêve, 'A. Couvreur. Portrait avec notice biographique', *Galerie de l'association internationale pour le progrès des sciences sociales*, 1864, pp. i-v; London *Times*, 24 April 1894; *Galignani's Messenger*, 16 November 1890.

5 'Literary Notes from Paris', The Contributor, *Australasian*, 29 July 1882, S.852, pp. 2–3.

6 'Monsieur Renan's Reminiscences', *Victorian Review*, 1 December 1883.

7 There are indications in her articles that she did not travel alone. Koozee, her travelling companion on previous trips, would have been unavailable after her marriage.

8 'A Trip through Central Europe. Hamburg', The Wanderer, *Australasian*, 2 December 1882, S.870, p. 3; 'A Trip through Central Europe. Berlin', The Wanderer, *Australasian*, 16 December 1882, S.872, pp. 2–3.

9 'A Trip through Central Europe. Dresden-Prague', The Wanderer, *Australasian*, 20 January 1883, S.877, pp. 3–4.

10 'A Trip through Central Europe. Vienna I', The Wanderer, *Australasian*, 3 February 1883, S.879, pp. 3–4; 'II', 17 February 1883, S.881, p. 3.

11 'A Trip through Central Europe. Buda-pest', The Wanderer, *Australasian*, 10 March 1883, S.884, p. 3.

12 Lecture given in June 1883 by Mme J. Tasma, 'Queensland. La dernière née des colonies australiennes, son bétail, son coton, son sucre', *Bulletin de la société de géographie commerciale de Paris*, Au Siège de la Société, Paris, 1883.

13 EAH diary, 17 February 1884; Jessie sailed on the *Mangana* for Launceston on 21 September 1883, staying in Tasmania for about two months.

Notes

14 VPRS 5336, Vol. 2—Divorce & Matrimonial Court Book, p. 12.
15 'To Australia by a Messageries Steamer I', The Tourist, *Australasian*, 11 August 1883, S.906, pp. 3–4; 'II', 18 August 1883, S.907, pp. 3–4.
16 *Victorian Review*, vol. IV, no. 1, August 1881.
17 ibid., IX, 1 December 1883, 'Monsieur Renan's Reminiscences'.
18 'William Shiels (1848–1904), premier and lawyer', *ADB* 11; Helen McCallum, 'William Shiels and Divorce Law Reform in Victoria 1883–1890', BA Hons thesis, ANU 1970, NLA MS 2441.
19 Margaret James, 'Marriage and Marital Breakdown in Victoria', Appendix D.
20 Letters to author from Bronwyn Merrett, Assistant Manager, Reference Services, PRO, Vic., 21 June 1990 stating that *Fraser v. Fraser* was listed in the contemporaneous index, but the file was not with the others of 1883; 23 August 1990, stating Divorce Case Files 1861–1917 were transferred to what was then the Archives Division of the State Library of Victoria in 1968, with no accompanying documentation. Letters to author from Prothonotary's Office, Supreme Court, 9 August 1990; 20 August 1990, 2 October 1990 from Macbeth Genealogical Services, which conducted a search of the files; from Mallesons Stephen Jaques, 7 July 1992; from State Library of Victoria, 13 February 1991; library holds some letters of Sir John Madden.
21 *Argus*, 14 December 1883.
22 *Age*, 14 December 1883. There was also a one-sentence report in the *Australasian*, 15 December 1883, and a longer one in the *Weekly Times*, 15 December 1883.
23 VPRS 5336.
24 There were thirty-seven petitions for divorce in Victoria in 1883, the highest number ever, and twenty-five decrees for divorce, also the highest ever; see James, Appendix D.
25 Birth certificate, Geelong 1880/614; Sands and McDougall, *Directory of Victoria*, 1883.
26 The Church of England rules would have prevented Fraser's marriage in a church if he had stated he was the guilty party in a divorce.
27 His children were Dora, Gladys Degraves and Charles White. Information from Bill Falkiner, Brisbane; death certificates; *Illustrated Australian News*, 1 September 1891; *Kyneton Guardian*, 28 June 1913; John Pacini, *A Century Galloped By. The First Hundred Years of the Victoria Racing Club*, Melbourne, 1984; Tim Hewat, *Golden Fleeces. The Falkiners of Boonoke*, Bay Books, Sydney, 1980; *Argus*, 27 June 1913.
28 EAH diary, 17 February 1884.
29 *Australasian*, 14 March 1885, Part I, Chapters I, II; 21 March 1885, Chapters III, IV; 28 March 1885, Part II, Chapters I, II; 4 April 1885, Chapters III, IV; 11 April 1885, Chapter V.
30 'A Letter from Florence', The Traveller, *Australasian*, 10 May 1884, S.945, p. 3; ibid., 24 May 1884, S.947, p. 3.
31 She describes attending an artists' ball with a companion in one of her Florence articles; a diary entry (JC diary, 5 November 1889) refers to a Mr Hirsch 'whom we met six years ago in Florence'.
32 *Lancet*, 8 November 1884. The Health Exhibition attracted over four million visitors in six months.

33 Jessie's usual outlet, the *Australasian*, does not appear to have published her articles on the Health Exhibition. The associated publication, the *Argus*, carried reports beginning 12 July 1884 by the Scientific Correspondent of the *Australasian* (not Jessie).

34 *British Medical Journal*, 19 January 1884.

35 See Goblet d'Alviella.

36 'A Latter-day Pilgrimage. I', The Traveller, *Australasian*, 23 August 1884, pp. 349–50; 'II', 30 August 1884, pp. 426–7; 'III', 6 September 1884, pp. 474–5; 'IV', 13 September 1884, p. 523.

37 The information about the 'proposal' is contained in a letter by Ethel Morris (née Huybers) to Ray Beilby, 29 August 1967, FL F232.

38 *British Australian*, 28 October 1897.

39 Sir Charles Dilke, *Problems of Greater Britain*, London, 1890 (NLA MC756 CIHM No. 6286,7), p. 396.

40 'A Letter from Paris', Society and Fashion, *Australasian*, 11 July 1885, p. 56.

41 Letter to author from J. Gencourt, Le Secrétaire Général, Association des Membres de l'Ordre des Palmes Académiques, Ministère de l'Education Nationale, 8 January 1992. Surviving records do not show the date on which Jessie received this honour. M. Gencourt states the award was made 'sans doute entre 1884 et 1889, plus vraissemblablement vers 1885-87 (Présidence de Jules GREVY)'.

42 EAH diary, 27 February 1885.

43 Marriage certificate 144/1885, District of Paddington, Co. Middlesex. Jessie's address was 26 Cornwall Road, and Auguste Couvreur's, 11 Kildare Terrace.

9 *I AM NOT BORN WITH A WIFE'S INSTINCTS*

1 *Queen*, 13 January 1894.

2 JC diary, 1889–90; obituaries, Auguste Couvreur, give lists of mourners and associations.

3 JC diary, 12 January 1889.

4 'The Political Situation in Belgium', London *Times*, 31 August 1894.

5 *Table Talk*, 12 September 1890; *Galignani's Messenger*, 16 November 1890.

6 An article on Treves in Italy appears to be the only one by Tasma in the *Australasian* between 1886 and 1889. 'What is to be seen at Treves', The Traveller, *Australasian*, 20 March 1886, pp. 572–3.

7 Letter to Mr Broadley, undated [?1890–91], FL F232.

8 'The Lady Barrister of Brussels', by 'A Lady Who Knows Her', *Pall Mall Gazette*, no. 6, December 1888.

9 'Lieb Liebchen, leg's Händchen aufs Herze mein', in Heinrich Heine, 'Book of Songs', *Poems selected from Heinrich Heine*, ed. Kate Freiligrath Kricker, Walter Scott, London, 1884. There are many translations of the poem, including one by Sir Robert Garran.

10 JC diary, 18 February 1889.

11 ibid., 18 January 1889; 30 January 1890.

12 ibid., 20 March 1889.

13 EAH diary, 17, 27 February 1884. Their creditors, mainly their bank and their

London agent, H. and A. Hawley, agreed to Huybers and Co's offer to pay 13 shillings in the pound at 3, 6, 9 and 12 months.

14   *Mercury*, 7 May 1887.
15   ibid., 6 August 1887; Roberts and Co., *Catalogue of the Library of* A. *Huybers*, Hobart, 1887; Memorial, Registrar of Deeds, Tasmanian Titles Office, No. 8800. Highfield was sold on 2 September 1887 for £1610.
16   JC diary, 18 January 1889.
17   ibid., 5 January 1889.
18   ibid., 4 March 1889.
19   *Mercury*, 17 July 1886; *Tasmanian Mail*, 23 September 1920; Greco, p. 5A.
20   JC diary, 4 March 1889.
21   Edith's first *Spectator* article was published on 19 March 1887.
22   Robert Baldick, *The Life of J.K. Huysmans*, The Clarendon Press, Oxford, 1955, p. 117 says Huysmans fell in love with Edith; Jane Clark, in 'Arthur José de Souza Loureiro 1853–1932', *Art and Australia*, vol. 23, no. 1, Spring 1985, that she had an affair with Huysmans.
23   Two of Edith's letters to Huysmans, dated 27 June 1890 and 7 May 1897, are reproduced in Daniel Habrekorn, *Lettres Correspondance à Trois Reunies et présentées*, les Editions Thot, Vanves, 1980, pp. 193–4, 228–9; both concern the fate of Villiers de L'Isle Adam's son, Totor, by his mistress Marie Dantine. Baldick, p. 119, mentions another letter dated in the late 1890s from Winchester, Massachusetts, in which Edith asked Huysmans's help in having a short story published in France.
24   Letter Edith to Willie, Richmond Hill, NY, 21 July 1908 (E. Jones).
25   Eugène Jean-Charles Reverdy was born in Paris on 2 March 1858. His uncle, Gustave Courbet, the forerunner of the Impressionists, was forced to flee from France after being found guilty of leading the destruction of the Colonne Vendôme as a member of the 1871 Commune, after the fall of Napoleon III. He died in Switzerland in 1877.
26   Edith Valerio, 'Gustave Courbet and his Country', *Art in America*, vol. 10, 1922.
27   'Art and Artists. Monsieur and Madame Reverdy', *Table Talk*, 15 September 1890.
28   JC diary, 18 July 1889.
29   ibid., 17 November 1889.
30   ibid., 6 April 1890.
31   ibid., 26 May 1890.
32   ibid., 14 June 1890.
33   ibid., 29 April 1890.
34   ibid., 7 June, 17 December 1890.
35   ibid., 14 June 1890.
36   ibid., 1, 6, 23 January 1889.
37   ibid., 28 March 1889.
38   ibid., 20 January 1889.
39   ibid., 18 February 1889.
40   ibid., 18 July 1889.
41   ibid., 26 July 1889.
42   ibid., 1 January 1890.

43 ibid., 20, 23, 26 July 1889.
44 ibid., 30 January 1890.
45 ibid., 4, 7, 9, 12 October 1889.
46 Jessie wrote on 12 September 1889 (JC diary), 'With my sisters-in-law it must always be thus far and no further in respect of the going out of my mind and heart towards them'.
47 JC diary, 13 December 1889.
48 ibid., 21 December 1889.
49 ibid., 24 October 1889.
50 ibid., 21 July 1891; *World*, 24 December 1890.
51 ibid., 3 December 1890.
52 ibid., 5 September 1890.
53 ibid., 14 September 1890.
54 ibid., 29 September 1890.
55 ibid., 9 November 1889.
56 ibid., 10 July 1890.
57 ibid., 24 July 1890.
58 ibid., 3, 17 December 1890.
59 ibid., 3 December 1890.
60 ibid., 21 July 1891; *Macbeth*, 1, 3.
61 ibid., 18, 31 January 1889.
62 ibid., 15 February 1889.
63 ibid., 18 February 1889; accounts of speech in *Compte-Rendu des actes de la société royale belge de géographie*, vol. 13, no. 1, 1889, January-February, pp. 12–13; *l'Indépendance belge*, 17 February 1889.
64 JC diary, 24 March 1889.
65 ibid., 21 March 1890. No report of this speech has been traced. A 'Conférence du travail' took place in Berlin in March 1890, but there are no reports of a speech by Tasma in its records (Conférence Internationale, Leipsig, 1890). There are also no reports of her speech in *l'Indépendance belge*, *Bulletin*, *Mémoires*, *Compu-Rendus* (letter, Carlos Van Lerberghe, Bibliothèque Royale, Brussels, 1992).
66 *Compte-Rendu des actes de la société royale belge de géographie*, vol. 16, no. 2, 1982 Mars et Avril, pp. 65–6; *l'Indépendance belge*, 24 March 1892.
67 JC diary, 17 May 1889.
68 The two-volume Tauchnitz (Leipsig) edition arrived just before they left Constantinople on 12 May.
69 *Les origines de la forme républicaine du government dans les Etats-Unis d'Amérique*, trs avec l'authorisation de l'auteur, sur la 3 edn rev. par Madame Auguste Couvreur. Avec une préface de Emile de Laveleye, Muquardt, Bruxelles, 1890.
70 ARB 1829–1898. NLA G18 987, 5, p. 166, 28 May 1891, Temple Bar. Authors' Ledgers 1868–99, Richard Bentley paid eight guineas for the articles.
71 JC diary, 17 May 1889.
72 ibid., 24 October 1889.
73 ibid., 24, 31 October, 16 November 1889.
74 'The Royal Wedding in Greece', *Argus* 17, 19, 20 December 1889.
75 JC diary, 5, 9 November 1889.
76 ibid., 21 December 1889.

Notes

10 TASMA IS SURPASSED BY FEW BRITISH NOVELISTS

1 *Home Notes*, 16 November 1896.
2 *Australasian Critic*, 1 October 1890.
3 REB, *European Mail*, 18 January 1889.
4 Although dated 1889, it was available for the Christmas market, and some reviews appeared late in 1888.
5 EAH diary, 14 April 1889.
6 Greco, p. 6; see also *Queen*, 13 January 1894.
7 Rolf Boldrewood, 'Heralds of Australian Literature', *Australian Association for the Advancement of Science Report of the 4th meeting*, Hobart, January 1892.
8 See *Queen*.
9 REB, *Pall Mall Gazette*, 1 February 1889.
10 ibid. (REB), *Spectator*, 2 February 1889.
11 ibid., *Times*, 1 June 1889.
12 ibid., *Guardian*, 30 January 1889.
13 ibid., *World*, 9 January 1889.
14 ibid., *Academy*, 12 January 1889.
15 ibid., *Glasgow Herald*, 3 January 1889.
16 ibid., *Athenaeum*, 5 January 1889.
17 ibid., London *Figaro* 9 March 1889.
18 ibid., A. Patchett Martin, *European Mail*, 18 January 1889, 10 January 1890.
19 ibid., *Saturday Review*, 29 December 1888; *Australasian*, 16 February 1889.
20 *Journal de Bruxelles*, 6 February 1889.
21 Gérard Harry, 'Un Roman Australien', *l'Indépendance belge*, 13 January 1889.
22 *Belgian News*, 20 January 1889; *Précurseur*, 11 February 1889; *Bulletin de la société de géographie commerciale*, 1889, vol. XI, no. 2.
23 Léo Quesnel, *La nouvelle revue*, 1 February 1889.
24 JC diary, 11 January 1889.
25 ibid., 10 January 1889.
26 ibid., 15 February 1889.
27 University College of London. Agreement between Trübner and Co., London, and Bernhard Tauchnitz, Leipzig, 5 March 1889; Asa Briggs, *Essays in the History of Publishing*, London, 1974, p. 292, quoting S.H. Steinberg.
28 JC diary, 21 March 1890. Jessie said there were four editions, but only three have been discovered: AKP NLA Mfm G14 936, Reel 27, 8, p. 313, G14 934, Reel 25, 5, p. 279 (Trübner Publication Account Books); G14 926, 5, p. 206 (KP Print and Paper Books); G14 928, 1, p. 486 (Kegan Paul Sheet Stack and Binding Books). Trübner's records show that surprisingly small numbers of all books, not only of Jessie's, were published. Further quantities of the book after the second edition, of from 50 to 250 copies, were bound and released according to demand.
29 *Galignani's Messenger*, 16 November 1890; *Illustrated Sydney News*, 25 April 1891.
30 JC diary, 7 October 1889; AKP, NLA Mfm G 14 936, Reel 27, 8, p. 316 (Trübner Publication Account Books).
31 JC diary, 30 January 1890.
32 REB, *Athenaeum*, 8 February 1890.
33 ibid. (REB), *Scottish Leader*, 30 January 1890.

34 ibid., *Literary World*, 7 February 1890.
35 ibid., *Lincolnshire Herald*, 24 February 1890.
36 ibid., *Pictorial World*, n.d.
37 ibid., *Glasgow Herald*, 30 January 1890.
38 ibid., *Indépendance belge*, 12 January 1890.
39 *Belgian News*, 3 March 1890.
40 Frank Arthur Mumby, *Publishing and Bookselling: A History from the Earliest Times to the Present Day*, Jonathan Cape, London, 1934, p. 305.
41 JC diary, 26 May 1890.
42 ibid., 4 March 1889.
43 ibid., 20 April 1890.
44 AKP, NLA Mfm G14 928, Reel 19, 1, pp. 141, 222, 431 (Kegan Paul Sheet Stock and Binding Books); G14 936, Reel 27, 8, pp. 315, 318 (Trübner Publication Account Books); G14 925, Reel 16, 3, p. 406, G 14 926, Reel 17, 4, p. 320 (KP Print and Paper Book); G14 932, Reel 23, 3, p. 435 (Royalties and Commercial Accounts); G14 926, Reel 17, 5, p. 37 (KP Print and paper Books); G14 912, Reel 32, 6, p. 366, 7, p. 82 (KP Publication Book). A one volume colonial edition of 2000 was published at the same time, or very shortly after the three-volume edition. G14 920, 17, p. 173 (Indian and Colonial Series); G14 921, Reel 12, 22, p. 18 (Royalty and Share).
45 REB, *Manchester Examiner*, 12 April 1890.
46 ibid. (REB), London *Times*, 2 May 1890.
47 ibid., *Manchester Examiner*.
48 ibid., *Scotsman*, 7 April 1890.
49 ibid., *Glasgow Herald*, 17 April 1890.
50 ibid., *Woman*, 19 April 1890.
51 ibid., *World*, 11 June 1890.
52 ibid., *Academy*, 24 March 1890.
53 ibid., *Daily News*, 31 May 1890.
54 ibid., London *Times*, 2 May 1890.
55 ibid., *Indépendance belge*, 20 August 1890.
56 ibid., *Pall Mall Budget*, n.d.
57 ibid., *Manchester Guardian*, 2 December 1890.
58 JC diary, 1 January 1890.
59 ibid., 30 January 1890.
60 ibid., 6 December 1890.
61 ibid., 29 April 1890.
62 *World*, 2 July 1890.
63 JC diary, 7 June 1890.
64 ibid., 7 June, 10 July 1890.
65 ibid., 4 July 1890.
66 *World*, 24 December 1890.
67 JC diary, 3 December 1890.
68 ibid., 21 July 1891.
69 *PPJ*, p. 193.
70 REB, *Academy*, 13 February 1892.
71 ibid. (REB), *Daily News*, 25 December 1891.
72 ibid., London *Times*, 25 December 1891.

73 ibid., *Athenaeum*, 8 December 1891.
74 ibid., *Lady's Pictorial*, 19 December 1891.
75 ibid., *Literary Opinion*, December 1891.
76 Published by Hutchinson and Co., London, 1889. Other contributors were B.L. Farjeon, who contributed the title story, C. Haddon Chambers (three stories), Edmund Stansfield Rawson, Edward Jenkins, H.B. Marriott Watson, and the editor, who wrote 'Traits of the Township', a semi-critical account of Bairnsdale, Vic. where he owned a newspaper from 1877–82.
77 Published by Trischler and Co., London, 1890. Other contributors were Mrs Campbell Praed (two stories), H.B. Marriott Watson, Hume Nisbet, Mrs Lance Rawson, Dr Mannington Caffyn, Reginald Clayton, E.S. Rawson, Robert Richardson, Arthur Patchett Martin and the editor.
78 Published by Griffith, Farran, Okeden and Welsh, London, 1891. Other contributors were Rosa Praed, Mrs Henry Day, Kathleen Caffyn, Mrs Lance Rawson, Margaret Thomas and the editor (review, *Sydney Morning Herald*, 23 May 1891).
79 Published by Griffith, Farran, Okeden & Welsh of London and Sydney, in 1891. Other contributors included Rosa Praed and Harriette Anne Patchett Martin, some veterans from previous Patchett Martin books including Hume Nisbet and H.B. Marriott Watson, Frederic E. Weatherly, Miss M. Senior Clark and Countess De La Warr.
80 *Gentlewoman*, Christmas number, 1891 to 7 May 1892.
81 *KWF*, p. 70. Lesbia Wiseman, who is described as related to the English Cardinal Wiseman, may be based on a woman writer who lived in Kyneton, Mrs Grace Langford, who was a niece of Cardinal Newman (REB *Leader*, n.d.). Mrs Langford was author of *Werona: A Romance of Australian Domestic Life* Remington, London, 1893.
82 REB, *Literary World*, 16 November 1892.
83 ibid. (REB), Sheffield *Daily Telegraph*, 18 November 1892.
84 ibid., *World*, November 1892.
85 ibid., *Vanity Fair*, 18 November 1892.
86 ibid., *Spectator*, November 1892.
87 ibid., *Natal Mercury*, n.d.
88 ibid., *Sydney Morning Herald*, 20 March 1893.
89 ibid., *Belgian News*, November 1892.
90 ibid., London *Times*, 22 December 1892.
91 *Table Talk*, 14 July 1893.
92 Letter Jessie Couvreur to Fauvette Erdos, March 1890 (R. Erdos).
93 ibid., 23 December [1893].
94 See Jane Clark, 'Arthur Loureiro'.
95 *Table Talk*, 1 December 1893. Reverdy held an exhibition of wood carvings before he left for Europe. The article implies he had had little success in Melbourne.
96 *Mercury*, vol. 15, 19 May 1893; Victorian death certificate 3198/1893.
97 Will, 26 July 1888 made at Caledonian Hotel, London, while visiting England; Letters of Administration, Perpetual Trustees, 15 June 1893.
98 *Argus*, 1 February 1894.
99 FMLB 1/138, 20 January 1892.

11 REMAIN AT THE HAGUE UNTIL FURTHER ORDERS

1 *l'Indépendance belge*, 24, 26, 27 April 1894; London *Times*, 24 April 1894; Goblet d'Alviella, 'Nécrologie Auguste Couvreur', *Société d'archéologie de Bruxelles annuaire*, vol. 16, Brussels, 1895; 'Nécrologie', *Société royale belge de géographie*, vol. 18, 1894.

2 The notice was in the name of 'Madame Auguste Couvreur née Jessie Huybers; Mesdemoiselles Delphine et Victorine Couvreur; Monsieur Ernest Couvreur et ses enfants; Madame veuve Huybers, ses enfants, beaux-enfants et petits-enfants'.

3 Charles Frederick Moberly Bell's position was officially assistant manager but he carried out the duties of manager and was later managing director (*History of the Times. The Twentieth Century Test 1884–1915*, The Times, London, 1947, p. 113). His letters to the paper's correspondents are filed in a series called the Manager's Letter Books (MLB).

4 Copies of the letters written to *Times* foreign correspondents by the foreign manager are filed in dusty, fragile, 100-year-old bound books known as the Foreign Manager's Letter Books (FMLB).

5 MLB 9/534, 27 April 1894.

6 FMLB 2/567, 5 July 1894; FMLB 3/642, 15 November 1896.

7 FMLB 2/606, 8 August 1894; FMLB 3/178, 14 October 1895.

8 FMLB 3/876, 11 June 1897.

9 FMLB 2/567, 5 July 1894.

10 FMLB 2/606, 8 August 1894.

11 MLB 9/649, 25 May 1894.

12 Jessie stayed with Mrs Bigelow at 10 Chelsea Embankment. She had met Mr Bigelow, the son of the former United States Minister, in Paris at the Hotel de la Grande Bretagne while visiting Athens in November 1889 (JC diary, 12 November 1889).

13 MLB 10/342, 29 October 1894.

14 FMLB 2/771, 6 December 1894.

15 FMLB 2/786, 20 December 1894.

16 FMLB 3/202, 4 November 1895; FMLB 3/736, 5 February 1897.

17 MLB 10/655, 3 January 1895.

18 FMLB 2/818, 17 January 1895.

19 FMLB 2/981, 3 April 1895.

20 London *Times*, 18 March, 4 June 1895.

21 FMLB 3/4, 30 May 1895.

22 FMLB 3/17, 10 June 1895.

23 *History of the Times*, p. 176.

24 ibid., pp. 161–76; E. Moberly Bell, *Flora Shaw*, Constable, London, 1948.

25 MLB 12/199, 14 May 1895.

26 London *Times*, 16 August 1895.

27 Neal Ascheron, *The King Incorporated. Leopold II in the Age of Trusts*, George Allen & Unwin, London, 1963, pp. 242–7; Barbara Emerson, *Leopold II of the Belgians, King of Colonialism*, Weidenfeld and Nicolson, London, 1979, pp. 236–7.

28 London *Times*, 16 September 1895.

29 FMLB 3/178, 14 October 1895.
30 MLB 13/268, 23 December 1895.
31 *History of the Times*, pp. 243–4.
32 London *Times*, 3 January 1896.
33 'A Resident of Pretoria on the Crisis', London *Times*, 9 January 1896.
34 FMLB 3/863, 30 May 1897.
35 London *Times*, 17 June 1897.
36 FMLB 3/642, 15 November 1896.
37 FMLB 3/318, 22 January 1896.
38 FMLB 3/178, 14 October 1895.
39 FMLB 3/525, 26 July 1896.
40 London *Times*, 10 November 1896.
41 ibid., 11 November 1896.
42 FMLB 3/636, 11 November 1896.
43 FMLB 3/642, 15 November 1896.
44 Greco, p. 88.
45 London *Times*, 25 October 1897.

12 I HAVE BEEN SO CAST DOWN BY MY LONG ILLNESS

1 Letter, Mrs Morris, Jessie's niece, to Ray Beilby, 30 October 1967, FL F232.
2 *Bulletin Communale*, Ville de Bruxelles I, 14 January 1895, pp.17–8, acceptance of legacy; the Ecole Couvreur still exists at 114 rue Terre-Neuve.
3 EAH diary, 20 April 1890.
4 Letter, Mrs Morris; R. Beilby to C. Hadgraft reporting visit to Mrs Morris, 10 May 1968, FL F232.
5 MLB 12/737, 25 September 1895.
6 EAH diary, 17 November 1895; information from Jacqueline Laude, Reverdy's grand niece, stating that Edith had two children by Reverdy indicates that this child was Reverdy's. Reverdy died in Ornans on 1 March 1937.
7 ARB G19 019, Reel 34, 66, pp. 250–4; 67, pp. 249–51 (Agreement and Memorandum Books). The contract was for publication of a one or two-volume novel. The rights to foreign editions were reserved to the author. Jessie's agent was A.P. Watt and Son, Hastings House, Norfolk Street, Strand, London. Bentley printed 750 copies, G18 986, 3, p. 43 (General Authors' Ledgers 1872–96); G19 007, Reel 22, 42, p. 430 (Publication Ledger 1883–7).
8 Frank Arthur Mumby, *Publishing and Bookselling: A History from the Earliest Times to the Present Day*, Jonathan Cape, London, 1934, p. 343. The vogue for three-volume novels ended in 1894, according to Mumby.
9 NCC, p. 400.
10 REC, *Daily Chronicle*, September 1895 (only month noted, not exact date on this and some following cuttings).
11 ibid. (REC), *Daily Telegraph*, September 1895.
12 ibid., *Standard*, 8 October 1895.
13 ibid., *World*, 28 August 1895.
14 ibid., *Scotsman*, August 1895.
15 ibid., *Academy*, 19 October 1895.

16 ibid., *Spectator*, September 1895.
17 ibid., *Athenaeum*, September 1895.
18 ibid., *St James Gazette*, September 1895.
19 ibid., *Queen*, 12 October 1895.
20 ibid., *Morning Post*, 30 September 1895.
21 EAH diary, 10 February 1898; letters, Jessie to Willie, 16 September 1897; Eddie to Willie, 27 October 1897 (E. Jones).
22 Dr E.W. Ringrose to Dr K. Huybers, 25 February 1992.
23 Letter Jessie to Willie, 16 September 1897 (E. Jones).
24 Death certificate No. 653/1897 Commune d'Ixelles.
25 Letter, Eddie to Willie Huybers, 27 October 1897 (E. Jones).
26 This phrase did not appear in Jessie's last will but it was probably an accurate representation of the extent of her estate.
27 EAH diary, 10 February 1898.
28 London *Times*, 25 October 1897. The *Times* obituary stated that Jessie died after an illness of only two days. This information seems to have been supplied by Edward Huybers to cover the fact that he had been sending dispatches for Jessie during her last illness.
29 REC, undated, unsourced obituaries.
30 ARB, G19 019, Reel 34, 67, pp. 249–51 (Agreement Memorandum Book) for a two volume work. The rights of translation were reserved to the author. Jessie received an advance of £42. When the work was published in a single volume, the royalties at 9d. per copy did not cover the advance. G18 986, 4, p. 37 (General Authors' Ledger); G19 007, Reel 22, 42, p. 411 (Publication Ledger 1893–7); G19 021, Reel 36, 71, p. 266 (Agreement and Public Register 1887–98).
31 REC, undated, unsourced reviews.
32 Copies of wills in French; letter, Charlotte to Willie, 17 August [1898] mentions three wills (E. Jones).
33 Letter, Edith to Willie, 22 December 1908.
34 Charlotte described the painting in her will as 'the admirable Portrait of my dear Father'.

EPILOGUE

1 EAH diary, 10 February 1898.
2 Death certificate, Queensland, 1897/4239/388.
3 Letter, Koozee to Willie, 6 September 1898 (E. Jones).
4 Melbourne *Punch*, 4 June 1896.
5 Some examples: 'Cooking for the Masses', 25 January 1902; 'Our Kitchens', 1 February 1902, 'Qualifications of a Cook', 8 February 1902; 'The Beginning and End of Dinner', 15 February 1902; 'The Horror of Housework', 22 February 1902; 'A Dinner of Herbs', 12 April 1902.
6 Newspaper cuttings, R. Erdos.
7 Letters Koozee to Fauvette Loureiro, from various addresses in Victorian Western District (R. Erdos).
8 Death certificate 5562/1907.

Notes

9   Letter, Edith to Willie, 22 December 1908 (E. Jones).
10 Death certificate 5829/1908; *Tasmanian Mail*, 8 August 1908.
11 Will, Charlotte Huybers; letter P.W. Tocknell, Assistant Manager Necropolis, Springvale to author, 24 August 1990.
12 Greco, p. 5B.
13 Letter, Edith to Willie, undated [?1906], Richmond Hill, NY.
14 EAH diary, 27 April 1913: 'Jack lives near Boston with his Greek friend'.
15 Published in Boston by Lothrop, Lee and Shepard, 1913. Demetrios was later on the staff of the Pennsylvania Academy of Fine Arts.
16 *Tasmanian Mail*, 23 September 1920; EAH diary, 17 March 1921.
17 For example, 'Gustave Courbet and His Country', vol. 10, 1922; 'Henri Marten and His Art', vol. 10, 1922; 'Emile Claus, His Art and His Country', vol. 12, 1924; 'The Art of Paul Landowski', vol. 16, 1927.
18 Letter, Huybers Memorial Fund Committee, undated (E. Jones).
19 Letter, Edith to Willie, Chichester Avenue, Richmond Hill, NY, 1 January 1904 (E. Jones).
20 EAH diary, 9 October 1941.
21 Correspondence with Ray Beilby, 1967, FL F272.
22 FBB, p. 5.

Bibliography

WORKS BY TASMA (BY DATE OF PUBLICATION)

Novels

Uncle Piper of Piper's Hill. An Australian Novel, 1 vol., Trübner & Co., London, 1889
—— , 2nd edn, 1889
—— , F.F. Lovell and Co., New York, 1889 (Lovell's international series No. 33)
—— , G. Munro, New York, 1889 (Seaside library No. 1217)
—— , Harper & Bros, New York, 1889 (Harper's Franklin Square library No. 652)
—— 2 vols, B. Tauchnitz, Leipzig, 1889
Uncle Piper of Piper's Hill. A Novel, E. A Petherick, Melbourne, William Heinemann, London, 1891 (Colonial edition) (Petherick's collection of favourite and approved authors No. 97)
—— , William Heinemann, London, 1892 (Popular edn)
Uncle Piper of Piper's Hill, eds Cecil Hadgraft and Ray Beilby, Nelson, Melbourne, 1969
Uncle Piper of Piper's Hill, Pandora, London, 1987 (intro. Margaret Harris)

A Sydney Sovereign and other Tales, Trübner & Co., London, 1890
—— , Lovell, New York, 1889

In Her Earliest Youth, 3 vols, Kegan Paul, Trench, Trübner & Co., London, 1890
In Her Earliest Youth. A Novel, 1 vol., Kegan Paul, Trench, Trübner & Co., London, 1890
—— , Indian and Colonial series, Kegan Paul, 1890
—— , Harper and Bros, New York, 1890 (Harper's Franklin Square library No. 670)
—— , F.F. Lovell and Co., New York, 1890 (Lovell's international series No. 66)
—— , Kegan Paul, Trench, Trübner & Co., London, 1891

The Penance of Portia James, 1 vol., William Heinemann, London: 1891

—— , J. W. Lovell Co., New York, 1891 (Lovell's international series No. 187)
—— , United States Book Co., New York, 1891
—— , E.A. Petherick & Co., Melbourne, William Heinemann, London, 1891 (Colonial edition) (Petherick's collection of favourite and approved authors No. 95)
—— , Heinemann and Balstier, Leipzig, 1891 (The English Library No. 69)
—— , Heinemann and Balstier, Leipzig, 1893 (The English Library No. 160)
—— , William Heinemann, London, 1894
—— , William Heinemann, London, 1899

A Knight of the White Feather, 2 vols, William Heinemann, London, 1892
The White Feather, Lovell, Coryell and Co., New York, 1892
A Knight of the White Feather, 1 vol., E.A. Petherick & Co., Melbourne, William Heinemann, London, 1893 (Petherick's collection of favourite and approved authors No. 111)
—— 1 vol., Heinemann and Balestier, Leipzig, 1893 (English Library No. 160)

Not Counting the Cost, 3 vols, R. Bentley, London, 1895
—— 1 vol., D. Appleton and Co., New York, 1895 (Appleton's Town and Country Library No. 175)

A Fiery Ordeal, 1 vol., R. Bentley and Son, London, 1897
—— , D. Appleton and Co., New York, 1898
—— , D. Appleton and Co., New York, 1898 (Appleton's town and country library No. 233)

Novels as serials

'The Pipers of Piper's Hill', The Novelist, *Australasian*, 7 January–12 May 1888
'In Her Earliest Youth', The Novelist, *Australasian*, 4 January–7 June 1890
'The Penance of Portia James', Feuilleton, *World*, 29 July–18 November 1891

Short stories

'Barren Love' in ed. Garnet Walch, *'Hash': A Mixed Dish for Christmas with Ingredients by various Australian Authors*, P.E. Reynolds, Melbourne, 1877
    also in *A Sydney Sovereign*, 1890
    eds Elizabeth Webby and Lydia Wevers, *Happy Endings. Stories by Australian and New Zealand Women*, Allen & Unwin, Sydney, 1987
'Malus Oculus' in ed. 'The Vagabond', *The 'Vagabond' Annual. Christmas 1877*, George Robertson, Melbourne, 1877
'How a Claim was Nearly Jumped in Gum-Tree Gully', *Australasian*, 19 January 1878, p. 70
    also in *A Sydney Sovereign*, 1890
    eds Cecil Hadgraft and Richard Wilson, *A Century of Australian Short Stories*, Heinemann, London, 1963
'Monsieur Caloche' in *Australasian*, 27 April, 4 May 1878
    also in *A Sydney Sovereign*, 1890

ed. Philip Mennell, *In Australian Wilds, and other Colonial Tales and Sketches*, Hutchinson and Co., London, 1889

ed. Colin Roderick, *Australian Round-Up. Stories from 1790 to 1950*, Angus and Robertson, Sydney, 1953

ed. Fiona Giles, *From the Verandah. Stories of Love and Landscape by Nineteenth Century Australian Women*, McPhee Gribble/Penguin Books, Melbourne, 1987

ed. Lynne Spender, *Her Selection: Writings by Nineteenth-Century Australian Women*, Penguin Books, Ringwood, Vic., 1988 (part only)

Connie Burns and Marygai McNamara, *Eclipsed. Two Centuries of Australian Women's Fiction*, Collins, Sydney, 1988

ed. Mary Lord, *The Penguin Best Australian Short Stories*, Penguin Books, Ringwood, Vic., 1991

'A Philanthropist's Experiment' in *Australasian*, 3 August 1878, pp. 134–5

also in *A Sydney Sovereign*, 1890

'The Rubria Ghost' in ed. F.R.C. Hopkins, *The Australian Ladies' Annual*, McCarron, Bird, Melbourne, 1878

also in *From the Verandah*, 1987

'Concerning the Forthcoming Melbourne Cup' in *The Australian Ladies' Annual*, 1878

'What an Artist Discovered in Tasmania' in ed. Garnet Walch, *Australasia: An Intercolonial Christmas Annual*, George Robertson, Melbourne, 1878

'L'amour aux Antipodes' in *La nouvelle revue* (Paris), August 1880

also in *l'Indépendance belge*, 11, 13, 16, 17, 18, 21, 23, 24 September 1880

'Mr Schenck's Pupil' in The Storyteller, *Australasian*, 14 March 1885, p. 522; 21 March 1885, p. 570; 28 March 1885, pp. 617–8; 4 April 1885, p. 666; 11 April 1885, pp. 713–4

'A Sydney Sovereign' in The Storyteller, *Australasian* 15, 22, 29 January, 5, 12, 19 February 1888

also in *A Sydney Sovereign*, 1890

'John Grantley's Conversion' in ed. Mrs Patchett Martin, *Under the Gum Tree. Australian 'Bush' Stories by Mrs Campbell Praed and others*, Trischler & Co., London, 1890

'A Wool-King's Widow' in Town and Country Tales, *World*, 2 July 1890

'His Modern Godiva' in Town and Country Tales, *World*, 23 July 1890

'The Lady of the Christmas Card' in Town and Country Tales, *World*, 24 December 1890

'An Antipodean Heiress' in Town and Country Tales, *World*, 22 July 1891

'An Old time Episode in Tasmania' in ed. H.A. Patchett Martin, *Coo-ee: Tales of Australian Life by Australian Ladies*, Griffith, Farran, Okeden and Welsh, London, 1891 (colonial edition)

also in ed. Dale Spender, *The Penguin Anthology of Australian Women's Writing*, Penguin Books, Ringwood, Vic., 1988

also in eds Ken Goodwin and Alan Lawson, *The Macmillan Anthology of Australian Literature*, Macmillan, South Melbourne, Vic., 1990

'Bertha and the Snake' in ed. A. Patchett Martin, *Over the Sea. Stories of Two Worlds*, Griffith, Farran, Okeden & Welsh, London, 1891

'Sick unto Death', Chapter XXIII, 30 April 1892 in 'The Fate of Fenella', *Gentlewoman*, 25 December 1891–6 May 1892

Bibliography

'Gran'ma'[s] Tale', *Queensland Pastoral News*, February–August 1936

Articles

'A Hint for the Paris Commissioners', The Lady's Column, *Australasian*, 24 November 1877, p. 743

'Fable for a Rainy Day', The Contributor, *Australasian*, 15 December 1877, pp. 742–3

'Holiday Impressions of Tasmania', The Tourist, *Australasian*, 30 March 1878, p. 391

'A Novel by M. Zola', The Contributor, *Australasian*, 1 June 1878, p. 680

'About Burial', *Melbourne Review*, vol. III, no. 11, July 1878

'A Passing Glimpse of Cape Town', 3 parts, The Traveller, Part I, *Australasian*, 6 September 1879, p. 295; II, 13 September 1879, p. 326; III, 20 September 1879, pp. 357–8

'Home Impressions. A Sermon, a Play and a Wedding', two parts, The Sketcher, *Australasian*, 11 October 1879, pp. 454–5; Concluded, 18 October 1879, pp. 487

'Notes from Paris. The Comedié Française in England, from a French Point of View', The Traveller, *Australasian*, 10 January 1880 pp. 38–9

'Notes from Paris', The Traveller, *Australasian*, 21 February 1880, p. 231

'Professor Nordenskiold's North-East Passage', two parts, The Traveller, *Australasian*, 12 June 1880, p. 744; Concluded, 19 June 1880, p. 774

'The Familistere of Guise', The Traveller, *Australasian*, 21 August 1880, pp. 230–1

'Art Gossip and the Paris Salon. No. I—Realism' (two parts), Fine Arts, *Australasian*, 11 September 1880, pp. 326–7; no other parts found

'A Communistic Gathering', The Sketcher, *Australasian*, 5 March 1881, p. 294

'Literary Notes from Paris', The Traveller, *Australasian*, 16 April 1881, p. 488

'A Zinc Foundry in Belgium', The Traveller, *Australasian*, 21 May 1881, p. 647

'Bordeaux, in its Relation with Australia', Part I, The Traveller, *Australasian*, 11 June 1881, p. 743; II, 18 June 1881, p. 775

'An Interview with the King of the Belgians', The Traveller, *Australasian*, 16 July 1881, p. 71

'The "Actualités" of Paris', The Traveller, *Australasian*, 30 July 1881, p. 136

'Les femmes qui tuent and les femmes qui volent', *Victorian Review*, vol. 4, no. 1, August 1881

'Autumn in Paris', The Traveller, *Australasian*, 14 January 1882, p. 39

'Professor Tyndall on Molecules', Scientific, *Australasian*, 15 April 1882, p. 455

'Literary Notes from Paris', The Contributor, *Australasian*, 29 July 1882, S.852, pp. 2–3

'A Trip through Central Europe. Hamburg' (six parts), The Wanderer, *Australasian*, 2 December 1882, S.870, p. 3

'A Trip through Central Europe. Berlin', The Wanderer, *Australasian*, 16 December 1882, S.872, pp. 2–3

'A Trip through Central Europe, Dresden-Prague', The Wanderer, *Australasian*, 20 January 1883, S.877, pp. 3–4

'A Trip through Central Europe, Vienna I', The Wanderer, *Australasian*, 3 February 1883, S.879, 3–4

'A Trip through Central Europe. Vienna II', The Wanderer, *Australasian*, 17 February 1883, S.881, p. 3

'A Trip through Central Europe, Buda-Pest', The Wanderer, *Australasian*, 10 March 1883, S.884, p. 3

'To Australia by a Messageries Steamer Part I', two parts The Tourist, *Australasian*, 11 August 1883, S.906, pp. 3–4; II, 18 August 1883, S.907, pp. 3–4

'Monsieur Renan's Reminiscences (Souvenirs d'enfance et de jeunesse), *Victorian Review*, 1 December 1883

'A Letter from Florence', two parts, The Traveller, *Australasian*, 10 May 1884, S.945, p. 3; 24 May 1884, S.947, p. 3

'A Latter-day Pilgrimage', four parts, The Traveller, *Australasian*, I, 23 August 1884; II, 30 August 1884, pp. 426–7; III, 6 September 1884, pp. 474–5; IV, 13 September 1884, pp. 523

'A Letter from Paris', Society and Fashion, *Australasian*, 11 July 1885, p. 56

'What is to be seen at Treves', The Traveller, *Australasian*, 20 March 1886, pp. 572–3

'The Lady Barrister of Brussels' (By a Lady Who Knows Her) [Madamoiselle Popelin], *Pall Mall Gazette, An Evening Newspaper and Review*, 6 December 1888

'The Royal Marriage in Greece', three parts, No. I, *Argus*, 17 December 1889; No. 2, 19 December 1889; No. 3, 20 December 1889

(Note: More articles and short stories by Tasma probably remain to be discovered)

Translation

Les origines de la forme républicaine du government dans les Etats-Unis d'Amérique, trs avec l'autorisation de l'auteur, sur la 3 ed. rev. par Madame Auguste Couvreur. Avec une préface de Emile de Laveleye, C. Muquardt, Bruxelles, F. Alcan, Paris, 1890, 197 pp. [Straus, Oscar Solomon, *The origins of the republican form of government in the United States of America*, with an introductory essay by Emile de Laveleye (tr. from the French edition), 2nd revised edn, G.P. Putnam's Sons, New York and London, 1901, first published 1885, edns 1887, 1901, 1926.]

Lectures

'L'Australie et les avantages qu'elle offre a l'emigration Française', 20 July 1880, *Bulletin de géographie commerciale de Paris*, Paris, 1880

'Queensland. La dernière née des colonies Australiennes, son bétail, son coton, son sucre', June 1883, *Bulletin de la société de géographie commerciale de Paris*, Au Siège de la Société, Paris, 1883

'Melbourne et le Bush Australien', 14 February 1889, *Compte-Rendu des actes de la société royale belge de géographie*, vol. 13, no. 1, January–February, 1889

—— ibid., *l'Indépendance belge*, 17 February 1889

'Le Tasmanie: Voyage par le cap Horn', 23 March 1892, *Compte-Rendu des actes de la société royale belge de géographie*, vol. 16, no. 2, March–April, 1892

(Note: There are shorter reports of many other lectures in newspapers)

GENERAL BIBLIOGRAPHY

Manuscripts and unpublished material

Archives of Kegan Paul, Trench, Trübner and Henry S. King 1853–1912, Chadwyck-Healey, Bishops Stortford, Herts, 1974, NLA G14 910–14 936

Archives of Richard Bentley and Son, 1829–98, Chadwyck-Healey, Bishops Stortford, Herts, 1974. NLA G20 811–14

Beilby, Ray, Biographical material, letters, research material on Tasma, FL MSS F232

Buchanan, Joan Matilda, 'Mrs Charles Meredith. A Biography 1812–1895', NLA MS 312

Couvreur, Jessie, Journal, 1889–1891, Brussels, 1 January 1889–11 July 1891, Original Renée Erdos. Microfilm ML Mfm FM 4/447; NLA Mfm G24 751; FL MSS F234

——— , Reviews of publications with other contributions to periodicals, FL MSS F233

Deakin, Catherine, Diary, NLA MS 1540

Erdos, Renée, Diaries Jessie Couvreur; letters, reviews, cuttings (reviews and biographical)

Falkiner, Bill, Letter

Fraser, Jessie, Diary, 1873, Windward, London (R. Erdos)

Fryer Library, F233, Copies of articles by Tasma

Hutchinson, Ben (comp.), 'Bibliography of Tasma' (Madame Jessie Catherine Couvreur), 1987

Huybers, Edith Charlotte, Diary, 1873–1875, London, Brussels, Paris, Melbourne, FL MSS F371

Huybers, Edward Alfred, Cuttings 1880–1900, FL MSS F372

——— Diary and autobiography, 1877–1937, FL MSS F373

——— 'From Birth to Borderland', autobiography, ML MSS 1423

——— 'The Philosopher of the Café Greco', autobiography, FL MSS F374

Huybers, Kenneth, Family letters, photographs etc.

James, Margaret, 'Marriage and Marital Breakdown in Victoria, 1860–1960', PhD Thesis, La Trobe University, March 1984, Family Information Centre, Institute of Family Studies

Jones, Enid, Family letters, Simeon family, to Charles Ogleby and Charlotte Huybers, letters to William Huybers, death records, wills, cuttings etc.

Jordens, Ann-Mari, 'Cultural Life in Melbourne 1870–1880', MA Thesis, University of Melbourne, 1967

Kyneton Historical Society, Collection of cuttings; A History of Kyneton series, published as series in Kyneton Guardian

London Times Archives, Manager's Letter Book 5: 14 January 1892–3 August 1892; 9: 3 January–28 August 1894; 10:29 August 1894–6 March 1895; 11: 6 March–8 April 1895; 12: 9 April–7 November 1895; 13: 7 November 1895–27 May 1896; 14: 28 May 1896–12 January 1897; 15: 12 January 1897–22 July 1897 (No. 16 is missing)

——— Foreign Manager's Letter Book 2: 29 August 1893–28 May 1895; 3: 29 May 1895–29 November 1897

McCallum, Helen, 'William Shiels and Divorce Law Reform in Victoria 1883–1890', BA Hons Thesis, ANU, 1970, NLA MS 2441

Roe, Jillian Isobel, 'A decade of assessment. Being a study in the intellectual life of the city of Melbourne between 1876 and 1886', MA Thesis, ANU, 1965
Smith, C.P., 'Men Who Made "The Argus" and "The Australasian" 1846–1925', LL MS 10727 MSB 312
Union Bank records, Group Archive, ANZ Bank, Melbourne, 1868–73

Official records

Birth, death, marriage certificates: England, Tasmania, Victoria, Queensland, Belgium
Census, 1841, 1851 United Kingdom
France. Ministère de l'Education Nationale. Records l'Ordre des Palmes Académiques
Land records: Tasmanian Titles Office; Victorian Lands Office
Victoria, *Acts of Parliament*, Divorce, 1859, 1860–1, 1864–65, 1889
Victoria, *Parliamentary Debates*, 1860–74, 1883
Victoria, Supreme Court Records
Victorian Public Records Series. Divorce and Matrimonial Court Book
Wills, probate records: England, Tasmania, Victoria

Articles, pamphlets

d'Alviella, Count Goblet, 'Nécrologie Auguste Couvreur', *Société d'archéologie de Bruxelles annuaire*, vol. 16, Brussels, 1895
Birkett, Winifred, 'Some Pioneer Australian Women Writers', in Flora S. Eldershaw, *The Peaceful Army A Memorial to the Pioneer Women of Australia 1788–1938*, Women's Executive Committee 150th Anniversary Celebrations, Sydney, 1938
Boldrewood, Rolf (T.A. Bowne), 'Heralds of Australian Literature', *Australian Association for the Advancement of Science*, Report of 4th Meeting, Hobart, January 1892
Cathedral Church of St David, Hobart, n.d., n.p.
Clark, Jane, 'Arthur José de Souza Loureiro 1853–1932', *Art and Australia*, vol. 23, no. 1, Spring 1985
Ecole Couvreur professionnelle et ménére, Brussels, 1913
Embling, Thomas, 'Premature Internments', *Victorian Review*, May 1882
Harris, Margaret, 'The Writing of Tasma, The Work of Jessie Couvreur', ed. Debra Adelaide, *A Bright and Fiery Troop. Australian Women Writers of the Nineteenth Century*, Penguin Books, Ringwood, Vic., 1988
Higgins, Susan, ' "That Singular Anomaly, the Lady Novelist" in 1888', *Australia 1888*, vol. 7, April 1981
Hutchinson, R.C., 'Mrs Hutchinson and the Female Factories of Early Australia', *Tasmanian Historical Research Association Papers and Proceedings*, vol. IX, no. 2, December 1963
Levett, John, 'The Tasmanian Public Library in 1850', in *Books, Libraries and Readers in Colonial Australia*, eds Elizabeth Morrison and Michael Talbot, Graduate School of Librarianship, Clayton, Vic., 1985
Mackay, Edward Alan, 'The First Flour Mills of Port Phillip', *Victorian Historical Magazine*, vol. XVI, no. 4, November 1937

Bibliography

McLaren, Ian F., ' "Como", an Historic Melbourne Home', Royal Historical Society of Victoria, 22 June 1957

Malone, Betty, ' "From Como House to Como City"—a Study in Diversity', Prahran's Heritage No. 4, Prahran Historical and Arts Society, 1989

Mickle, D.J., 'Origins of the name "Yarraman" and some Yarraman history', Gippsland Gate, vol. 5, no. 4, June 1976

National Trust of Australia (Victoria) Photographic Committee Tour 72, 'Kyneton and District Tour', 9–11 March 1991

Nield, James Edward, 'On the Advantages of Burning the Dead', Transactions and Proceedings of the Royal Society of Victoria, vol. 11, 1874

Sève, Edouard, 'A. Couvreur. Portrait avec Notice Biographique', Galerie de l'Association Internationale pour le progrès des Sciences Sociales, 1864

Shaw, A.G.L., 'The Origins of the Probation System in Van Diemen's Land', Historical Studies, Australia and New Zealand, vol. 6, no. 21, November 1953

A Short Guide to the Cathedral Church of St David, plus notes 1803–42 and 1842–63

Stephenson, B., 'History of Malmsbury', Typescript [1924? or 1927?]

Sussex, Lucy, 'Tasma's First Publication', Australian Literary Studies, vol. 15, no. 3, May 1992

Valerio, Edith, 'Gustave Courbet and his Country', Art in America, vol. 10, 1922

'British Novelists in Belgium. "Tasma" at Home', Galignani's Messenger, 16 November 1890

'Some Australian Women. Part II "Tasma" ', Illustrated Sydney News, 25 April 1891

' "Tasma" (Mme Auguste Couvreur)', Queen, the Lady's Newspaper, 13 January 1894

'Well-known Women. Madame Couvreur (Tasma)', Home Notes, 14 November 1896

Newspapers, periodicals

Annuaire, Société d'archéologie de Bruxelles, 16, 1895
Annual Register, 1894
Australasian, 1878–90, 1897, 1900
Australasian Sketcher, 1873
Australian Journal 1863–66, 1869
Brisbane Courier, 1933
British Australasian, 1897
British Medical Journal, 1884
Bulletin, 1991
Bulletin communal (Brussels) 1874, 1885, 1895
Galignani's Messenger (Paris), 1890
Gentlewoman, 1891–2
Hobart Mercury, 1860–93
Hobart Town Courier, 1852–3
Home Notes, 1896
Illustrated Australian News, 1888, 1891
Illustrated Melbourne Post, 1865
Illustrated Sydney News, 1891, 1894
Illustrated Tasmanian Mail, formerly Tasmanian Mail, 1908, 1920, 1934–5
l'Indépendance belge, 1880–3, 1889–92
Kyneton Guardian, 1857–1900, 1913

Kyneton Observer, 1867
Lancet, 1884
Launceston Examiner, 1884
London Times, 1873, 1887, 1894–7
Melbourne Age, 1873, 1883
Melbourne Argus, 1867, 1873–84, 1889, 1894, 1913
Melbourne Leader
Melbourne Herald, 1971
Melbourne Review, 1878–9
La nouvelle revue (Paris), 1879–89
Pall Mall Budget, 1889–1890
Pall Mall Gazette, 1889–1891
Queen, The Lady's Newspaper, 1894
Queensland Pastoral News, 1936
Spectator (London), 1886–90
Table Talk, 1888, 1890–3, 1899
Victorian Review, 1881–3
Weekly Times, 1883
World: A Journal for Men and Women (London), 1890–7

Books

Adam, Juliette (Lamber), *My Literary Life*, D. Appleton and Co., New York, 1904 NLA Mfm 1424, Reel 625, No. 4991, History of Women series.

Adelaide, Debra, *Australian Women Writers. A Bibliographic Guide*, Pandora, London, 1988

Ascherson, Neal, *The King Incorporated. Leopold II in the Age of Trusts*, George Allen & Unwin, London, 1963

Aspinall, Clara, *Three Years in Australia*, L. Booth, London, 1862

Australian Dictionary of Biography, 1–6, Melbourne University Press, Carlton, Vic., 1966–76

Baldick, Robert, *The Life of J.-K. Huysmans*, The Clarendon Press, Oxford, 1955

Bell, E. Moberly, *Flora Shaw (Lady Lugard D.B.E.)*, Constable, London, 1947

Bennett, Daphne, *Emily Davies and the Liberation of Women 1830–1921*, André Deutsch, London, 1990

Bibliographie nationale, Dictionnaire des ecrivans belges, 1830–1880, P. Weiussenbrugh, Bruxelles, 1886

Biographie coloniale belge, 14, Bruxelles, 1955

Biographie nationale, L'Académie royale des sciences, des lettres et des beaux-arts de Belgique, Bruxelles, vol. 43, suppl. 5, 1983–84

Bradstock, Margaret and Wakeling, Louise, *Rattling the Orthodoxies, A Life of Ada Cambridge*, Penguin Books, Ringwood, Vic., 1991

Branca, Patricia, *Women in Europe since 1750*, Croom Helm, London, 1978

Brand, Ian, *The Convict Probation System: Van Diemen's Land 1839–1854*, Blubber Head Press, Hobart, 1990

Bremner, G. A., *They're Racing at Kyneton. A History of the Kyneton District Racing Club, 1866–1974*, n.p., Kyneton

British Library, *The British Library General Catalogue of Printed Books to 1975*, K.G. Saur, London, 1983

Burke's *Peerage, Baronetage, Knightage*, Harrison and Sons, London, 1910

Byrne, Desmond, *Australian Writers*, Richard Bentley, London, 1896

'The Captain', *In Old Days and These*, Monotone Art Printers, Hobart, 1930

—— *Old Landmarks of Hobart Town*, Hobart, J. Walch, 1931

Clark, Jane and Whitelaw, Bridget, *Golden Summers. Heidelberg and Beyond*, International Cultural Corporation of Australia, Melbourne, 1985

Clarke, Patricia, *Pen Portraits, Women Writers and Journalists in Nineteenth-Century Australia*, Allen & Unwin, Sydney, 1988

—— and Spender, Dale (eds), *Life Lines. Australian Women's Letters and Diaries, 1788–1840*, Allen & Unwin, Sydney, 1992

Cooper, John Butler, *The History of Prahran 1836–1924*, Modern Printing Co., Melbourne, 1924

Cooper, John Butler, *The History of St Kilda 1840–1930*, vols I & II, Printers Pty Ltd, Melbourne, 1931

Crow, Duncan, *The Victorian Woman*, George Allen and Unwin, London, 1971

Cunningham, Gail, *The New Woman and the Victorian Novel*, Macmillan, London, 1978

Curl, James Stevens, *A Celebration of Death*, Constable, London, 1980

Debrett's *Peerage, Baronetage, Knightage and Companionage*, Dean and Son, London, 1911, 1918

Demetrios, George, illust. John Huybers, *When I was a Boy in Greece*, Lee and Shepard, Boston, 1913

Deuel, Leo, *Memoirs of Heinrich Schliemann. A documentary portrait drawn from his autobiographical writings, letters and excavation reports*, Harper and Row, New York, 1977

Dilke, C. W., *Greater Britain: a record of travel in the English speaking countries during 1886–7* (2nd edition), London, 1889

—— *Problems of Greater Britain*, London, 1890 (NLA MC756 CIHM, No. 6286, 7)

Eastman, Hugh Malcolm, *Memoirs of a Sheepman*, Halstead Press, Deniliquin, NSW Sydney, 1953

Eglise et enseignement actes du colloque du 1o anniversaire de l'Institut d'histoire du Christianisme de l'université libre de Bruxelles, l'Université de Bruxelles, Bruxelles, 1880–84

Emerson, Barbara, *Leopold II of the Belgians. King of Colonialism*, Weidenfeld and Nicolson, London, 1979

Evans-Pritchard, E.E., *The Sociology of Comte. An Appreciation*, Manchester University Press, Manchester, 1970

Falkiner, Suzanne, *The Writers' Landscape: Wilderness, Settlement*, Simon and Schuster, East Roseville, NSW, 1992

Foster, Joseph, *Men-at-the-Bar*, Reeves and Turner, London, 1885

Fox, Shirley, *An Art Students's Reminiscences of Paris in the Eighties*, Mills and Boon, London, 1909

Garryowen, *The Chronicles of Early Melbourne, 1835 to 1851*, vol. 2, Fergusson and Mitchell, Melbourne, 1888

Giordano, Margaret and Norman, Don, *Tasmanian Literary Landmarks*, Shearwater Press, Hobart, 1984

Gott, Ted, *The Enchanted Stone, the Graphic Worlds of Odilon Redon*, National Gallery of Victoria, Melbourne, 1990

Green, Frank C., *The Tasmanian Club 1861–1961*, n.p., Hobart, 1961

Green H.M., *A History of Australian Literature*, Angus and Robertson, Sydney, 1961

Greenhalgh, Paul, *Ephemeral Vistas. The Expositions Universelles, Great Exhibitions and World's Fairs 1851–1939*, Manchester University Press, Manchester, 1988

Griffin, Graeme M. and Tobin, Des, *The Australian Response to Death*, Melbourne University Press, Melbourne, 1982

Habrekorn, Daniel, *Lettres Correspondance à Trois Réunies et présentées*, Les Editions Thot, Vanves, 1980

Hadgraft, Cecil and Beilby, Ray, *Australian Writers and their Work. Ada Cambridge, Tasma and Rosa Praed*, Oxford University Press, Melbourne, 1979

Hay, Bertine, *History of the Fraser and Agnew Families*, priv. pub., 1972

Hergenham, Laurie (ed.), *The Penguin New Literary History of Australia*, Penguin Books, Ringwood, Vic., 1988

Hewat, Tim, *Golden Fleeces. The Falkiners of Boonoke*, Bay Books, Sydney, 1980

Hibbins, G. M., *A History of the City of Springvale. Constellation of Communities*, City of Springvale/Lothian, Port Melbourne, Vic., 1984

History of Kyneton 1836–1900, compiled from the files of the *Kyneton Observer* (1856–1862), the *Kyneton Guardian* (1836 et seq.), *Kyneton Guardian* (1934–5)

Horstman, Allen, *Victorian Divorce*, Croom Helm, London, 1985, pp. 105–6

Humphreys, H.M. (compiler), *Men of the Time in Australia*, Vic. series, 2nd edn, McCarron, Bird, Melbourne, 1882

James, John Stanley ('The Vagabond', 'Julian Thomas'), *The Vagabond Papers*, ed. Michael Cannon, Hyland House, Melbourne, 1969

Jones, Lewis and Peggy, *The Flour Mills of Victoria 1840–1990. An Historical Record*, Flour Millers' Council of Victoria, Melbourne, 1990

Jullian, Philippe, *Dreams of Decadence*, Phaidon, London, 1971

Keay, Carolyn, *Odilon Redon*, Academy Editions, London, 1977

Laver, James, *The First Decadent, being the Strange Life of J.K. Huysmans*, Faber and Faber, London, 1954

——, *French Painting and the Nineteenth Century*, B.T. Batsford, London, 1937

Lee, Sidney (ed.), *Dictionary of National Biography*, Smith Elder, London, 1897

Library of Congress, *National Union Catalog, Pre-1956 Imprints*, Mansell Information, London, 1974

Lodewycks, K A., *The Belgians in Australia*, Boolarong Publications, Brisbane, 1988

Love, Harold, *James Henry Nield. Victorian Virtuoso*, Melbourne University Press, Melbourne, 1989

McGuire, Frank, *A Brief History of the City of Mordialloc*, Community Committee for Victoria's 150th Anniversary, Mordialloc, 1985

Marvin, F.S., *Comte. The Founder of Sociology*, Chapman and Hall, London, 1936

Mennell, Philip, *Dictionary of Australasian Biography*, Hutchinson, London, 1892

——, *In Australian Wilds, and other Colonial Tales and Sketches*, Hutchinson, London, 1889

Miller, E. Morris, *Australian Literature 1795–1938*, Sydney University Press, Sydney, 1973

Morton, Thomas, *Speed the Plough: a Comedy in Five Acts*, Mathew Carey, Philadelphia, 1807 NLA Mfm 13147

Bibliography

Mumby, Frank Arthur, *Publishing and Bookselling: A History from the Earliest Times to the Present Day*, Jonathan Cape, London, 1934

Norman, L., *Pioneer Shipping of Tasmania*, Shearwater Press, Hobart, 1989

—— *Sea Wolves and Bandits*, J. Walch, Hobart, 1946

O'Connor, Lillian, *Pioneer Women Orators*, Columbia University Press, New York, 1954

Pacini, John, *A Century Galloped by. The First Hundred Years of the Victoria Racing Club*, Victoria Racing Club, Melbourne, 1984

[Phillips, John], *Reminiscences of Australian Early Life, by a Pioneer*, A.P. Marsden, London, 1893

Poe, Edgar Allan, 'The Premature Burial' in *Selected Tales*, ed. John Curtis, Penguin Books, Harmondsworth, UK, 1956

Prevost, M., d'Amat, Roman and de Morembert, H. Tribout (eds), *Dictionnaire de Biographie Française*, Paris

Rae-Ellis, Vivienne, *Louisa Anne Meredith. A Tigress in Exile*, Blubber Head Press, Hobart, 1979

Raitt, A.W., *The Life of Villiers de L'Isle-Adam*, The Clarendon Press, Oxford, 1981

Randell, J.O., *Pastoral Settlement in Northern Victoria, Vol. I, The Coliban District*, Queensberry Hill Press, Melbourne, 1979

—— *Pastoral Settlement in Northern Victoria, Vol. II, The Campaspe District*, Chandos Publishing Co., Burwood, Vic., 1982

Richardson, John, *Highgate. Its History since the Fifteenth Century*, Historical Publications Ltd, New Barnet, Herts, 1983

Ridge, George Ross, *Joris-Karl Huysmans*, Twayne's World Authors Series, New York, 1968

Robb, E. M., *Early Toorak and District*, Robertson and Mullens, Melbourne, 1934

Ronald, Robert B., *The Riverina: People and Properties*, F.W. Cheshire, Melbourne, 1960

Rotberg, Robert I., *The Founder. Cecil Rhodes and the Pursuit of Power*, Oxford University Press, New York, 1988

Sands and McDougall, *Directory of Victoria*, Sands and McDougall, Melbourne, 1860–1913

Saunders, David (ed.), *Historic Buildings of Victoria*, Jacaranda Press, Brisbane, 1966

Schreiner, Olive intro. Doris Leesing, *The Story of an African Farm*, Hutchinson, London, [1883] 1987 edn

de Serville, Paul, *Pounds and Pedigrees. The Upper Class in Victoria 1850–80*, Oxford University Press, Melbourne, 1991

[Shaw, Flora L.] The *Times* Special Correspondent, *Letters from Queensland*, Macmillan, London, 1893, reprinted from the *Times*, December 1892, January, February 1893

—— *The Story of Australia*, Horace Marshall and Son, London, 1897, in series The Story of the Empire, ed. Howard Angus Kennedy

Smith, James (ed.), *Cyclopaedia of Victoria*, Cyclopaedia Co, London, 1903

Spender, Dale, *Writing a New World: Two Centuries of Australian Women Writers*, Pandora, London, 1988

Stephens, Winifred, *Madame Adam (Juliette Lamber) La Grande Française. From Louis Philippe until 1917*, Chapman and Hall, London, 1917

Stevens, Roslyn (compiler), *History of Malmsbury*, n.p, 1987

Stone, Carolyn R. and Tyson, Pamela, *Old Hobart Town and Environs 1802–1855*, Pioneer Design Studio, Lilydale, Vic., 1978

Tate, Audrey, *Ada Cambridge. Her Life and Work 1844–1926*, Melbourne University Press, Carlton, Vic., 1991

Thomas, Julian (John Stanley James), *The Vagabond Papers*, ed. Michael Cannon, Hyland House, Melbourne, 1969

Thompson, Kenneth, *Auguste Comte: The Foundation of Sociology*, Thomas Nelson, London, 1976

The Times, *The History of* The Times, vol. 3, *The Twentieth Century 1884–1912*, *The Times*, London, 1947

Who's Who in Australia, International Press Services, Sydney, 1929

Wilde, William H., Hooton, Joy and Andrews, Barry, *The Oxford Companion to Australian Literature*, Oxford Univerity Press, Melbourne, 1985

NEWSPAPER REPORTS OF LECTURES

FL F372 1. Société de géographie commerciale de Paris, 21 December 1880; 2. Société de géographie d'Anvers, n.d. [March 1881]; 3. Arts, Sciences & Littérature, n.d. [Artistic and Literary Circle, Brussels, 25 March 1881]; 4. Lettres, sciences et arts n.d. [Artistic and Literary Circle, Brussels, 25 March 1881]; 5. Belgique n.d. [received by King, 20 March 1881]; 6. Chronique de la ville, n.d. [received by King, 20 March 1881]; 7. La France—25 Mars 1881 [Artistic and Literary Circle, Brussels, 25 March 1881]; 8. Soirées populaires, n.d.; 9. Anvers, 17 Mars, [Artistic Circle, Antwerp, 16 March 1881]; 10. Cercle artistique et littéraire [Artistic and Literary Circle, Brussels, 25 March 1881]; 11. Untitled [Cercle des anciens normalistes, late March 1881]; 12. En Australie. Causerie populaire [Philotechnique Association Boulogne-sur-Seine, 31 March 1881]; 13. Madame Tasma aux soirées populaires, n.d. [Popular evenings, Brussels, April 1881]; 14. Association philotechnique conférence, n.d. [Philotechnique Association, Boulogne-sur-Seine, 31 March 1881]; 15. untitled, n.d., Echo du Parlement; 16. Au Cercle, n.d. [Artistic and Literary Circle, Brussels, winter 1881–2]; 17. Arts, Sciences et Lettres, n.d. [Artistic Circle, Ghent, winter 1881–2]; 18. untitled [Artistic and Literary Circle, Brussels, winter 1881–82]; 19. untitled, n.d. [received by King, 20 March 1881]; 20. Société de géographie, *Précurseur*, Anvers, Mars 1889; 21. Nouvelles du monde, [Talk given to Geographic Society, Paris, December 1880]; 22. untitled [received by King, 20 March 1881]; 23. untitled [Artistic and Literary Circle, Brussels, winter 1881–2]; 24. untitled [Note on unspecified speech]; 25. *Indépendance belge*, 24 March 1892 [Royal Belgian Society of Geography—Tasmania and *Windward*]; 26. Roubaix, *Journal de Roubaix*, April 1893 [Lecture at Roubaix 1892–3].

REVIEWS OF BOOKS (FROM BOOK OF CUTTINGS AND LOOSE CUTTINGS KEPT BY TASMA)

Uncle Piper of Piper's Hill

Scots Observer, 29 December 1888; *Saturday Review*, 29 December 1888; *Graphic*, 2

Bibliography

March 1889; *Scotsman*, Edinburgh, 17 December 1888; *Morning Post*, 29 December 1888; *Athenaeum*, 5 January 1889; *Pall Mall*, 11 January 1889; *Academy*, 12 January 1889; *Glasgow Herald*, 3 January 1889; *European Mail* (Patchett Martin), 10 January 1889; *Brighton Gazette and Sussex Telegraph*, 27 December 1889; *World*, 9 January 1889 (P. and Q.); *Times*, 1 June 1889; *Empire*, 12 July 1889; *Belgian News*, 20 January 1889; *Spectator*, 2 February 1889; *European Mail*, 18 January 1889; *Manchester Guardian*, 21 January 1889; *Bookseller*, January 1889; *Pall Mall*, n.d.; *The Whitehall Review*, 27 December 1888; *The Guardian*, 30 January 1889; *British Australasian*, 13 February 1889; *Linconshire Herald*, 31 August 1889; *Problems of Greater Britain*, Sir Charles Dilke [extract from book]; *The South Australian Register*, 30 January 1889; *The London Figaro*, 9 March 1889; *Illustrated London News*, 9 March 1889; *Australasian* (Melbourne), 16 February 1889; *British Australasian*, n.d.; *Belgian News*, n.d.; *Pall Mall Gazette*, 1 February 1889; *Liverpool Courier*, 7 March 1889; *Journal de Bruxelles*, 6 February 1889; 'Un Roman Australien' by Gérard Harry, *Indépendance belge*, 13 January 1889; *Précurseur*, 11 February 1889; *Kolnische Zeitung*, 2 February 1889; 'Australasie et Océanie', *Bulletin de la Société de Géographie Commerciale*, 1889, XI, no. 2; Trübner's monthly list.

A Sydney Sovereign

Scotsman, 20 January 1890; *Scottish Leader*, Edinburgh, 20 January 1890; *Manchester ?*, n.d.; *Glasgow Herald*, 30 January 1890; *Literary World*, 7 February 1890; *Lincolnshire Herald*, 6 February 1890; *Athenaeum*, 8 February 1890; *Bookseller*, 6 February 1890; *Scots Observer*, 8 February 1890; *Saturday Review*, 15 February 1890; *Hobart Mercury*, 24 February 1890; *Australasian*, 8 March 1890; *Belgian News*, 3 March 1890; *Pictorial World*, n.d; *South African Empire*, 13 June 1890

In Her Earliest Youth

Manchester Examiner, 12 April 1890; *Athenaeum*, 12 April 1890; *Times*, 2 May 1890; *Scotsman*, 7 April 1890; *Glasgow Herald*, 17 April 1890; *Woman*, 19 April 1890; *Saturday Review*, 19 April 1890; *Academy*, 24 March 1890; *Daily News*, 31 May 1890; *Spectator*, 31 May 1890; *World*, 11 June 1890; 'Bibliographie' (French lang.) quoting *Times*, n.d.; *Pall Mall Budget*, n.d.; *Manchester Guardian*, 2 December 1890; *Illustrated London News*, 31 May 1890; *Manchester Guardian*, 13 August 1890; *Indépendance belge*, 20 August 1890; *Sydney Morning Herald*, 11 September 1891; *Hood's Literary News*, Hobart, October 1890

The Penance of Portia James

Sunday Sun, 19 July 1891 (preview); *Athenaeum*, 8 December 1891; *Lady's Pictorial*, 19 December 1891; *Belgian News*, 12 December 1891; *Anti-Jacobean*, December 1891; *Literary Opinion*, December 1891; *Indépendance belge*, 27 December 1891; *Pictorial World*, December 1891; *Daily News*, 26 December 1891; *Times*, 26 December 1891; *Harok*, 8 December 1891; *National Observer*, 2 January 1892; *Academy*, 13 February 1892

A Knight of the White Feather

Spectator, November 1892; *World*, November 1892; *Speaker*, November 1892; *Vanity Fair*, 18 November 1892; *Belgian News*, November 1892; *Pall Mall*, n.d.; *Literary World*, 16 November 1892; *Manchester Examiner*, 16 November 1892; *Lady*, n.d.; *Times*, 22 December 1892; *World*, 23 December 1892; *Sheffield Daily Telegraph*, 18 November 1892; *Yorkshire Post*, 7 December 1892; *Guardian*, 30 November 1892; *Daily Chronicle*, n.d.; *Sydney Morning Herald*, 20 March 1893; unknown, n.d.; *Natal Mercury*, n.d.; *Pioneer Mail*, n.d.; *Academy*, 31 December 1892

Not Counting the Cost

Globe, September 1895; *Athenaeum*, September 1895; *Daily Chronicle*, September 1895; *Daily Telegraph*, September 1895; *Scotsman*, August 1895; *World*, August 1895; *Standard*, 8 October 1895; *Pioneer Mail*, Allahabad, c. 14 October 1895; *Guardian*, 2 October 1895; *Saturday Review*, 9 November 1895; *Queen*, 12 October 1895; *Academy*, 19 October 1895; *Spectator*, September 1895; *Morning Post*, 30 September 1895; *Daily News*, September 1895; *Pall Mall Gazette*, September 1895; *St James Gazette*, September 1895

A Fiery Ordeal

unnamed, n.d. (3 cuttings)

Index

Barrington, Sir Fitzwilliam, 4, 118
Barton Vale, 165
Bay of Biscay, 38, 111
Bay of Phaelus, 108
Baynton, Thomas, 24
Bechuanaland, 141
Belgian News, 119, 125, 181, 182, 183
Belgium, 72, 73–6, 82, 93, 96, 100,
    109, 133, 134, 135, 136–7, 139–40,
    142, 143, 154, 178
Bell, Sir Charles Frederick Moberly,
    131, 132–3, 134–5, 137, 138–9,
    140–1, 147, 184
Bell, Henri, 15
Bendigo, Vic., 5, 26
Benson, Lucy *see* Fraser, Lucy
Benson, Dr William, 91
Bentley, Richard & Son, 111, 148,
    154, 180, 185, 186
Berardi, Gaston, 96
Berardi, Léon, 96
Berardi, Madame, 116
Berlin, 85, 140, 176
Berry, Sir Graham, 69, 100, 173
'Bertha and the Snake', 124
Bibliothèque Nationale, Paris, 72
Bibliothèque Royale Albert I, Brussels,
    72, 156
Bidencope, Joseph, 36
Biotsfort (Brussels), 106, 108
Blairgowrie, 58–9, 60, 115, 160, 172
Bloy, Léon, 101
boarding schools, 3, 5; *see also*
    education
Boers, 141, 142
Boldrewood, Rolf, 24, 115, 162, 181
Bordeaux, 73–4, 86, 174
Boston, 128, 148, 187
Boulogne-sur-Seine, 76
Boyd, Benjamin, 27
Bright, John, 83
Brisbane *Courier*, 162
British Army, 78th Highlanders, 15;
    80th Regiment, 16
British Guiana, 141
Broadley, Alexander Meyrick, 98, 122
Bromby, Bishop Charles Henry, 19
Brontë, Charlotte, 117, 171

Brown, Sylvester John, 24
Browne, Mabel Gore, 10
Browne, Sir Thomas Gore, 10
Bruges, 74
Brussels, xiii, 5, 45–8, 50, 68, 71, 76,
    95, 96–7, 105–6, 114, 116, 117,
    127, 130, 142, 145–7, 156, 160, 171
Buckland, Rev John Richard, 9
Budapest, 85, 86, 176
Bulletin, xi, xvi, 162
Bulloo Downs Station, 78
Bulloo River, 157
Buls, Charles, 96, 105–6, 111, 130, 147
Burdekin River, 22, 27
Burgess, Murray, 12–13
burial, 6, 63–4, 172–3; *see also*
    cremation
Burke, Robert O'Hara, 79
Burnaby, Capt F.G., 173
Burnewang West Station, 25–6
bushrangers, 13, 16, 73, 111, 115, 159
bush tradition, xi, 63
Butler, Charles, 10

Cabana, Kew, 79
Cabanel, Alexandre, 70
Cambridge, Ada, xii, 24, 66, 167
Campaspe River, 23, 24, 25, 167
Campaspe School, 25
Canterbury, England, 93, 178
Cape Horn, 39, 111, 170
Cape Town, 69, 173
Carandini, Marie, 24
Carlsruhe, 17, 22–3, 24
Catani, Ugo, 79
Catholic Church, 71, 78, 83, 86, 92–3
Census (England, 1841), 163;
    (England, 1851), 5, 164;
Cercle des anciens normalistes,
    Brussels, 76, 175
Cercle artistique et littéraire, Brussels,
    76, 175
Chance, Rebecca, 12–13, 128, 165
children, 123, 126–7, 154; *see also*
    Tasma, views on children
Chirol, Sir Valentine, 134, 140, 142
Christian Science Monitor, 159
Clark, Rev. Charles, 69

problems, 104, 105, 131, 145–6, 153, 186; foreign correspondent, xii–xiii, 131–44, 147, 148, 153, 155, 184–5; illness, 144, 145, 148, 151–2, 153; imagination, 9, 45; journalist, 60, 84, 112; lecturer, xii, xiv–xv, 9, 28, 39, 68–9, 71, 72–7, 79, 86–7, 88, 94, 109–11; marriage (first), xv, 14, 18, 19, 20–1, 22, 23, 24–6, 28–9, 31–3, 34, 55, 57–8, 65–6, 79–80, 119, 120; marriage (second), xv, 81, 84, 93, 94–5, 96–7, 98, 104–8, 109, 112, 128–9, 130, 145–6, 185; marriage ties, 48–9, 53, 92, 105, 123, 150–1; 'New Woman', xiii, 71, 94, 123; novelist, xi, xii, xiv, xv, xvi, 7, 11, 16, 18–19, 20, 32–3, 98, 114–26, 148–51, 155; personality, xv, 11, 25, 55, 160; pseudonym, 59–60, 73, 116, 123; radical views, xiii, 18, 44, 93, 97; relations with men, xv, 48–9, 53, 61–2, 72, 80–1, 105–8, 112, 151; short story writer, 41–2, 60, 63, 76–7, 92, 113, 117–19, 122, 148, 159; social life, 104–5; teacher, 9, 25–6, 34, 40, 46; translator, xv, 111, 180; writer of articles, 62–4, 78, 79, 84–6, 88–9, 92–3, 94, 97–8, 112; writing career, 10–11, 58, 59–60, 67, 118; writing career (difficulty in writing), 121, 122, writing career (doubts on ability), 118, 122; writing carer (payments from writing), 117, 119, 121, 122, 123, 134–5, 139; views on children, 29–30, 123, 126–7; views on death, burial/cremation, eternity, 6–7, 63–4, 99, 154; views on marriage, 84, 92, 94; views on motherhood, 29, 102–3; views on religion, 10, 20, 24, 30, 71, 78, 84, 93, 154; views on socialism 71, 93; views on women's right to education, xiii, 84; youth 10–12, 13; *see also* titles of novels
Tasmania, 2, 5, 11, 14–16, 17, 43, 72–3, 97, 154, 155, 174; *see also* Aboriginal people
'Tasmania. Voyage by Cape Horn', 111, 170
Tasmanian Club, 10, 165, 169
Tasmanian Mail, 187
Tasmanian Racing Club, 64
Tauchnitz, Bernard (Leipsig), 111, 117, 180, 181
Tets, Comte de, 111
Thargomindah, 78, 152, 157
Thatcher, Richmond, 66
three-volume novels, 119, 121, 148, 185
Tooringabby Station, 27, 66
Transvaal, 138, 140–1, 147
Treves, 178
Tricoupis, Charilaos, 111
Tricoupis, Miss, 111, 112
Troye, Capt. de, 3
Trübner & Co., 114, 117, 119, 181
Trübner, Nicholas, 119
Trucanini, 162
Türe, General, 107
Tyndall, Prof. John, 79, 175
Twamley, 11

Uncle Piper of Piper's Hill, xi, xiv, xvi, 16, 18, 24, 31, 42, 57, 59, 91–2, 94, 98, 111, 114–17, 119, 120, 121, 123, 124, 126, 127, 149, 154, 181
Uncle Tom's Cabin, 116
Under the Gum Tree : Australian 'Bush' Stories, 124, 183
Union Bank, 27–8, 167, 168
'l'Union des femmes', 71
United States, xv, 111, 159, 180
Universal Review, 101

'The Vagabond', 60, 78, 92, 172
The Vagabond Annual, 60
Valerio, Edith *see* Reverdy, Edith
Valerio, Pierre, 128, 148, 160
Vanderbilt, Cornelius, 111
Vanderkindere, M., 96, 130
Van Diemen's Land *see* Tasmania
Vanity Fair, 125, 183
Vasco, Louis *see* Loureiro, Vasco

Index